Total Quality

Management, Organization, and Strategy

James W. Dean, Jr.
University of Cincinnati

James R. Evans
University of Cincinnati

West Publishing Company

Minneapolis/St. Paul   New York   Los Angeles   San Francisco

WEST'S COMMITMENT TO THE ENVIRONMENT

In 1906, West Publishing Company began recycling materials left over from the production of books. This began a tradition of efficient and responsible use of resources. Today, up to 95% of our legal books and 70% of our college texts and school texts are printed on recycled, acid-free stock. West also recycles nearly 22 million pounds of scrap paper annually—the equivalent of 181,717 trees. Since the 1960s, West has devised ways to capture and recycle waste inks, solvents, oils, and vapors created in the printing process. We also recycle plastics of all kinds, wood, glass, corrugated cardboard, and batteries, and have eliminated the use of Styrofoam book packaging. We at West are proud of the longevity and the scope of our commitment to the environment.

Production, Prepress, Printing and Binding by West Publishing Company.

 TEXT IS PRINTED ON 10% POST CONSUMER RECYCLED PAPER    PRINTED WITH SOY INK™

To our families . . .

Jan, Noelle, and Bridget
Beverly, Kristin, and Lauren

Contents

PREFACE   vii

PART I   **Introduction to Total Quality**   **1**

CHAPTER 1   Introduction   3
CHAPTER 2   Approaches to Total Quality   33
CHAPTER 3   Tools and Techniques for Quality Planning and Improvement   67

PART II   **Total Quality and Organization Theory**   **101**

CHAPTER 4   Quality in Customer-Supplier Relationships   103
CHAPTER 5   Designing Organizations for Quality   127
CHAPTER 6   Total Quality and Organizational Change   147

PART III   **Total Quality and Organizational Behavior**   **173**

CHAPTER 7   Quality Teamwork   175
CHAPTER 8   Empowerment and Motivation   197
CHAPTER 9   Quality Leadership   217

PART IV   **Total Quality and Strategic Management**   **237**

CHAPTER 10   Total Quality and Competitive Advantage   239
CHAPTER 11   Strategic Planning and Total Quality Implementation   259

BIBLIOGRAPHY   283

Preface

The need for students to learn and understand the principles of total quality has become increasingly obvious in recent years. Several chief executives of Fortune 500 companies recently wrote an open letter to colleges and universities in *Harvard Business Review*, strongly urging them to incorporate total quality into the curriculum. Organizations that hire college graduates are demanding that their new employees understand not only the importance of providing quality products and services to customers, but also the principles and tools of total quality management (TQM). Students starting their working lives unfamiliar with total quality will indeed be one step behind.

It is difficult for students to learn about TQM on their own, because there are so many different approaches to the topic. Although these approaches are similar, each has its own jargon and acronyms, which makes trying to penetrate the subject for the first time a difficult experience. Furthermore, most books about TQM are not written with the needs and experiences of students in mind.

This book has three objectives:

- to familiarize students with the basic principles and methods associated with total quality management;
- to show students how these principles and methods have been put into effect in a variety of organizations; and
- to illustrate the relationship between TQM principles and the theories and models studied in management courses.

The book presents the basic principles and tools associated with TQM and provides many cases that can be used as the basis for class discussion. The cases focus on large and small companies in manufacturing and service industries in North and South America, Europe, and Asia.

This book is organized so that it can be used as a supplement to textbooks for courses in management, organization theory, organizational behavior, and/or strategic management. The book can also be used as a free-standing introduction to TQM in an elective course on quality management. Students who have had the basic courses in management will be familiar with the various theories to which TQM is compared in the book.

Organization of the Book

Unlike most books on TQM, this one is organized according to traditional management topics. This organization helps students to see the parallels between TQM and management theories in areas such as organizational design and leadership. TQM is often presented as new or different, which it clearly is not. Many TQM ideas are based on management theories that are familiar to teachers and students. The organization of this book enables students to appreciate the ways in which TQM really is different.

The book has four parts. Part I, Introduction to Total Quality Management, presents the core principles of TQM and begins to explain how they relate to familiar management concepts. This section also explains many of the most common TQM techniques students are likely to encounter. Part II, Total Quality and Organization Theory, introduces the idea of customer-supplier relations and shows how TQM relates to topics such as organization-environment relations, organizational design, and change.

Part III, Total Quality and Organizational Behavior, discusses the themes of teamwork and empowerment and relates TQM to the topics of groups, motivation, and leadership. Part IV, Total Quality and Strategic Management, deals with the impact of TQM on both the content and process of competitive strategy. The bibliography at the end of the book provides a number of references for students who wish to deepen their understanding of various aspects of TQM.

Because the topics in this book are presented in different orders in different courses, we have tried to make each chapter as free-standing as possible. In most cases students should read Part I first as an introduction to TQM. After that the chapters can be covered in virtually any order, thus giving instructors a great deal of flexibility.

Acknowledgments

We are extremely grateful to the following reviewers who provided excellent feedback and suggestions for improvement on earlier drafts of the book:

> Charles Schrader, Iowa State University
> Stephen Beckstead, Utah State University
> Arthur L. Darrow, Bowling Green State University
> Allen Bluedorn, University of Missouri-Columbia
> John Alderson, East Arkansas Community College
> Uttarayan Bagchi, University of Texas at Austin
> David A. Waldman, Concordia University
> Cynthia Lengnick-Hall, Wichita State University.

In addition, we would like to thank Carole Barnett, Richard Buck, Richard Garula, Gerry Kaminski, Dick McKeever, Todd Molfenter, Barbara Reckers, Ann Schooley, and Charles Seeley, all of whom also contributed to this project in various ways. Finally, we greatly appreciate the help of our editors at West: Esther Craig and Richard Fenton.

We have come to believe, like many business and academic leaders, that quality is an absolute essential not only for competitive success in business, but also for meaningful work and integrity in many aspects of life. If this book helps students to contribute to the quality of their organizations' products and services and to understand the importance of quality in all their endeavors, then our efforts will have been worthwhile.

James W. Dean, Jr.
James R. Evans

To Students

One of the ideas you'll learn about in this book is continuous improvement, which means relentlessly trying to improve the quality of something over a long period of time. We would like to improve the quality of this book in the next edition, and we would like you to help us do so.

If you have an idea for how we could make this book better, write to us at the address below. For example, if a certain section is hard to understand or not very interesting, let us know. Once you start reading this book, you will probably pay more attention to the quality of the products and services you receive. If you have a particularly interesting experience that relates to TQM, tell us about it. This book contains quite a few cases; one of the cases in the next edition could be yours. If we use your idea, example, or case, we'll put your name in the book, and send you a free copy when it is published.

We hope you enjoy the book, and we also hope to hear from you.

James W. Dean, Jr.
James R. Evans

College of Business Administration
University of Cincinnati
Cincinnati, OH 45221-0020

PART I

Introduction to Total Quality

CHAPTER 1

Introduction

Chapter Outline

A Brief History
The Concept of Quality
    Quality in Manufacturing
    Quality in the Service Sector
Principles of Total Quality Management
    Customer Focus
    Strategic Planning and Leadership
    Continuous Improvement
    Empowerment and Teamwork
TQM and Traditional Management Practices
Current Practices
    Critics and Debate
Review and Discussion Questions
Cases

In this chapter we will introduce you to the basic principles of total quality. Specifically, we will

- provide reasons why attention to quality is imperative in today's global economy,
- discuss major issues facing manufacturing and service organizations,
- provide an overview of the key elements of total quality management,
- compare and contrast total quality management with traditional management practices, and
- discuss current practices and the ongoing debate of the value of total quality.

One of the most celebrated turnarounds in American business occurred at Xerox. Xerox experienced rapid growth through the 1960s after introducing its 914 copier, called "the most successful business product ever introduced." They reached $1 billion in revenue faster than any other company. They could sell all they produced. They had little competition. And they thought they knew what the customer needed.

In the 1970s Japanese competitors entered the market with cost-competitive machines. Customers now had a choice. As Xerox began to lose market share, the company realized that a tremendous amount of change would be required to compete successfully. Xerox began a process of benchmarking—comparing their products and processes with those of others—to gauge how much improvement was needed. The results shocked top management. Xerox had ten times as many assembly line rejects as their Japanese competitors, twice the product lead time, nine times as many suppliers, and seven times as many defects per hundred machines. Most startling was that their unit manufacturing cost equalled the selling price of their overseas competition.

In 1983 President David Kearns convened the company's top 25 managers. As a result of this meeting, they agreed to focus on quality as the main strategy for running their business. Their agenda for the future was summarized in the Xerox Quality Policy:

- Xerox is a quality company.
- Quality is the basic business principle for Xerox.
- Quality means providing our external and internal customers with innovative products and services that fully satisfy their requirements.
- Quality improvement is the job of every Xerox employee.

Xerox established an initiative called Leadership Through Quality, a 34-step strategy designed to instill quality as the basic business principle throughout the company, ensure that all employees focus on their customers, and pursue quality improvement.

Profitability increased annually as the quality process took root. Between 1986 and 1990 return on assets increased from 7.8 percent to 14.6 percent, and revenues increased from $9.42 billion to $12.69 billion. In 1989 Xerox Business Products and Systems won the Malcolm Baldrige National Quality Award in recognition of its achievements in implementing quality throughout the organization.

Total quality—a comprehensive, organization-wide effort to improve the quality of products and services—applies not only to large manufacturers such as Xerox. All organizations—large and small, manufacturing and service, profit and not-for-profit—can benefit from applying the principles of total quality.

A BRIEF HISTORY

To understand the importance of quality in business today, we need to review some history. Before the Industrial Revolution, skilled craftspeople served both as manufacturers and inspectors, building quality into their products through their considerable pride in their workmanship. Customers expected quality, and craftspeople understood it.

The Industrial Revolution changed everything. Thomas Jefferson brought Honoré Le Blanc's concept of interchangeable parts to America. Eli Whitney mistakenly believed that this idea would be easy to carry out. The government awarded him a contract in 1798 to supply 10,000 muskets in two years. He designed special machine tools and trained unskilled workmen to make parts according to a standard design, measure them, and compare them to a model. Unfortunately, Whitney grossly underestimated the effect of variation in the production process and its impact on quality. It took more than 10 years to complete the project, perhaps the first example of cost-overrun in government contracts! This same obstacle—variation—continues to plague American managers to this day.

Frederick W. Taylor's concept of "scientific management" greatly influenced the nature of quality in manufacturing organizations. By focusing on production efficiency and decomposing jobs into small work tasks, the modern assembly line destroyed the holistic nature of manufacturing. To ensure that products were manufactured correctly, independent "quality control" departments assumed the tasks of inspection. Thus, the separation of good from bad product became the chief means of ensuring quality.

Statistical approaches to quality control had their origins at Western Electric when the inspection department was transferred to Bell Telephone Laboratories in the 1920s. The pioneers of quality control—Walter Shewhart, Harold Dodge, George Edwards, and others—developed new theories and methods of inspection to improve and maintain quality. Control charts, sampling techniques, and economic analysis tools laid the foundation for modern quality assurance activity and influenced the thinking of two of their colleagues, W. Edwards Deming and Joseph M. Juran.

Deming and Juran introduced statistical quality control to Japanese workers after World War II as part of General MacArthur's rebuilding program. Although this was not much different than what was being done in America, there was one vital difference. They convinced top Japanese managers that quality improvement would open new world markets and was necessary for the survival of their nation. The managers believed in, and fully supported, the concept of quality improvement. The Japanese were in an ideal position to embrace this philosophy. The country was devastated from the war, and they had few natural resources with which to compete, except their people. During the next 20 years, while the Japanese were improving quality at an unprecedented rate, quality levels in the West remained stagnant.

Western manufacturers had little need to focus on quality. America had a virtual monopoly in manufacturing, and the post-war economy was hungry for nearly any kind of consumer good. Top managers focused their efforts on marketing, production quantity, and financial performance.

During the late 1970s and early 1980s, many businesses in the United States lost significant market share to other global competitors, Japan in particular. For example, U.S.-made computers purchased in the United States dropped from 94 percent in 1979 to 66 percent in 1989. In 1980 domestic automobile manufacturers commanded a 71.3 percent share of the U.S. market; by 1991 this declined to 62.5 percent. Although the U.S. auto industry has made remarkable progress in slowing and even reversing this trend in recent years, other industries such as machine tool, electronics, and steel have been devastated. Fueling the competitive crisis were the facts that consumers became increasingly quality-conscious and that the technological complexity of modern electronics made sophisticated consumer products more difficult to make.

By 1987 *Business Week* posed a stern warning to American management:[1]

> Quality. Remember it? American manufacturing has slumped a long way from the glory days of the 1950s and '60s when "Made in U.S.A." proudly stood for the best that industry could turn out. . . . While the Japanese were developing remarkably higher standards for a whole host of products, from consumer electronics to cars and machine tools, many U.S. managers were smugly dozing at the switch. Now, aside from aerospace and agriculture, there are few markets left where the U.S. carries its own weight in international trade. For American industry, the message is simple. Get better or get beat.

The "quality revolution" in America can be traced to 1980, when NBC aired a white paper entitled "If Japan Can . . . Why Can't We?" This program introduced the 80-year-old Deming, who was virtually unknown in the United States, to corporate executives across America. Ford Motor Company was among the first to invite Deming to help transform its operations. Within a few years, Ford's earnings were the highest for any company in automotive history, despite a 7 percent drop in U.S. car and truck industry sales, higher capital spending, and increased marketing costs. In 1992 the media celebrated the fact that the Ford Taurus outsold the Honda Accord to become the leader in domestic sales. Former CEO Donald Petersen stated:

> The work of Dr. Deming has definitely helped change Ford's corporate leadership. . . . Dr. Deming has influenced my thinking in a variety of ways. What stands out is that he helped me crystallize my ideas concerning the value of teamwork, process improvement and the pervasive power of the concept of continuous improvement.

America woke up to quality during the 1980s as most major companies embarked on extensive quality improvement campaigns. In 1984 the U.S. government designated October as National Quality Month. In 1987—some 34 years after Japan established the Deming Prize—Congress established the Malcolm Baldrige National Quality Award, spawning a remarkable interest in quality among American business. (Chapter 2 discusses the Baldrige Award.)

By the end of the decade Florida Power and Light became the first non-Japanese company to win Japan's coveted Deming Prize for quality. After the publicity that quality received from the manufacturing sector, the quality movement shifted to services, particularly health care, government, and education.

By 1991 *Business Week* was calling quality "a global revolution affecting every facet of business.... For the 1990s and far beyond, quality must remain the priority for business." Dr. Joseph Juran, one of the premier leaders in the quality movement, observed:

> I have become optimistic for the first time since the quality crisis descended on the United States. I now believe that, during the 1990s, the number of U.S. companies that have achieved stunning results will increase by orders of magnitude. I also believe that, during the 1990s, the United States will make great strides toward making 'Made in the USA' a symbol of world class quality.[2]

Quality in the twentieth century has evolved from a narrow focus on control to one that permeates all aspects of the modern business enterprise. Quality is a requirement to compete successfully in today's global marketplace.

THE CONCEPT OF QUALITY

People define quality in many ways. Some think of quality as superiority or innate excellence; others view it as a lack of manufacturing or service defects. Today most managers agree that the main reason to pursue quality is to satisfy customers. The American National Standards Institute (ANSI) and the American Society for Quality Control (ASQC) define quality as "the totality of features and characteristics of a product or service that bears on its ability to satisfy given needs." The view of quality as the satisfaction of customer needs is often called *fitness for use*. In highly competitive markets, merely satisfying customer needs will not achieve success. To beat the competition, organizations often must *exceed* customer expectations. Most progressive organizations now define quality as follows:

Quality is meeting or exceeding customer expectations.

One example of creating satisfied customers is the rock and roll band, the Grateful Dead (see box).

Managers of manufacturing and service functions deal with different types of quality issues. The following sections provide a brief overview of these issues. Although the details of quality management differ between manufacturing and service industries, the customer-driven definition eliminates these artificial distinctions and provides a unifying perspective.

The Grateful Dead Exceeds Customer Expectations[3]

The Grateful Dead have been going strong for over a quarter century and command one of the most loyal followings of any musical group. Their customer focus is evident in many of their practices. For example, instead of barring recording equipment from their concerts, a standard practice designed to protect record sales, the band sets aside a special area in concert halls to accommodate fans' equipment. The quality of lighting and sound exceeds that of most other bands. They keep the ticket prices at or below the average price of other rock concerts. The concerts can be nearly twice as long as other performers—up to 3-1/2 hours, and no songs are repeated during a four-night stand in one city. Tickets can be obtained by mail instead of waiting in long lines. When tickets are received, fans also receive a list of inexpensive hotels, restaurants, and camping facilities in the area. The Dead have a loyal customer base—known affectionately as "Deadheads." And their quality focus has paid off handsomely: estimates of ticket revenues in 1992 were over $30 million.

Quality in Manufacturing

Manufactured products have several quality dimensions,[4] including the following:

1. Performance: a product's primary operating characteristics.
2. Features: the "bells and whistles" of a product.
3. Reliability: the probability of a product's surviving over a specified period of time under stated conditions of use.
4. Conformance: the degree to which physical and performance characteristics of a product match preestablished standards.
5. Durability: the amount of use one gets from a product before it physically deteriorates or until replacement is preferable.
6. Serviceability: the ability to repair a product quickly and easily.
7. Aesthetics: how a product looks, feels, sounds, tastes, or smells.
8. Perceived quality: subjective assessment resulting from image, advertising, or brand names.

Most of these dimensions revolve around the design of the product. In designing the Lexus automobile for instance, Toyota bought several competitors' cars—including Mercedes, Jaguar, and BMW—and put them through grueling test-track runs before taking them apart.[5] The chief engineer decided that he could match Mercedes on performance and reliability, as well as on luxury and status features. He developed 11 performance goals. The final design had a drag coefficient smaller than any other luxury car (resulting in higher aerodynamic performance), a lighter weight, a more fuel-efficient engine, and a lower noise level. Sturdier materials were used for seat edges to maintain their appearance longer. The engine was designed with more torque than German models to give the car the quick start that Americans prefer. Ford's director of North American interior design called the instrument cluster "a work of art."

Quality control in manufacturing is usually based on conformance, specifically *conformance to specifications*. Specifications are targets and tolerances determined by designers of products and services. *Targets* are the ideal values for which production strives; *tolerances* are acceptable deviations from these ideal values. For example, a computer chip manufacturer might specify that the distance between pins on a computer chip should be .095 ± .005 inches. The value .095 is the target, and ±.005 is the tolerance. Any pin distance between .090 and .100 would be acceptable.

A lack of defects has constituted quality in manufacturing for many years. Many studies comparing domestic and foreign products focus on statistical measures of defects. However, the lack of defects alone will not satisfy or exceed customer expectations. Many top managers have stated that good quality of conformance is simply the "entry into the game." A better way to achieve distinction and delight customers is through improved product design. Thus, manufacturers are turning their attention toward improved design for achieving their quality and business goals.

Quality in Services

Today services account for more than 75 percent of the U.S. workforce. The importance of quality in services cannot be underestimated, as statistics from a variety of studies reveal:[6]

- The average company never hears from more than 90 percent of its unhappy customers. For every complaint it receives, the company has at least 25 customers with problems, about one-fourth of which are serious.

- Of the customers who make a complaint, more than half will do business again with that organization if their complaint is resolved. If the customer feels that the complaint was resolved quickly, this figure jumps to about 95 percent.

- The average customer who has had a problem will tell 9 or 10 others about it. Customers who have had complaints resolved satisfactorily will only tell about 5 others.

- It costs six times more to get a new customer than to keep a current customer.

So why do many companies treat customers as commodities? In Japan the notion of customer is equated with "honored guest." Service clearly should be at the forefront of a firm's priorities.

Many of the key dimensions of product quality apply to services. For instance, "on time arrival" for an airline is a measure of service performance; frequent flyer awards and "business class" sections represent features. Banks and hotels have specifications that employees should greet customers using their names or that receptionists should answer telephones within three rings.

Many service organizations have well-developed quality assurance systems. Most of them, however, are based on manufacturing analogies and tend to be more product-oriented than service-oriented. For example, a typical hotel's quality assurance system focuses on technical specifications such as properly made-up rooms. However, service organizations have special requirements that manufacturing systems cannot fulfill. The most important dimensions of service quality include the following:[7]

- Time: How much time must a customer wait?
- Timeliness: Will a service be performed when promised?
- Completeness: Are all items in the order included?
- Courtesy: Do front-line employees greet each customer cheerfully?
- Consistency: Are services delivered in the same fashion for every customer, and every time for the same customer?
- Accessibility and convenience: Is the service easy to obtain?
- Accuracy: Is the service performed right the first time?
- Responsiveness: Can service personnel react quickly and resolve unexpected problems?

Service organizations must look beyond product orientation and pay significant attention to customer transactions and employee behavior. Several points that service organizations should consider are as follows:[8]

- The quality characteristics that a firm should control may not be the obvious ones. Customer perceptions are critical although it may be difficult to define what the customer wants. For example, speed of service is an important quality characteristic, yet perceptions of speed may differ significantly among different service organizations and customers. Marketing and consumer research can play a significant role.
- Behavior is a quality characteristic. The quality of human interaction is vital in every transaction that involves human contact. For example, banks have found that the friendliness of tellers is a principal factor in retaining depositors.
- Image is a major factor in shaping customer expectations of a service and in setting standards by which customers evaluate that service. A breakdown in image can be as harmful as a breakdown in delivery of the service itself. Top management is responsible for shaping and guiding the image that the firm projects.

- Establishing and measuring service levels may be difficult. Service standards, particularly those relating to human behavior, are often set judgmentally and are hard to measure. In manufacturing, it is easy to quantify output, scrap, and rework. Customer attitudes and employee competence are not as easily measured.

- Quality control activity may be required at times or in places where supervision and control personnel are not present. Often work must be performed at the convenience of the customer. This calls for more training of employees and self-management.

These issues suggest that the approach to managing quality in services differs from that used in manufacturing. However, manufacturing can be seen as a set of interrelated services, not only between the company and the ultimate consumer, but within the organization. Manufacturing is a customer of product design; assembly is a customer of manufacturing; sales is a customer of packaging and distribution. If quality is meeting and exceeding customer expectations, then manufacturing takes on a new meaning, far beyond product orientation. Total quality provides the umbrella under which everyone in the organization can strive to create customer satisfaction. The Baldrige Award criteria, discussed in chapter 2, do not distinguish between manufacturing and service, even though awards are given in both categories.

PRINCIPLES OF TOTAL QUALITY MANAGEMENT

In the early 1980s Polaroid conducted an internal survey of its operations and identified several major areas of concern:[9]

1. Quality was often ensured too late in the production cycle—at final assembly, rather than in the design and development stages.
2. Customer needs and satisfaction were not well understood.
3. Quality was not an important issue until it became a problem.
4. Management seemed willing to sacrifice quality when costs or scheduling conflicted.
5. Operators were not sufficiently trained in their jobs and in quality issues.
6. Quality problems were experienced with vendors.
7. Quality costs appeared high.

These issues are not quality problems; they are design problems, marketing problems, manufacturing problems, human resource problems, supplier relations problems, and financial problems. They encompass the management of operations throughout the firm. Polaroid's response was a comprehensive and integrated management strategy centered on quality.

Today the term *total quality management (TQM)* conveys a total, company-wide effort that includes all employees, suppliers, and customers, and that seeks continuously to improve the quality of products and processes to meet the needs and expectations of customers. TQM has become the basic *business strategy* for firms that aspire to meet the needs of their customers.

There probably are as many different approaches to TQM as there are businesses. Although no program is ideal, successful programs share many characteristics. The basic attributes of TQM are (1) customer focus, (2) strategic planning and leadership, (3) continuous improvement, and (4) empowerment and teamwork.

Customer Focus

The customer is the judge of quality. Quality systems must address all product and service attributes that provide value to the customer and lead to customer satisfaction and loyalty. Many factors influence value and satisfaction throughout the customer's overall purchase, ownership, and service experiences. This includes the relationship between the company and customers—the trust and confidence in products and services—that leads to loyalty. This concept of quality includes not only the product and service attributes that meet basic requirements, but also those features that enhance the product and differentiate it from competing offerings. This is often referred to as the "service bundle" or "service package." A business can achieve success only by understanding and fulfilling the needs of customers.

TQM is an important element of business strategy that is directed toward market-share gain and customer retention. It demands constant sensitivity to emerging customer and market requirements, and measurement of the factors that drive customer satisfaction. TQM also requires an awareness of developments in technology and rapid and flexible response to customer and market needs. Such requirements extend well beyond merely reducing defects and complaints or meeting specifications. Nevertheless, defect and error reduction and elimination of causes of dissatisfaction contribute significantly to the customers' views of quality and so are important parts of TQM. In addition, the company's approach to recovering from defects and errors is crucial to its improving both quality and relationships with customers.

A company must remain close to the customer, knowing what work the customer does and how the customer uses its products. Customer opinion surveys and focus groups can help companies understand customer requirements and values. New techniques, such as toll-free telephone numbers, enable firms to obtain customer feedback. Several companies require their sales and marketing executives to meet with random groups of key customers on a regular basis. Other companies bring customers and suppliers into internal product design and development meetings. The Coca Cola Company is one example of good customer relationship management (see box).

Coke Stays Close to the Customer[10]

While companies concerned about quality try to minimize problems that cause customer dissatisfaction, all companies occasionally receive complaints from customers. Often the response to such complaints can make the difference between keeping and losing a loyal customer. The Coca-Cola Company's Industry & Consumer Affairs department is responsible for all consumer contacts with the company's headquarters in Atlanta. The mission of the department is "to protect and enhance Coca-Cola's trademarks and image by providing a communications link between consumers and company management." The department's 60 employees handle over 500,000 contacts each year, both by mail and via the Company's toll-free hotline (1-800 GET COKE). Most of the contacts are inquiries about the product.

If a customer does call with a complaint, Coca-Cola sends the customer a letter apologizing for the problem, as well as coupons that allow the customer to replace the unacceptable product. As Roger Nunley, Director of Industry & Consumer Affairs puts it, "We strive to exceed customer expectations *every time*. We want our customers to be excited and pleased with our response." In certain circumstances, the local Coca-Cola bottler may also follow up with the customer.

A Service Quality Survey is mailed to the customer two weeks after the initial contact. The survey asks the customer to rate the quality of the response, as well as the quality of the phone agent or letter-writer (for example, how courteous or professional the company representative was). The survey also asks whether the customer will continue to purchase products of the Coca-Cola Company. According to the Company's most recent data, 90 percent of customers were satisfied with how their complaint was handled, but in the spirit of continuous improvement, the Company aspires to 100 percent satisfaction.

Internal customers—the recipients of any work output, such as the next department in a manufacturing process or the order-picker who receives instructions from an order entry clerk—are also crucial to assuring quality for the external customers who purchase the product. Failure to meet the needs of internal customers will likely affect external customers. Employees must view themselves as customers of some employees and suppliers to others.

Strategic Planning and Leadership

Achieving quality and market leadership requires a long-range strategy. Improvements do not happen overnight. The success of Japanese manufacturers evolved over several decades. Planning and organizing improvement activities take time and require major commitments on the part of all members of the organization. Strategies, plans, and budget allocations need to reflect long-term commitments to customers, employees, stockholders, and suppliers. They also must address training, employee development, supplier development, technology evolution, and other factors that bear upon quality. A key part of the long-term commitment is regular review and assessment of progress toward long-term goals.

Leadership for quality is the responsibility of top management. Senior leadership must create clear quality values and high expectations and build them into the way the company operates. Reinforcement of the values and expectations requires the substantial personal commitment and involvement of senior management. The leaders must take part in the creation of strategies, systems, and methods for achieving excellence. The systems and methods need to guide all activities and decisions of the company and encourage participation and creativity by all employees. Through their regular personal involvement in visible activities—such as planning, reviewing company quality performance, serving on improvement teams, and recognizing employees for quality achievement—the senior leaders serve as role models, reinforcing the values and encouraging leadership in all levels of management.

If commitment to quality is not a priority, any initiative is doomed to failure. Lip service to quality improvement is the kiss of death. The CEO of Motorola, one of the first Baldrige winners, had quality as the first agenda item at every top management meeting. He frequently left after quality was discussed, sending the message that once quality was taken care of, financial and other matters would take care of themselves. The Budd Company, a major automobile body component supplier, has a Corporate Quality Council made up of top executives and managers. The council sets quality policy and reviews performance goals within the company. Quality should be a major factor in strategic planning and competitive analysis processes.

Many of the management principles and practices required in a TQM environment may be contrary to long-standing practice, as discussed later in this chapter. Top managers, ideally starting with the CEO, must be the organization's TQM leaders. The CEO should be the focal point providing broad perspectives and vision, encouragement, and recognition. The leader must be determined to establish TQM initiatives and committed to sustain TQM activities through daily actions in order to overcome employees' inevitable resistance to change.

Unfortunately, many organizations do not have the commitment and leadership of their top managers. This does not mean that these organizations cannot develop a quality focus. Improved quality can be fostered through the strong leadership of middle managers and the involvement of the workforce. In many cases, this is where quality begins. In the long run, however, an organization cannot sustain quality initiatives without strong top management leadership.

Continuous Improvement

Continuous improvement is part of the management of all systems and processes. Achieving the highest levels of quality and competitiveness requires a well-defined and well-executed approach to continuous improvement. Such improvement needs to be part of all operations and all work unit activities in a company. Improvements may be of several types:

- enhancing value to the customer through new and improved products and services;
- reducing errors, defects, and waste;
- improving responsiveness and cycle time performance; and
- improving productivity and effectiveness in the use of all resources.

Thus, improvement is driven not only by the objective to provide better quality, but also by the need to be responsive and efficient—both of which confer additional marketplace advantages. To meet all of these objectives, the process of continuous improvement must contain regular cycles of planning, execution, and evaluation. This requires a basis—preferably a quantitative basis—for assessing progress and for deriving information for future cycles of improvement. Quality must be *measured*.

Improving Products and Services   Careful research is required to determine the needs of customers, and those needs must be reflected in the design of products and services. A Japanese professor, Noriaki Kano, suggests that three classes of customer needs exist:

- Dissatisfiers—those needs that are *expected* in a product or service, such as a radio, heater, and required safety features in an automobile. Such items generally are not stated by customers but are assumed as given. If they are not present, the customer is dissatisfied.
- Satisfiers—needs that customers say they want, such as air conditioning or a compact disc player in a car. Fulfilling these needs creates satisfaction.
- Delighters/exciters—new or innovative features that customers do not expect. When first introduced, antilock brakes and air bags were examples of exciters. Newer concepts still under development, such as collision-avoidance systems, offer other examples. The presence of such unexpected features, if valued, leads to high perceptions of quality.

The importance of this classification is realizing that although satisfiers are relatively easy to determine through routine marketing research, special effort is required to elicit customer perceptions about dissatisfiers and delighters/exciters. Over time delighters/exciters become satisfiers as customers become used to them (as is the case today with antilock brakes and air bags), and eventually satisfiers become dissatisfiers (customers are dissatisfied if they are not provided). Therefore, companies must innovate continually and study customer perceptions to ensure that their needs are being met. Scandinavian Airlines is one organization that set about to delight its customers (see box).

Designing and Improving Work Processes   Quality excellence derives from well-designed and well-executed work processes and administrative systems that stress prevention. Improvements in the quality of product design may lead to major reductions in scrap and defects later in the production process and, hence, to lower costs.

Fast response to customers is a major quality attribute. Success in competitive markets increasingly demands shorter product and service introduction cycles and faster response to customers. Reductions in cycle and response time can occur when work processes are designed to meet both quality and response goals. Response time reduction should be a major focus in all quality improvement processes of work units. Therefore, all designs, objectives, and work unit activities must measure cycle time and responsiveness. Major improvements in response time may require that work processes and paths be simplified and shortened. Since response time improvements often drive simultaneous im-

---

Scandinavian Airlines Improves its Products and Services

Improving the design of its service system transformed Scandinavian Airlines System (SAS) in Sweden. When president and CEO Jan Carlzon took over SAS in 1980, the company was suffering from the effects of an oil shock, two years of financial losses, and high labor costs. These factors prevented the company from competing on price alone with U.S. and Asian airlines.

Carlzon set about creating a quality image by instituting low standby fares for passengers under age 27; re-configuring airplanes to give more comfort and amenities to business-class passengers; training and empowering employees to handle problems swiftly, competently, and without excessive "red tape"; and improving ground service. In the latter category, changes included providing better express check-in service, new business facilities such as computers and fax machines, and automatic delivery of luggage to hotels owned by or linked to SAS's full-service travel agency.

To attain their quality objectives, Carlzon stressed the need to have behavioral change take place at the "moment of truth" where the employee comes into contact with the customer during the process of delivering the company's service.[11]

provements in quality and productivity, it is highly beneficial to consider response time, quality, and productivity objectives together.

Measurement as a Basis for Improvement Meeting quality and performance goals of the company requires that process management be based upon reliable information, data, and analysis. The quality of products, internal processes, and customer satisfaction must be measured. Facts and data needed for quality assessment and improvement include customer identification, product and service performance, operations records, market surveys, competitive comparisons, supplier lists, employee-related data, and cost and financial figures. Statistical reasoning with factual data is the basis for problem solving and continuous improvement. Facts, data, and analysis support such company purposes as planning, reviewing company performance, improving operations, and comparing quality with that of competitors

A company should select data and indicators that best represent the factors that determine customer satisfaction and operational performance. A system of indicators tied to customer and company performance requirements provides a clear and objective basis for directing all activities of the company toward common goals.

A company must also establish measures based on facts to assess quality improvement. Reporting of information must be timely and accurate. A systematic process to constantly measure and evaluate quality is essential. Traditional information systems focus on financial accounting, sales, marketing, purchasing, and scheduling measures. Quality measures should be part of the reports that are regularly provided to middle and upper management. However, line workers and supervisors also need quality reports so that they can help identify, analyze, and solve problems.

Analyzing the costs of poor quality is one approach that many firms use to identify improvement opportunities. The cost of poor quality includes such items as inspection costs, costs of scrap and rework, customer returns and warranty claims, and other related expenses. The next boxed example illustrates the effective use of such information.

Empowerment and Teamwork

All functions at all levels of an organization must focus on quality to achieve corporate goals. Teamwork can be viewed in three ways:

1. Vertical—teamwork between top management and lower-level employees. Employees are empowered to make decisions that satisfy customers without a lot of bureaucratic hassles, and barriers between levels are removed.
2. Horizontal—teamwork within work groups and across functional lines (often called cross-functional teams). A product development team might consist of designers, manufacturing personnel, suppliers, salespeople, and customers.

Travenol Laboratories Studies Quality Costs[12]

Travenol Laboratores, Inc. instituted a program to incorporate quality costs and decision support systems to assist mangers in discovering significant improvement opportunities in one of its northern Illinois manufacturing facilities. A committee consisting of the plant manager, the engineering manager, and the controller meets each month to identify areas of opportunity for improving quality and reducing costs. They use a computerized system to track trends in quality-related costs.

The system has a high degree of flexibility to allow managers to view monthly or year-to-date data, total costs, costs divided by the value of production or machine hours, and other statistics. Once the committee has found an area of opportunity, it assigns a diagnostic team consisting of technical and operations staff to investigate the problem. The diagnostic team seeks to discover causes and remedies, evaluates the quality and economic impact of various alternatives, and recommends courses of action to the committee.

---

3. Interorganizational—partnerships with suppliers and customers. Rather than dictating specifications for purchased parts, a company might develop specifications jointly with suppliers to take advantage of the suppliers' manufacturing capabilities.

Vertical Teamwork   Everyone must participate in quality improvement efforts. The person in any organization who best understands his or her job and how it can be improved is the one performing it. Employees must be empowered to make decisions that affect quality and to develop and implement new and better systems. This often represents a profound shift in the philosophy of senior management, as the traditional philosophy is that the workforce should be "managed" to conform to existing business systems.

Companies can encourage participation by recognizing team and individual accomplishments, sharing success stories throughout the organization, encouraging risk taking by removing the fear of failure, encouraging the formation of employee involvement teams, implementing suggestion systems that act rapidly, provide feedback, and reward implemented suggestions, and providing financial and technical support to employees to develop their ideas.

Mariott and American Express[13] are two examples of companies that exemplify the empowering and rewarding of employees for service quality. At Marriott customer service representatives are called "associates" and have wide discretion to call on any part of the company to help customers. Indeed, they earn lush bonuses for extraordinary work. At American Express cash awards of up to $1,000 have been given to "Great Performers" such as Barbara Weber, who in 1986 cut through miles of State Department and Treasury Department red tape to refund $980 of stolen traveler's checks to a customer stranded in Cuba.

Employees need training in quality skills related to performing their work and to understanding and solving quality-related problems. Training brings all employees to a common understanding of goals and objectives and the means to attain them. Training usually begins with awareness of quality management principles and is followed by specific skills in quality improvement. Training should be reinforced through on-the-job applications of learning, involvement, and empowerment.

Increasingly training and participation need to be tailored to a more diverse workforce. All employees, from the CEO on down, must be suitably trained and involved in quality activities. Managers must view training as a continuous effort, not a one-time project. This requires a commitment of significant resources that many firms are reluctant to make.

Horizontal Teamwork   Problem solving and process improvement are best performed by cross-functional work teams. General Motors, for example, is trying to eliminate the practice of competing internally in order to promote teamwork. One manager characterized GM as one of the most fiercely internally competitive companies that ever existed. GM developed a system called the Quality Network that is made up of joint union-management Quality Councils at the corporate, division, and plant levels. This system, which is common across all of General Motors, encourages teamwork and cooperation. Plants hold periodic "corporate analysis meetings" during which production is shut down briefly for thorough audits of the quality system. Hundreds of plant-level work teams with thousands of workers focus on ways to improve quality and productivity.

Interorganizational Partnerships   Partnerships must be created both internally and externally. Companies should seek to build partnerships that serve mutual and larger community interests. Partnerships might include those that promote labor-management cooperation such as agreements with unions, cooperation with suppliers and customers, and linkages with educational organizations. Teamwork and participation, involving everyone in the organization as well as suppliers and customers, lead to creativity and innovation.

TQM AND TRADITIONAL MANAGEMENT PRACTICES

TQM is quite different from traditional management practices. "Traditional management" means the way things are usually done in most organizations in the absence of a TQM focus. Many "traditional" organizations have been applying TQM principles all along, so not all of these comments pertain to every organization. The nature of TQM differs from common management practices in many respects. Among the key differences that will be explored in greater depth throughout this book are the following:[14]

1. Strategic Planning and Management

In traditional management, financial and marketing issues such as profitability, return on investments, and market share drive strategic planning. Quality planning activities are delegated to the "quality control" department. Long-term quality initiatives are viewed as being costly and not contributing to the ultimate performance measure—profit. Quality planning and strategic business planning are indistinguishable in TQM. Quality goals are the cornerstone of the business plan. Measures such as customer satisfaction, defect rates, and process cycle times receive as much attention in the strategic plan as financial and marketing objectives.

2. Changing Relationships with Customers and Suppliers

In traditional management, quality is defined as adherence to internal specifications and standards. Quality is measured only by the absence of defects. Inspection of people's work by others is necessary to control defects. In TQM, quality is defined as products and services beyond present needs and expectations of customers. Innovation is required to meet and exceed customers' needs.

Traditional management places customers outside of the enterprise and within the domain of marketing and sales. TQM views everyone inside the enterprise as a customer of an internal or external supplier, and a supplier of an external or internal customer. Marketing concepts and tools can be used to assess internal customer needs and to communicate internal supplier capabilities.

In traditional management, suppliers are pitted against each other to get the lowest price. The more competing suppliers there are, the better it is for the customer company. In TQM, suppliers are partners with their customers. The aim of the partnership is innovation, reduction in variation of critical characteristics of supplied materials, lower costs, and better quality. The aim may be enhanced by reducing the number of suppliers and establishing long-term relationships.

3. Organizational Structure

Traditional management views an enterprise as a collection of separate, highly specialized individual performers and units, loosely linked by a functional hierarchy. Lateral connections are made by intermediaries close to the top of the organization. TQM views the enterprise as a system of interdependent processes, linked laterally over time through a network of collaborating (internal and external) suppliers and customers. Each process is connected to the enterprise's mission and purpose through a hierarchy of micro- and macroprocesses. Every process contains subprocesses and is also contained within a higher process. This structure of processes is repeated throughout the hierarchy.

In traditional management, hierarchical "chimney" organization structures promote identification with functions and tend to create competition, conflict, and adversarial relations between functions. In TQM formal and informal mechanisms encourage and facilitate teamwork and team development across the entire enterprise.

Traditional managers oversee departments or functions that do not know they are interdependent, and each department acts as if it were the whole. Problems are seen as the result of individual people or departments not doing their best. TQM managers run interdependent systems and processes and exercise managerial leadership through participative management in carrying out their roles as mentors, facilitators, innovators, and so on. Quality results from the enterprise's systems. People working in the system cannot do better than the system allows. The vast majority of problems will be prevented and improvement will be promoted when people understand where they fit in and have the knowledge to maximize their contribution to the whole. Only management can foster an environment that nurtures a team-oriented culture that can prevent problems and continually improve.

4. Organizational Change

Once a traditional organization has found a formula for success, it keeps following it. Management's job is to prevent change, to maintain the status quo. In TQM the environment in which the enterprise interacts is changing constantly. If the enterprise continues to do what it has done in the past, its future performance relative to the competition will deteriorate. Management's job, therefore, is to provide the leadership for continual improvement and innovation in processes and systems, products, and services. External change is inevitable, but a favorable future can be shaped.

5. Teamwork

In traditional management, individuals and departments work for themselves. Individuals are driven by short-term performance measures, have narrowly defined jobs, and rarely see how they fit into the whole process or system. Little communication and cooperation exists between design and manufacturing, manufacturing and marketing, and sales/service and design. In TQM individuals cooperate in team structures such as quality circles, steering committees, and self-directed work teams. Departments work together toward system optimization through cross-functional teamwork.

The adversarial relationship between union and management is inevitable in traditional management. The only room for negotiation is in areas such as wages, health, and safety. In TQM the union is a partner and a stakeholder in the success of the enterprise. The areas for partnership and collaboration are broad, particularly in education, training, and meaningful involvement of employees in the improvement of processes that they affect and that affect their work.

6. Motivation and Job Design

Traditional management motivates employees through fear of punishment. People are motivated to perform in order to avoid failure and punishment, rather than to contribute something of value to the enterprise. Employees are afraid to do anything that would displease the boss or not be in compliance with company regulations. The system makes people feel like losers. TQM managers provide leadership rather than overt intervention in the processes of their subordinates, who are viewed as process managers rather than functional specialists. People are motivated to make meaningful contributions to what they believe is an important and noble cause, of value to the enterprise and society. The system enables people to feel like winners.

In traditional management, competition is inevitable and inherent in human nature. Performance appraisal, recognition and reward systems place people in an internally competitive environment. Individualism is reinforced to the detriment of teamwork. Competitive behavior—one person against another or one group against another—is not a natural state in TQM. TQM reward systems recognize individual as well as team contributions and reinforce cooperation.

7. Management and Leadership

Traditional management views people as interchangeable commodities, developed to meet the perceived needs of the enterprise. People are passive contributors with little autonomy—doing what they are told and nothing more. TQM views people as the enterprise's true competitive edge. Leadership provides people with opportunities for personal growth and development. People are able to take pride and joy in learning and accomplishment, and the ability of the enterprise to succeed is enhanced. People are active contributors, valued for their creativity and intelligence. Every person is a process manager presiding over the transformation of inputs to outputs of greater value to the enterprise and to the ultimate customer.

In traditional management, control is achieved by preestablished inflexible responsive patterns given in the book of rules and procedures. People are customers of a "book" that prescribes appropriate behaviors. In TQM control is achieved by shared values and beliefs in the organization, knowledge of mission, purpose, and customer requirements.

The principles of total quality management are embodied in the business philosophy of many leading companies such as Procter & Gamble (see box).

Procter & Gamble Embraces TQM[15]

P&G focuses on delivering superior consumer satisfaction using four basic principles:

- *Really know our customers and consumers.* Know those who resell our products and those who finally use them—and then meet and exceed their expectations.
- *Do right things right.* This requires hard data and sound statistical analysis to select the "right things" and to direct continual improvement in how well we do those things.
- *Concentrate on improving systems.* In order to achieve superior customer and consumer satisfaction and leadership financial goals, we must continually analyze and improve the capability of our basic business systems and sub-systems.
- *Empower people.* This means removing barriers and providing a climate in which everyone in the enterprise is encouraged and trained to make his or her maximum contribution to business objectives.

The *P&G Statement of Purpose* captures the "what," "how," and expected "results" of their quality efforts.

We will provide products of superior quality and value that best fill the needs of the world's consumers.

We will achieve that purpose through an organization and a working environment that attracts the finest people; fully develops and challenges our individual talents; encourages our free and spirited collaboration to drive the business ahead; and maintains the Company's historic principles of integrity, and doing the right thing.

Through the successful pursuit of our commitment, we expect our brands to achieve leadership share and profit positions that, as a result, our business, our people, our shareholders, and the communities in which we live and work, will prosper.

CURRENT PRACTICES

Despite all the publicity that TQM has generated, a 1991 study by Ernst and Young and the American Quality Foundation showed some sobering results.[16] While 55 percent of U.S. firms use quality information to evaluate business performance monthly or more frequently, 70 percent of Japanese firms follow this practice. Almost 20 percent of U.S. businesses review quality less than annually or not at all; the comparable figure in Japan is 2 percent and in Germany, 9 percent. Japanese and German firms place significantly more emphasis on the customer. In Japan 58 percent of the businesses always or almost always translate customer expectations into the design of new products and services, compared to 40 percent in Germany and only 22 percent in the United States. Japanese firms also use technology twice as much as U.S. companies in meeting customer expectations. Japan dramatically leads the other countries in the routine use of process improvement methods. In the study, 47 percent of Japanese firms indicated that they always or almost always use process simplification, compared to 12 percent in the United States. Surprisingly, Japan does not organize the majority of its workforce into quality-related teams, but it does have the highest rate of employee participation in regularly scheduled meetings about quality.

The study also indicates some future directions: 21 percent of U.S. companies expect to increase the number of employees in quality-related teams, and 51 percent of the U.S. companies plan to use quality performance as a criterion for compensating senior management. However, as singer Paul Simon declares, "the nearer your destination, the more you're slip-sliding away." The CEO of Xerox once stated, "Quality is a moving target." As we improve, so will our competitors. In fact, the ability of Japan to achieve world competitiveness did not come from our lack of quality improvement, but because of their higher *rate* of improvement. To close the widening gap, U.S. business must increase its quality improvement more rapidly. This includes not only the workplace, but also education. American business schools are *just beginning* to incorporate quality principles into their curricula; in Japan, elementary schools teach statistical process control.

Critics and Debate

Much criticism has arisen regarding TQM. In reference to Douglas Aircraft—a troubled subsidiary of McDonnell Douglas Corporation—*Newsweek* stated, " . . . the aircraft maker three years ago embraced 'Total Quality Management,' a Japanese import that had become the American business cult of the 1980s. . . . At Douglas, TQM appeared to be just one more hothouse Japanese flower never meant to grow on rocky ground."[17] Other articles in *The Wall Street Journal* ("Quality Programs Show Shoddy Results," May 14, 1992) and the *New York Times* ("The Lemmings Who Love Total Quality," May 3, 1992) suggest that total quality approaches are passing fads that are inherently flawed.

Perhaps it is unfortunate that a three-letter acronymn was chosen to represent such a powerful management concept. It is equally unfortunate that many people point to such headlines as a generalized condemnation of TQM. Reasons for failure are rooted in organizational approaches and systems, many of which this book addresses. Our purpose here is to provide a solid link between concepts of total quality and the traditional management areas of organization theory, organizational behavior, and strategy. When any company begins to think of how to improve, it will be led to the various approaches that are united under the TQM concept. Today, total quality is a matter of survival.

SUMMARY

Quality—meeting and exceeding customer expectations—is a major concern to all manufacturing and service organizations. Foreign competition has made companies focus on quality as a key business strategy. "Total quality management" denotes a comprehensive effort involving everyone in an organization to meet customer needs and continuously improve products and services.

The key elements of TQM are customer focus, strategic planning and leadership, continuous improvement, and empowerment and teamwork. Total quality represents a radical change from traditional management practices. In this sense, an organization that pursues total quality must address issues of organizational and behavioral change. The remainder of this book develops these concepts further and ties them together with theories of management, organization, and strategy.

REVIEW AND DISCUSSION QUESTIONS

1. Explain why quality became the most important issue facing American business in the 1980s. In addition to the economic competition from Japan, what other factors may have contributed to the importance that quality has assumed?

2. Cite several examples in your own experience in which your expectations were met, exceeded, or not met in purchasing goods or services. How did you regard the company after your experience?

3. How might the definition of quality apply to your college or university? Provide examples of who some customers are and how their expectations can be met or exceeded.

4. Think of a product with which you are familiar. Describe the eight "multiple quality dimensions" for this product that are listed in this chapter.

5. What might the eight "multiple quality dimensions" mean for a college or university? For a classroom?

6. Explain the differences between manufacturing and service organizations and their implications for quality.

7. Describe the key elements of "total quality management."

8. How might you apply the concepts of total quality to your personal life? Consider your relations with others and your daily activities such as being a student, belonging to a fraternity or professional organization, and so on.

9. Why is a customer focus a critical element of TQM?

10. Make a list of your personal "customers." What steps might you take to understand their needs and remain "close" to them?

11. Cite an example in which you did not purchase a product or service because it lacked "dissatisfiers" as defined in the chapter. Cite another example in which you received some "exciters/delighters" that you did not expect.

12. In what ways might the lack of top management leadership in a quality effort hinder or destroy it?

13. Explain the various areas within an organization in which continuous improvement may take place.

14. Why is measurement important in a TQM effort?

15. Examine some process with which you are familiar. Make a list of ways that the process can be measured and improved. What difficulties might you face in implementing these ideas?

16. Describe the three ways of viewing teamwork.

17. Describe some possible ways in which vertical, horizontal, and interorganizational teamwork can be applied at a college or university.

18. What does empowerment mean? How might an employee really know that he or she is truly empowered?

19. Have you ever felt restricted in your work because of a lack of empowerment? Can you cite any experiences in which you noticed a lack of empowerment in a person who was serving you? Why is this such a difficult concept to implement in organizations?

20. Explain the key differences between "traditional" management practices and those in a TQM environment.

21. Prepare a self-assessment questionnaire designed to determine if an organization follows traditional management practices or a TQM approach. You might consider applying it to some organization.

CASES

Hillshire Farm/Kahn's[18]

In 1971, Consolidated Foods Incorporated (later to be renamed Sara Lee) acquired Quality Packing Company, the forerunner of Hillshire Farm, to complete the meat product lines for their Kahn's division and compete in the smoked sausage market. In 1988 Hillshire Farm merged with Kahn's to gain economies of scale and buying power.

Milton Schloss, president of Kahn's at the time of the acquisition, wanted to produce smoked sausage products that were equal to or superior to the market leader, Eckridge. Hillshire Farm later surpassed Eckridge as the leader in the smoked sausage market.

As president of Hillshire Farm and Kahn's, Schloss was a firm believer in "managing by walking around." He made a habit of making a daily tour of the plant and asking employees "what's new?" One day an employee asked him if he really meant it. This surprised Schloss, and he arranged to meet privately with the employee early the next morning. The employee arrived with a balsa wood model of a new plant layout he had been working on at home. Recognizing the superiority of his ideas, Schloss asked him why he had not come forward sooner. The employee said that nobody had ever asked him. The design was implemented and portions are still in place at Hillshire Farm in Cincinnati. This event was a catalyst for further quality efforts.

Drawing from a similar program at Procter & Gamble, Hillshire Farm developed a system called Deliberate Methods Change (DMC) to seek ways for continually improving their processes. Using DMC, semivoluntary groups of salaried employees met to improve current processes. By emphasizing the positive aspects of improvement and refusing to place blame on workers for process design flaws, these groups built trust among the workforce.

Schloss was a firm believer in quality within the meat industry, and especially at Hillshire Farm. He used customer complaints—or more accurately, what customers found unacceptable—as the basis for defining quality. Schloss personally answered all customer complaints promptly, something that was unheard of at the time. Frequently customers were so surpised to hear from the company president that they apologized for their complaints. However, Schloss listened carefully to understand the nature of the complaint so that he could improve product quality. Also, he believed that a phone call from the company president would allow Hillshire Farm to keep the customer for life.

Schloss took a variety of steps to show his commitment and improve quality. He kept the plant grounds free of litter, freshly painted all the walls, and kept the grass and the shrubbery neatly trimmed. In this way he communicated to employees the attitude they should adopt when they entered the building. Schloss also required that all telephone calls be answered after two rings and that the caller not be kept on hold for long.

The company defined four dimensions of quality—taste, particle definition, color, and packaging—and kept all employees continually informed of the company's quality standards. The accounting and finance departments judged quality according to how promptly and accurately they could make invoices and payments. Marketing and sales were responsible for identifying the features of the product that the customer perceived as most valuable and differentiable and for convincing the customer of Hillshire Farm's leadership in these features.

Schloss personally saw to it that these activities were performed throughout the company. He believed that management must act immediately on new ideas and suggestions. Getting commitment from supervisors was the most difficult task. Management had to explain the "hows and whys" behind the changes, motivate the workers, and recognize the top performers.

When Bill Geoppinger became the CEO at Hillshire Farm and Kahn's, he realized that a great challenge lay ahead. He had inherited an organization that, although focused on quality, was essentially an autocracy. Employees were used to management making the decisions and Geoppinger realized that it would be difficult to make significant changes because of the cultural tradition.

To implement a total quality effort successfully, Geoppinger realized that the corporate culture would have to change, to become more open, flexible, and responsive. He brought in a new management team that emphasized total quality and team approaches and discontinued many of the personal initiatives devised by Milton Schloss. The 1988 merger of Hillshire Farm and Kahn's further served to change the corporate culture. Empowerment of employees became a priority. Management held regular meetings with line employees to give them the opportunity to share their concerns. He encouraged line employees to participate as members of DMC teams. This open culture and focus on empowerment was adapted to all aspects of the business including accounting, finance, and marketing. However, the total quality effort is most visible in production operations.

In 1991 the Deli Select Line implemented statistical process control (SPC). The company was the market leader in this product category and wished to keep its competitive advantage in this low-margin business. The division was relatively new and had new employees who could be empowered with little resistance. Before implementing SPC, the only data they collected was yield, the "efficient use of inputs." The team decided that yield improvement would be a good objective for improving costs. However, they could not sacrifice quality for yield, so they also monitored defect rates. They tracked defect rates by monitoring product specifications of the output and tracking customer complaints.

Calculating product defects was challenging. They had to quantify customers' perceptions of quality from complaint records. Through team efforts, they defined specifications for the product and its packaging. The product was inspected from the customer's point of view, as seen through the package window. Because they continually monitored incoming meat quality in identifying yields, they felt that this amount of inspection was sufficient.

To track defect rates, they pulled a box of finished products at random every hour and inspected for product and packaging characteristics. Points were assigned based on severity and graphed on a control chart. Improvements in defects and yields were both realized using SPC. By statistically tracking customer complaints, they could determine which factors were the greatest cause of concern. For example, fat is a major concern because it is highly visible in darker meat products.

Discussion Questions

1. Based on the facts presented in this case, assess the company in the areas of
   - customer focus
   - strategic planning and leadership
   - continuous improvement
   - empowerment and teamwork

2. List strengths and areas for improvement that you would suggest in each of these categories. Would you state that Hillshire Farm/Kahn's has fully adopted TQM? Why or why not? What steps would you recommend that the company take next?

The Case of the Stalled Quality Program[19]

A manufacturer of electrical parts installed a quality management program that never quite got off the ground. A conversation with two employees, a supervisor and an inspector who was not part of the management team, follows:

SUPERVISOR: We have some problems in inspection. With a certain inspector, we have a large rejection rate. At first, we thought there was something wrong with process variability. So we went in and did all kinds of troubleshooting and found nothing. Having found no assignable cause, we were at a loss and we had to move the inspector to a different position.

INSPECTOR: Our inspection job is made up of two components: one part is visual and is somewhat subjective and the other part uses measuring instruments and is usually objective, provided the instruments are well-calibrated. I have never had any problems with anybody on the second part. Whenever a disagreement arose, we could resolve our differences after recalibrating the measuring instrument. However, I have always had disagreement with the supervisor and other inspectors on the subjective part of the evaluation process. Their (other inspectors) overall rejection rate has been consistently lower than mine. Whenever I go on vacation or am absent, the overall defect rate in my shift goes down. I was constantly blamed for the high defective rates that were produced in my shifts.

CONSULTANT: So how did you go about proving to your supervisor that you had a legitimate point?

Inspector: I did an informal study. I studied the final rejection rate downstream. I divided the data into two parts: the rejection rate for which I was the inspector and the rejection rate for which other inspectors were responsible. I actually collected data, analyzed it, and prepared a report for my supervisor. What I found and reported tells the whole story. The nonconforming rates downstream were a good 10 percent higher for items passed in other shifts. I tried to stress the fact that the visual part of the inspection in the other shifts was not done properly, giving a false sense of productivity only to lead to a higher number of nonconforming items downstream. All my data and reasoning fell on deaf ears and I was shifted from my position to a lesser job with fewer responsibilities.

If you were the consultant to this company, what would you tell the senior management?

ENDNOTES

1. "The Push for Quality," *Business Week*, June 8, 1987, p. 131.

2. J. M. Juran, "Strategies for World-Class Quality," *Quality Progress*, March 1991, pp. 81–85.

3. Stratton, Brad, "Dead Quality," Editorial comment, *Quality Progress,* June 1991, p. 5; Horne, Kim, "Quality and the Dead," Letter to the Editor, *Quality Progress,* November 1991, p. 6.

4. David A. Garvin, "What Does 'Product Quality' Really Mean?", *Sloan Management Review*, Vol. 26, No. 1, (1984), pp. 25–43.

5. "A New Era for Auto Quality," *Business Week,* October 2, 1990, pp. 84–96.

6. Karl Albrecht and Ronald E. Zemke, *Service America*, Homewood, Ill.: Dow Jones-Irwin, 1985.

7. A Parasuraman, V.A. Zeithaml, and L.L. Berry, "SERVQUAL: A Multiple-Item Scale for Measuring Consumer Perceptions of Service Quality," *Journal of Retailing,* Vol. 64, No. 1, Spring 1988, pp. 12–40.

8. King, Carol A. "Service Quality Assurance is Different," *Quality Progress,* Vol. 18, No. 6, June 1985, pp. 14–18.

9. Harold S. Page, "A Quality Strategy for the '80s," *Quality Progress,* Vol. 16, No. 11, November 1983, pp. 16–21.

10. Based on personal communication from Roger Nunley, Director, Industry & Consumer Affairs, Coca-Cola, the Service Quality Survey, and the Industry & Consumer Affairs Department Overview.

11. Kenneth Labich. "An Airline that Soars on Service," *Fortune,* December 31, 1990, pp. 94–96.

12. Adapted from Joseph J. Tsiakals, "Management Team Seeks Quality Improvement From Quality Costs," *Quality Progress,* Vol. 16, No. 4, April 1983, pp. 26–27.

13. Bro Uttal. "Companies that Serve You Best." *Fortune,* December 7, 1987, p. 101.

14. Adapted in part from Ed Baker, "The Chief Executive Officer's Role in Total Quality: Preparing the Enterprise for Leadership in the New Economic Age," *Proceedings of the William G. Hunter Conference on Quality,* Madison Wis., 1989.

15. "Total Quality at Procter & Gamble," The Total Quality Forum, Cincinnati, Ohio, August 6–8, 1991.

16. American Quality Foundation and Ernst & Young, *International Quality Study: Top Line Findings,* 1992.

17. "The Cost of Quality," *Newsweek,* September 7, 1992, pp. 48–49.

18. Appreciation is given to Dr. Reginald Bruce and his students at the University of Cincinnati for this case.

19. Reprinted from *Industrial Engineering* magazine, October 1991, Copyright 1991, Institute of Industrial Engineers, Norcross, GA 30092.

CHAPTER 2

Approaches to Total Quality

Chapter Outline

The Need for New Management Approaches
Approaches to Total Quality
The Deming Management Philosophy
    Profound Knowledge
    Deming's Fourteen Points for Management
The Juran Philosophy
The Crosby Philosophy
Frameworks for Total Quality
    The Malcolm Baldrige National Quality Award
    ISO 9000
Review and Discussion Questions
Cases

In 1987, *Business Week* warned that "unless the United States gets its manufacturing operations back in shape--and fast--it could lose any hope of maintaining the foundation on which tomorrow's prosperity rests."[1] Over the past few decades, the United States lost its dominance in many manufacturing and service industries to Japan and other global competitors.

The inability to compete successfully in a global market has affected the U.S. economy greatly. More than 5 million American workers lost their jobs during the second half of the 1980s. In the early 1990s General Motors and other firms announced massive layoffs and plant closings. At the same time, Japanese and other foreign investors purchased scores of failing American companies, built new factories in the U.S., and made them successful with a total quality approach to managing operations. Clearly, we need to understand the elements of their management practices that breed success.

This chapter introduces you to several philosophies and approaches to quality that are being used to guide total quality initiatives. The objectives of this chapter are

- to define the need for new management practices based on quality,
- to describe the Deming philosophy and compare it to traditional management approaches,
- to discuss the quality management philosophies of Juran and Crosby,
- to provide an overview of the Malcolm Baldrige National Quality Award and ISO 9000 certification as frameworks for total quality.

THE NEED FOR NEW MANAGEMENT APPROACHES

A major study conducted in the late 1980s by the MIT Commission on Industrial Productivity cited five basic reasons why many American companies have lost their ability to compete:[2]

1. Outdated strategies   Firms neglected manufacturing, because business strategies were driven by marketing and finance. Many firms did not invest in the human and physical capital necessary to sustain a competitive manufacturing capability.

2. Short time horizons   American business was (and in many cases, still is) preoccupied with short-term financial results. Companies have not made sufficient investment in research and development, facilities, and the training and education of the workforce. Short-term focus has overshadowed long-term issues such as a firm's ability to satisfy the true needs of customers and stay in business.

3. Technological weaknesses in development and production   Although many companies have made significant technological advances, they did not develop them into affordable and reliable manufactured goods or design effective manufacturing systems to produce them. Foreign competitors took ideas invented here and developed cost-effective processes to produce them quickly with high quality to meet consumer demands.

4. Neglect of human resources   U.S. firms have tended to view labor as a cost rather than a productive and critical resource. The importance of well-trained, well-motivated, and flexible workers has frequently been underestimated.

5. Failures of cooperation Many organizational barriers exist within firms that separate research and development, design, manufacturing, and marketing. These barriers are often bolstered by short-term, protective interests and excessive specialization.

The MIT commission's findings point to *poor management practices* as the key factor in our lack of competitiveness. Japanese startups in the U.S. support this assertion (see box). Sony claims that the production lines in its San Diego plant have the same rate of productivity as those in its Japanese factories. Workers are different, but management standards are the same. A Honda executive has stated that "the quality and productivity of workers depend on management. When Detroit changes its management system, we'll see more powerful American companies."

Japanese- and American-style management differ significantly. Japanese managers often rely on the input of subordinates in determining and clarifying goals and implementing work tasks. Small group problem-solving flourishes in this environment and provides increased motivation. Such participation employs the collective resources of the entire organization.

Today workers require extensive technical skills; the ability to learn, communicate, and adapt to new working conditions and technology; and the ability to work effectively in groups and to handle continuous change. Typical U.S. companies have not taken full advantage of the entire workforce because of their style of management.

American companies typically focus on major innovations rather than on gradual improvements. American management must increase its efforts to adopt a philosophy based on commitment to continuous improvement (without sacrificing important innovations) through the participation of all employees. This is the essence of total quality.

Toyota Management Overhauls Failing GM Plant

In working with General Motors on a joint venture, the New United Motor Manufacturing, Inc. (NUMMI), Toyota transformed a failing California assembly plant into GM's most efficient factory, producing the Toyota Corolla and the Geo Prizm. Before GM closed the plant in 1982, it was a battleground between inflexible managers and a workforce whose rate of absenteeism was 20 percent. Toyota quickly turned it around by hiring the best of the former workforce and replacing GM's 100 job classifications with teams of multiskilled workers. Absenteeism dropped to less than 2 percent. Productivity grew to twice the average level in GM plants. This occurred without any special technology or automation; the difference is in the way Toyota managers organize and operate the plant.

APPROACHES TO TOTAL QUALITY

Despite all the rhetoric, most firms in the United States and Europe have not come anywhere near fully adopting total quality. Adoption requires significant changes in organization design, work processes, and culture. Organizations use a variety of approaches. Some emphasize the use of quality tools, such as statistical process control or quality function deployment, but have not made the necessary fundamental changes in their processes and culture. Although these firms will realize limited improvements, the full potential of total quality is lost due to a lack of complete understanding by the entire organization.

Others have adopted a problem-solving focus in which they identify defects in both production and customer service and work to correct them through quality circles or other team approaches. Although improvements are achieved, they are sporadic and limited. The lack of involvement by management prevents the development of a culture focused on the customer.

A third approach emphasizes error prevention and "building in" quality. Although this approach is customer-focused, firms that follow it may overlook many opportunities for continuous improvement. Still other companies focus on continuous improvement coupled with innovations in work processes and organization strategy. Single approaches, such as statistical process control or quality circles, can have some short-term success, but do not seem to work well over time.

Total quality requires a comprehensive effort that encompasses all of these approaches. A total change in thinking, not a new collection of tools, is needed. Unfortunately it is easy to focus on tools and techniques but very hard to understand and achieve the necessary changes in human attitudes and behavior.

The biggest dangers lie in the lack of complete understanding and the tendency to imitate—the easy way out. The "one best model" of TQM for one organization may not mesh with another organization's culture. Most successful companies have developed unique approaches to fit their own requirements. Research has shown that imitation of the TQM efforts of one successful organization may not lead to good results in another. To use one of Deming's often-quoted phrases, "There is no instant pudding."

Companies use TQM for two basic reasons:

1. to react to competitive threats, and
2. as an opportunity to improve.

Most firms—even Baldrige Award winners—have moved toward TQM for the first reason. Xerox, for example, saw its market share fall from 90 percent to less than 15 percent in a decade; Milliken faced increased competition from Asian textile manufacturers; Zytec Corporation found itself in financial difficulties because of reliance on a single customer. Although not facing dire crises, future threats were also the impetus for the TQ efforts of Federal Express, Solectron, and IBM Rochester.

When faced with a threat to survival, companies have less difficulty embracing TQM. Since a cultural change is necessary, it is more difficult to gain support for TQM when a crisis is not imminent. Some firms such as IBM Rochester—which embarked on TQM even when it was not facing a crisis—suggest that a crisis mentality, whether real or perceived, is necessary to effect change. To rally the troops, management might have to "manufacture" a crisis.

Total quality requires a set of guiding principles. Three individuals—W. Edwards Deming, Joseph M. Juran, and Philip B. Crosby—are the recognized experts or "gurus" of total quality. Among these three, Deming has generated the most interest—and controversy. A discussion of his philosophy, which is actually more about management than quality, follows.[3]

THE DEMING MANAGEMENT PHILOSOPHY

Deming was trained as a statistician and worked for Western Electric during its pioneering era of statistical quality control development in the 1920s and 1930s. During World War II he taught quality control courses as part of the national defense effort. Although Deming taught many engineers in the U.S., he was not able to reach upper management. After the war, Deming was invited to Japan to teach statistical quality control concepts. Top managers there were eager to learn, and he addressed 21 top executives who collectively represented 80 percent of the country's capital. They embraced Deming's message and transformed their industries. By the mid-1970s, the quality of Japanese products exceeded that of Western manufacturers, and Japanese companies had made significant penetration into Western markets.

Deming's contributions were recognized early by the Japanese. The Deming Application Prize was instituted in 1951 by the Union of Japanese Scientists and Engineers in recognition and appreciation for his achievements in statistical quality control. Deming also received the nation's highest honor, the Royal Order of the Sacred Treasure, from the emperor of Japan.

Deming was virtually unknown in the United States until 1980 when NBC aired a white paper entitled "If Japan Can...Why Can't We?" This program made Deming a household name among corporate executives, and companies such as Ford invited him to assist them in revolutionizing their quality approaches.

Deming's philosophy is based on improving products and services by reducing uncertainty and variability in the design and manufacturing processes. In Deming's view, variation is the chief culprit of poor quality. In mechanical assemblies, for example, variations from specifications for part dimensions lead to inconsistent performance and premature wear and failure. Likewise, inconsistencies in service frustrate customers and damage a firm's image. To achieve reduced variation, he advocates a never-ending cycle of product design, manufacture, test, and sales, followed by market surveys, then redesign, and so forth.

Deming stresses that higher quality leads to higher productivity, which in turn leads to long-term competitive strength. The Deming "chain reaction," shown in Figure 2.1, summarizes this view. This theory states that improvements in quality lead to lower costs because of less rework, fewer mistakes, fewer delays and snags, and better use of time and materials. Lower costs, in turn, lead to productivity improvements. With better quality and lower prices, the firm can achieve a higher market share and thus stay in business, providing more and more jobs. Deming states emphatically that top management has the overriding responsibility for quality improvement.

The Deming philosophy of quality and management is complex; indeed, several books have been written in an effort to explain and interpret it. Many of the principles are very basic yet difficult to put into practice. Deming has summarized his philosophy in what he calls "A System of Profound Knowledge."

Profound Knowledge

Profound knowledge consists of four parts: (1) appreciation for a system, (2) some knowledge of the theory of variation, (3) theory of knowledge, and (4) psychology.

Systems   A system is a set of functions or activities within an organization that work together to achieve organizational goals. For example, a McDonald's restaurant can be viewed as a system. It consists of the order-taker/cashier subsystem, grill and food preparation subsystem, drive-through subsystem, and so on.

The components of any system must work together for the system to be effective. When parts of a system interact, the system as a whole cannot be understood or managed solely in terms of its parts. To run any system, managers must understand the interrelationships among all subsystems and the people that work in them. One example is performance appraisal. The following are some of the factors within a system that affect the individual performance of an employee:

- training received
- information and resources provided
- leadership of supervisors and managers
- disruptions on the job
- management policies and practices

However, most performance appraisals do not recognize these factors.

Management must have an *aim*, a purpose to which the system continually strives. Deming believes that the aim of any system is for everybody—stockholders, employees, customers, community, the environment—to gain over the long term. Stockholders can realize financial benefits, employees can

Figure 2.1   **The Deming Chain Reaction**

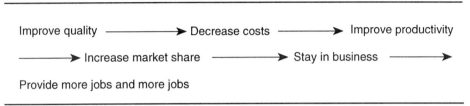

have opportunities for training and education, customers can receive products and services that meet their needs and create satisfaction, the community can benefit from business leadership, and the environment can benefit from socially-responsible management.

Deming emphasizes that management's job is to *optimize* the system. By making decisions that are best for only a small part of the system (often encouraged by competition), we *suboptimize*. Suboptimization results in a loss to everybody in the system. For example, a common practice is to purchase materials or services at the lowest bid. Inexpensive materials may be of such inferior quality that they will cause excessive costs in adjustment and repair during manufacture and assembly. Although purchasing's track record will look good, the system will suffer.

This theory applies to managing people also. Pitting individuals or departments against each other for resources is self-destructive. The individuals or departments will perform to maximize their expected gain, not that of the firm as a whole. Employees must cooperate with each other. Likewise, sales quotas or arbitrary cost reduction goals do not motivate people to improve the system and, ultimately, customer satisfaction; workers will only perform to meet the quotas and goals.

Variation   The second part of Profound Knowledge is some understanding of statistical theory, particularly as it applies to variation. Just as no two snowflakes are exactly alike, no two outputs from any production process are exactly alike. A production process contains many sources of variation. Different lots of material will vary in strength, thickness, or moisture content, for example. Cutting tools will have inherent variation in strength and composition. During manufacturing, tools will experience wear, machine vibrations will cause changes in settings, and electrical fluctuations will cause variations in power. Operators may not position parts on fixtures consistently.

The complex interaction of all these variations in materials, tools, machines, operators, and the environment cannot be understood. Variation due to any individual source appears random; however, their combined effect is stable and can usually be predicted statistically. Factors that are present as a natural part of a process are called *common causes of variation.*

Common causes generally account for about 80 to 90 percent of the observed variation in a production process. The remaining 10 to 20 percent result from *special causes of variation*, often called *assignable causes*. Special causes arise from external sources that are not inherent in the process. A bad batch of material purchased from a supplier, a poorly trained operator, excessive tool wear, or miscalibration of measuring instruments are examples of special causes. Special causes result in unnatural variations that disrupt the random pattern of common causes. Hence they are generally easy to detect using statistical methods, and it is usually economical to remove them.

A system governed only by common causes is said to be *stable*. Understanding a stable system and the differences between special and common causes of variation is essential for managing any system. Management can make two fundamental mistakes in attempting to improve a process:

1. To treat as a special cause any fault, complaint, mistake, breakdown, accident, or shortage when it actually came from common causes.
2. To attribute to common causes any fault, complaint, mistake, breakdown, accident, or shortage when it actually came from a special cause.

In the first case, tampering with a stable system will actually increase the variation in the system. In the second case, we can miss the opportunity to eliminate unwanted variation by assuming that it is not controllable. Changing a system on the basis of a special cause can damage the system and add cost. Variation should be minimized. The producer and consumer both benefit from reduced variation. The producer benefits by having less need for inspection, less scrap and rework, and higher productivity. The consumer is assured that all products have similar quality characteristics; this is especially important when the consumer is another firm using large quantities of the product in its own manufacturing or service operations.

Variation increases the cost of doing business. An example was published in the Japanese newspaper *Asahi* comparing the cost and quality of Sony televisions at plants in Japan and San Diego.[4] The color density of all the units produced at the San Diego plant was within specifications, although the density of some of those shipped from the Japanese plant was not (Figure 2.2). However, the average loss per unit at the San Diego plant was $0.89 greater than that of the Japanese plant. This was because units out of specification at the San Diego plant were adjusted within the plant, adding cost to the process. Furthermore, a unit adjusted to just within specifications was more likely to generate customer complaints than a unit that was closer to the original target value, therefore incurring higher field service costs. Figure 2.2 shows that fewer U.S.-produced sets met the target value for color density. The distribution of quality in the Japanese plant was more uniform around the target value, and even though some units were out of specification, the total cost was less.

The only way to reduce variation due to common causes is to change the technology of the process—the machines, people, materials, methods, or measurement system. The process is under the control of *management*, not the production operators. Pressuring operators to perform at higher quality levels may not be possible and may be counterproductive.

Figure 2.2 Variation in U.S.- versus Japanese-made Television Components

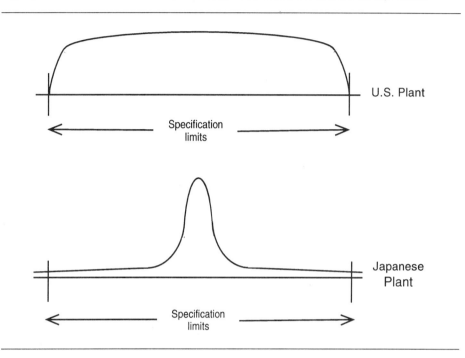

Variation due to special causes can be identified through the use of control charts, which are introduced in Chapter 3. The responsibility for using control charts to identify special causes of variation and to make the necessary corrections should lie with the production operators and their immediate supervisors.

Theory of Knowledge   The third part of Profound Knowledge is the Theory of Knowledge—a branch of philosophy concerned with the nature and scope of knowledge, its presuppositions and bases, and the general reliability of claims to knowledge. Deming was influenced greatly by Clarence Irving Lewis, author of *Mind and the World*.[5] Lewis stated, "There is no knowledge without interpretation. If interpretation, which represents an activity of the mind, is always subject to the check of further experience, how is knowledge possible at all? . . . An argument from past to future at best is probable only, and even this probability must rest upon principles which are themselves more than probable."

Deming emphasizes that there is no knowledge without theory and that experience alone does not establish a theory. To copy an example of success without understanding it with the aid of theory may lead to disaster. Experience only *describes*; it cannot be tested or validated. Theory establishes a cause-and-effect relationship that can be used for prediction. Theory leads to questioning and can be tested and validated—it explains *why*. Many companies have jumped on the latest fads advocated by popular business consultants. Methods that have sustained success are grounded in theory. Managers have a responsibility to learn and apply theory.

Psychology   Psychology helps us to understand people, interactions between people and circumstances, interactions between leaders and employees, and any system of management. People differ from one another. A leader must be aware of these differences and use them to optimize everybody's abilities and inclinations.

Many managers operate under the supposition that all people are alike and treat them as interchangeable components of a process. However, people learn in different ways and at different speeds and perform at different levels. Leaders have an obligation to make changes in the system of management that will bring improvement. People have an innate need for relationships with other people and for self-esteem and respect. Circumstances provide some people with dignity and self-esteem and deny them to other people. People inherit the right to enjoy work. Psychology helps us to nurture and preserve people's positive innate attributes.

Little in Deming's system of Profound Knowledge is original: The concept of common and special causes of variation was developed by Walter Shewhart in the 1920s; behavioral theories to which Deming subscribes were developed in the 1960s; systems theory was refined by management scientists from the 1950s through the 1970s; and scientists in all fields have long understood the relationships among prediction, observation, and theory. Deming's contribution was in tying together some basic concepts. He recognized the synergy among these diverse subjects and developed them into a theory of management.

Deming's Fourteen Points for Management

The 14 Points for Management, listed in Table 2.1, have been the subject of considerable controversy and debate. They have their basis in Profound Knowledge. Many companies have studied and applied them to their organizations.

1. Management Commitment   Businesses should not exist simply for profit; their true purpose should be to serve their customers and employees. To do this, they must take a long-term view and invest in innovation, training, and research. Japanese companies spend considerably more on research and development than those in the United States. Japanese firms are willing to give up short-term profits knowing that they will achieve a high market share several years in the future. Thus, an organization needs a clear mission and statement of purpose.

2. Learn the New Philosophy   American management has been built on the Taylor system which has led to numbers-driven production, quotas, and

---
Table 2.1 Deming's 14 Points for Management[6]

---

1. Create and publish to all employees a statement of the aims and purposes of the company or other organization. The management must demonstrate constantly their commitment to this statement.

2. Learn the new philosophy, top management and everybody.

3. Understand the purpose of inspection, for improvement of processes and reduction of cost.

4. End the practice of awarding business on the basis of price tag alone.

5. Improve constantly and forever the system of production and service.

6. Institute training.

7. Teach and institute leadership.

8. Drive out fear. Create trust. Create a climate for innovation.

9. Optimize toward the aims and purposes of the company the efforts of teams, groups, staff areas.

10. Eliminate exhortations for the workforce.

11. (a) Eliminate numerical quotas for production. Instead, learn and institute methods for improvement.

    (b) Eliminate MBO (Management by Objective). Instead, learn the capabilities of processes and how to improve them.

12. Remove barriers that rob people of pride of workmanship.

13. Encourage education and self-improvement for everyone.

14. Take action to accomplish the transformation.

---

adversarial work relationships. Old methods of management create mistrust, fear, and anxiety with a focus on "satisficing" rather than on "optimizing." Eliminating defects is not good enough. Defect-free production is taken for granted in Japan. Achieving competitive success in today's global economy requires a customer-driven approach based on mutual cooperation between labor and management and a never-ending cycle of improvement. Everyone, from the boardroom to the stockroom, must learn the new philosophy.

3. Understand Inspection Routine inspection acknowledges defects but does not add value to the product. Instead, it encourages defects because "someone else" catches and fixes the problems. This procedure increases costs and decreases productivity. Workers must take responsibility for their own work and be able to take appropriate action to assure good quality. Managers need to understand how variation affects their processes and to take steps to reduce the causes of variation. Inspection should be used as an information-gathering tool for improvement, not as an end in itself.

4. End Price Tag Decisions   Purchasing decisions traditionally have been driven by cost through competitive bidding, not by quality. Costs due to inferior materials and components increase costs in later stages of production and can far exceed the "savings" realized through competitive bidding. The purchasing department is a supplier to the production department and must understand its new role. Suppliers themselves are part of the whole system.

Deming urges businesses to establish long-term relationships with a few suppliers, leading to loyalty and enhanced opportunities for improvement. Management has always justified multiple vendors for reasons such as protection against strikes or natural disasters but has ignored hidden costs such as increased travel to visit suppliers, loss of volume discounts, added setup charges resulting in higher unit costs, and higher inventory and administrative expense. More importantly, using multiple suppliers increases the variation in purchased items and, hence, in the final product.

In contrast, a reduced supply base decreases variation and reduces scrap, rework, and the need to adjust to this variation. Long-term relationships between suppliers and customers allow the supplier to produce in greater quantities and reduce unit costs, foster improved communication, and enhance opportunities for process improvements.

5. Improve Constantly   Western management has typically thought of improvement in the context of large, expensive innovations such as robotics and computer-integrated manufacturing. The success of Japanese manufacturers, however, is due primarily to continuous, small, incremental improvements in design and production. Improved design results from understanding customer needs and from continual market surveys and other sources of feedback. Improved production is achieved by reducing the causes of variation in order to establish a stable, predictable production process. Statistical methods provide one means for doing this. Improvement should go beyond production, encompassing transportation, engineering, maintenance, sales, service, and administration—all areas of the organization.

6 Institute Training   Employees need the proper tools and knowledge to do a good job, and it is management's responsibility to provide these. In addition to specific job skills, all employees should be trained in statistical tools for quality problem solving and continuous improvement. Training not only improves quality and productivity, but also enhances workers' morale by showing them that the company is dedicated to helping them and is investing in their future. Deming notes that in Japan, entry-level managers spend 4 to 12 years on the factory floor and in other activities to learn the problems of production. At Honda of America in Marysville, Ohio, all employees start out on the production floor regardless of their job classification.

7. Institute Leadership   The job of management is leadership and guidance, not supervision and work direction. Supervisors should be coaches, not policemen, and supervision should provide the link between management and the workforce. Leadership can help to eliminate fear and encourage teamwork.

8. Drive Out Fear   Fear in work manifests in many ways: fear of reprisal, fear of failure, fear of the unknown, fear of change. Many workers fear punishment or reprisals for not meeting quotas and for problems of the system that are beyond their control. Managers compete against each other to protect their own jobs or to receive higher performance ratings. Fear encourages short-term, selfish thinking, not long-term improvement for the benefit of all.

9. Optimize Team Efforts   Barriers between individuals and departments lead to poor quality, because "customers" do not receive what they need from their "suppliers." This is often the result of internal competition for raises or performance ratings. Teamwork helps to break down barriers between internal customers and suppliers. The focus should be on meeting customer needs and improving processes. Teamwork is an important means of achieving a company's goals.

Perhaps the biggest barrier to team efforts in the U.S. is between unions and management. With some notable exceptions, the history of management-labor relations in the U.S. has been largely adversarial. Lack of sensitivity to worker needs, exploitation of workers, and poor management practices and policies have freqently resulted in strained relations. Labor also bears its share of the blame. It has had tended to resist any management effort to reduce rigid, rule-based tasks, preferring to adhere to structured approaches that stem from the Taylor principles. Unions, as Deming has said, are a part of the system and must work within the system.

10. Eliminate Exhortations   Motivation can be better achieved through trust and leadership than slogans. Slogans calling for improved quality usually assume that poor quality results from a lack of motivation. Workers cannot improve solely through motivational methods when the system in which they work constrains their performance. On the contrary, they will become frustrated and their performance will decrease further.

11. Eliminate Quotas and MBO (Management by Obiective   Numerical quotas reflect short-term perspectives and do not encourage long-term improvement, particularly if rewards or performance appraisals are tied to meeting quotas. Workers may short-cut quality to reach the goal. If the quota is met, they have no incentive to continue production or to improve quality. Arbitrary management goals without a method for achieving them have no meaning. Further, variation in the system makes year-to-year or quarter-to-quarter comparisons meaningless. The typical American MBO system focus on results, not processes, and encourages short-term behavior. Management must understand the system and the variation within it and seek to improve it in the long-term.

12. Remove Barriers to Pride in Workmanship   The Taylor system has promulgated the view of workers as a "commodity." Factory workers are given monotonous tasks, provided with inferior machines, tools, or materials, told to run defective items to meet sales pressures, and report to supervisors who know nothing about the job. Salaried employees are expected to work evenings and weekends to make up for cost-cutting measures that resulted in layoffs of their colleagues. Many are given the title of "management" so that overtime need not be paid. Management assumes it is smarter than workers and does not use the workers' knowledge and experience to the fullest extent. The key to the loss of pride in workmanship is the loss of control.

Deming believes that one of the biggest barriers to pride in workmanship is performance appraisal. Performance appraisals

- destroy teamwork by promoting competition among employees for limited resources;
- foster mediocrity since objectives typically are driven by numbers and what the boss wants;
- focus on short-term results and discourage risk taking; and
- are not focused on serving the customer.

Deming suggests that there are three categories of performance: the majority who work within the system, those outside the system on the superior side, and those outside the system on the inferior side. Statistical methods provide the means of making this classification. Superior performers should be compensated specially; inferior performers need extra training or a different job.

13. Institute Education   "Training" in number 6 refers to job skills; education refers to self-development. Firms have a responsibility to develop the value and self-worth of the individual. Investing in people is a powerful motivation method.

14. Take Action   The TQM philosophy is a major cultural change and many firms find it difficult. Top management must institute the process and include everyone in it.

One of the first American companies that has embraced the Deming philosophy is Ford Motor Company (see box).

THE JURAN PHILOSOPHY

Joseph M. Juran joined Western Electric in the 1920s during its pioneering days in the development of statistical methods for quality. He spent much of his time as a corporate industrial engineer. In 1951 Juran wrote, edited, and published the *Quality Control Handbook*, now in its fourth edition.

Ford Becomes a Deming Company

Dr. Deming came to Ford in 1981 to meet with the president, Donald Petersen, and other company officials who were stimulated by the program "If Japan Can . . . Why Can't We?" Deming began by giving seminars for top executives and meeting with various employees, suggesting changes corresponding to his 14 Points. Ford managers visited Nashua Corporation, the first American company to incorporate Deming's philosophy, to learn how statistical methods were used there. Chief executives from many of Ford's major suppliers visited Japan. Petersen himself took a course on statistical methods. The 14 Points became the basis for a transformation in Ford's management.

Ford's quality commitment is evident from its "Guiding Principles:"

- *Quality comes first.* To achieve customer satisfaction, the quality of our products and services must be our number one priority.
- *Customers are the focus of everything we do.* Our work must be done with customers in mind, providing better products and services than our competition.
- *Continuous improvement is essential to our success.* We must strive for excellence in everything we do: in our products, in their safety and value--and in our services, our human relations, our competitiveness, and our profitability.
- *Employee involvement is our way of life.* We are a team. We must treat each other with trust and respect.
- *Dealers and suppliers are our partners.* The company must maintain mutually beneficial relationships with dealers, suppliers, and our other business associates.
- *Integrity is never compromised.* The conduct of our company worldwide must be pursued in a manner that is socially responsible and commands respect for its integrity and for its positive contributions to society. Our doors are open to men and women alike without discrimination and without regard to ethnic origin or personal beliefs.

Petersen has stated that "The work of Dr. Deming has definitely helped change Ford's corporate leadership. It is management's responsibility to create the environment in which everyone can contribute to continuous improvement in processes and systems... Dr. Deming has influenced my thinking in a variety of ways. What stands out is that he helped me crystallize my ideas concerning the value of teamwork, process improvement, and the pervasive power of the concept of continuous improvement.

Juran taught quality principles to the Japanese in the 1950s just after Deming and was a principal force in their quality reorganization. Like Deming, he concludes that we face a major crisis due to the loss of sales to foreign competition and the huge costs of poor quality. To solve this crisis, new thinking about quality that includes all levels of the managerial hierarchy is required. Upper management in particular requires training and experience in managing for quality.

Juran's programs are designed to fit into a company's current strategic business planning with minimal risk of rejection. This is in contrast to Deming who proposes sweeping cultural change. Juran contends that employees at different levels of an organization speak in different "languages." (Deming believes statistics should be the common language.) Top management speaks in the language of dollars, workers speak in the language of things, and middle management must be able to speak both languages and translate between dollars and things. Thus, to get top management's attention, quality issues must be cast in the language they understand—dollars. Juran advocates the accounting and analysis of quality costs to focus attention on quality problems. At the operational level, Juran's focus is on increasing conformance to specifications through elimination of defects, supported extensively by statistical tools for analysis. Thus, his philosophy fits well into existing management systems.

Juran defines quality as "fitness for use." (Deming advocates no specific definition.) This is broken down into four categories: quality of design, quality of conformance, availability, and field service. Quality of design focuses on market research, the product concept, and design specifications. Quality of conformance includes technology, manpower, and management. Availability focuses on reliability, maintainability, and logistical support. Field service quality comprises promptness, competence, and integrity.

Juran views the pursuit of quality on two levels: (1) the mission of the firm as a whole is to achieve high product quality, and (2) the mission of each individual department in the firm is to achieve high production quality. Like Deming, Juran advocates a never-ending spiral of activities that includes market research, product development, design, planning for manufacture, purchasing, production process control, inspection and testing, followed by customer feedback. Because of the interdependence of these functions, the need for competent companywide quality management is great. Senior management must play an active and enthusiastic leadership role in the quality management process.

Juran's prescriptions focus on three major aspects of quality called the *Quality Trilogy* (a registered trademark of the Juran Institute): quality planning--the process for preparing to meet quality goals, quality control--the process for meeting quality goals during operations, and quality improvement--the process for breaking through to unprecedented levels of performance.

Quality planning begins with identifying customers, both external and internal, determining their needs, and developing product features that respond to customer needs. Like Deming, Juran asks people to know who uses their products, whether in the next department or in another organization. Quality goals are then established that meet the needs of customers and suppliers alike at a minimum combined cost. The process that can produce the product that meets customers' needs and can meet the quality goals under operating conditions must be designed. Strategic planning for quality should be similiar to the firm's financial planning process. The process should determine short–term and long-term goals, set priorities, compare results with previous plans, and mesh the plans with other corporate strategic objectives.

Quality control involves determining what to control, establishing units of measurement so that data may be objectively evaluated, establishing standards of performance, measuring actual performance, interpreting the difference between actual performance and the standard, and taking action on the difference. In many ways this parallels Deming's emphasis on identifying sources of variation and improving the work system.

Unlike Deming, Juran specifies a detailed program for quality improvement. The quality improvement process involves proving the need for improvement, identifying specific projects for improvement, organizing to guide the projects, diagnosing the causes, providing remedies for the causes, proving that the remedies are effective under operating conditions, and providing control to hold improvements. At all times, hundreds or even thousands of quality improvement projects should be under way in every area of the firm.

Juran's assessment of most companies is that quality control is far and away the top priority among the trilogy and most companies feel they are strong in this category. Quality planning and quality improvement, however, are not important priorities and are significantly weaker in most organizations. He feels that more effort needs to be placed on quality planning and even more on quality improvement.

Juran supports these conclusions with several case examples in which Japanese firms using the same technology, materials, and processes as American firms had much higher levels of quality and productivity. He explains that since the 1950s the Japanese have implemented quality improvement projects at a far greater pace than their Western counterparts. The result is that sometime in the 1970s Japanese product quality exceeded Western quality and continues to improve at a greater pace.

Japanese efforts at quality improvement were supported by massive training programs and top management leadership. Training in managerial quality-oriented concepts as well as training in the tools for quality improvement, cost reduction, data collection, and analysis is one of the most important components of Juran's philosophy. Juran maintains that the Japanese experience leaves little doubt as to the significance of the return on quality training in competitive advantage, reduced failure costs, higher productivity, smaller inventories, and better delivery performance.

THE CROSBY PHILOSOPHY

Philip B. Crosby was corporate vice president for quality at International Telephone and Telegraph (ITT) for 14 years after working his way up from line inspector. After leaving ITT, he established Philip Crosby Associates in 1979 to develop and offer training programs. He is also the author of several popular books. His first book, *Quality is Free*, sold about one million copies.

The essence of Crosby's quality philosophy is embodied in what he calls the Absolutes of Quality Management and the Basic Elements of Improvement. Crosby's Absolutes of Quality Management are as follows:

Quality means conformance to requirements not elegance. Crosby dispells the myth that quality is simply a feeling of "excellence." Requirements must be clearly stated so that they cannot be misunderstood. Requirements are communication devices and are ironclad. Once a task is done, one can take measurements to determine conformance to requirements. The nonconformance detected is the absence of quality. Quality problems become nonconformance problems—that is, variation in output. Setting requirements is the responsibility of management.

There is no such thing as a quality problem. Problems must be identified by the individuals or departments that cause them. There are accounting problems, manufacturing problems, design problems, front-desk problems, and so on. Quality originates in functional departments, not in the quality department, and the burden of responsibility for such problems lies with the functional departments. The quality department should measure conformance, report results, and lead the drive to develop a positive attitude toward quality improvement. This is similar to number 3 of Deming's points.

There is no such thing as the economics of quality: it is always cheaper to do the job right the first time. Crosby supports the premise that "economics of quality" has no meaning. Quality is free. What costs money are all the actions that involve not doing jobs right the first time. The Deming Chain Reaction provides a similar message.

The only performance measurement is the cost of quality. The cost of quality is the expense of nonconformance. Crosby notes that most companies spend 15 to 20 percent of their sales dollars on quality costs. A company with a well-run quality management program can achieve a cost of quality that is less than 2.5 percent of sales, primarily in the prevention and appraisal categories. Crosby's program calls for measuring and publicizing the cost of poor quality. Quality cost data are useful in calling problems to management's attention, selecting opportunities for corrective action, and tracking quality improvement over time. Such data provide visible proof of improvement and recognition of achievement. Juran also supports this theme.

The only performance standard is Zero Defects. Crosby feels that the Zero Defects (ZD) concept is widely misunderstood and resisted. Zero Defects is not a motivational program. It is as follows:

> Zero Defects is a performance standard. It is the standard of the craftsperson regardless of his or her assignment. . . . The theme of ZD is *do it right the first time*. That means concentrating on preventing defects rather than just finding and fixing them.
>
> People are conditioned to believe that error is inevitable; thus they not only accept error, they anticipate it. It does not bother us to make a few errors in our work . . . To err is human. We all have our own standards in business or academic life—our own points at which errors begin to bother us. It is good to get an A in school, but it may be OK to pass with a C.
>
> We do not maintain these standards, however, when it comes to our personal life. If we did, we should expect to be shortchanged every now and then when we cash our paycheck; we should expect hospital nurses to drop a constant percentage of newborn babies...We as individuals do not tolerate these things. We have a dual standard: one for ourselves and one for our work.
>
> Most human error is caused by lack of attention rather than lack of knowledge. Lack of attention is created when we assume that error is inevitable. If we consider this condition carefully and pledge ourselves to make a constant conscious effort to do our jobs right the first time, we will take a giant step toward eliminating the waste of rework, scrap, and repair that increases cost and reduces individual opportunity.[7]

Juran and Deming, on the other hand, would argue that it is pointless, if not hypocritical, to exhort a line worker to produce perfection since the overwhelming majority of imperfections are due to poorly designed manufacturing systems beyond the workers' control.

Crosby's Basic Elements of Improvement include *determination, education*, and *implementation*. By determination, Crosby means that top management must be serious about quality improvement. The Absolutes should be understood by everyone; this can be accomplished only through education. Finally, every member of the management team must understand the implementation process.

Unlike Juran and Deming, Crosby's program is primarily behavioral. He places more emphasis on management and organizational processes for changing corporate culture and attitudes than on the use of statistical techniques. Like Juran and unlike Deming, his approach fits well within existing organizational structures.

Crosby's approach, however, provides relatively few details about how firms should address the finer points of quality management. The focus is on managerial thinking rather than on organizational systems. By allowing managers to determine the best methods to apply in their own firm's situations, his approach tends to avoid some of the implementation problems experienced by firms that have adopted the Deming philosophy.

Crosby's philosophy has not earned the respect of his rivals.[8] Although they agree that he is an entertaining speaker and a great motivator, they say he lacks substance in the methods of achieving quality improvement. Nevertheless, hundreds of thousands have taken his courses in-house or at his Quality College in Winter Park, Florida.

FRAMEWORKS FOR TOTAL QUALITY

The philosophies of Deming, Juran, and Crosby provide fundamental principles on which total quality is based. Business firms tend to be highly individualized. As a result, it is difficult to apply one specific philosophy. Company leaders must understand the differences and commonalities in the three philosophies and tailor an approach that fits their unique culture. The most successful firms, such as Xerox and Motorola, have done this. Aspects of implementation are addressed further in chapter 11.

These philosophies do not provide a comprehensive framework for how to implement total quality within an organization or a means of assessing total quality efforts relative to one's peers or world-class companies. Awards and certification procedures fill this important role. The two most prominent frameworks are the Malcolm Baldrige National Quality Award and ISO 9000 registration.

The Malcolm Baldrige National Quality Award

Recognizing that American productivity was declining, President Reagan signed legislation mandating a national study/conference on productivity in October 1982. The American Productivity and Quality Center (formerly the American Productivity Center) sponsored seven computer networking conferences in 1983 to prepare for a White House Conference on Productivity. The final report on these conferences recommended that "a National Quality Award, similar to the Deming Prize in Japan, [should] be awarded annually to those firms that successfully challenge and meet the award requirements. These requirements and the accompanying examination process should be very similar to the Deming Prize system to be effective."

The Baldrige Award, named after the Secretary of Commerce who was killed in an accident shortly before the Senate acted on the legislation, was signed into law on August 20, 1987. Its purposes are to

- help stimulate American companies to improve quality and productivity for the pride of recognition while obtaining a competitive edge through increased profits;
- recognize the achievements of those companies that improve the quality of their goods and services and provide an example to others;

- establish guidelines and criteria that can be used by business, industrial, governmental, and other enterprises in evaluating their own quality improvement efforts; and
- provide specific guidance for other American enterprises that wish to learn how to manage for high quality by making available detailed information on how winning enterprises were able to change their cultures and achieve eminence.

The Award Examination is based upon criteria designed to provide a standard of excellence for organizations seeking to reach the highest levels of overall quality performance and competitiveness. The examination addresses all key requirements to achieve quality excellence as well as the important interrelationships among these key requirements.

Figure 2.3 illustrates the dynamic relationships among the seven categories of criteria. This framework has four basic elements.

1. Senior executive leadership drives the system, creating the values, goals, and systems, and guides the sustained pursuit of quality and performance objectives.
2. The system comprises a set of well-defined and well-designed processes for meeting the company's quality and performance requirements.
3. Measures of progress provide a results-oriented basis for channeling actions to deliver ever-improving customer value and company performance.
4. The basic goal of the quality process is the delivery of ever-improving value to customers.

To win the award, companies must excel in seven areas:

1. *Senior Executive Leadership* This category examines senior executives' *personal* leadership and involvement in creating and sustaining a customer focus and clear and visible quality values. Leadership drives the management system that guides all activities of the company toward quality excellence. Upper management should set goals and plans for integrating quality principles and practices into their organization. The company's customer focus and quality values must be integrated into day-to-day leadership, management, and supervision of all company units. Management must ensure that everyone in the organization has a clear understanding of their competitive environment. Leadership requires communicating quality values throughout the organization and establishing a measurement system to determine how well these quality values are adopted.

   The organization also has a responsibility to share its quality effort with the public, including the community, business, trade, school, and government organizations. Quality leadership must include business

Figure 2.3 Malcolm Baldrige National Quality Award Criteria Framework

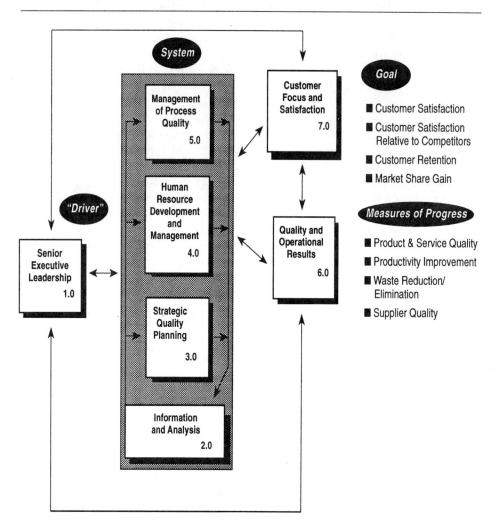

ethics, public health and safety, environmental protection, waste management, and other regulatory requirements.

2. *Information and Analysis*   This category examines the scope, validity, use, and management of data and information to drive quality excellence and improve competitive performance. Sound criteria must be used for the selection of data to support quality programs. The company's base of data must be used to support the firm's overall operational and planning objectives. The company must demonstrate how the data,

information, and analysis support a responsive, prevention-based approach to quality and customer satisfaction built upon "management by fact." Processes must be in place to ensure the consistency, standardization, review, update, and timely access of data. Competitive benchmark measures must be defined so that the organization can accurately assess its position against the industry as a whole and its competitors. A plan must exist to improve these benchmarks.

3. *Strategic Quality Planning*   This category examines the company's planning process for achieving or retaining quality leadership and integrating quality improvement planning into the overall business plan. The planning process defines how the plan will be implemented and how resources will be committed to its key elements. Also examined are the company's short- and long-term plans to achieve and/or sustain a quality leadership position. This includes measures to determine if suppliers can meet quality requirements and the impact that quality requirements will have on the organization.

4. *Human Resource Development and Management*   The areas examined in this category are the effectiveness of the company's efforts to develop and realize the full potential of the workforce, including management, and to maintain an environment conducive to full participation, quality leadership, and personal and organizational growth. The organization must encourage employee involvement, empowerment, teamwork, and innovation. A quality education and training program is necessary for quality improvement, and the effectiveness of such programs must be measured. A performance measurement system must be in place so that employees know how they are doing. They need to be recognized for their achievements and to be involved in the formation of performance measures by which they are evaluated. The company must be able to evaluate whether the performance measures are obtaining the desired results.

Employee well-being and morale are important to quality. Health, safety, satisfaction, and ergonomics are fundamental to working conditions that are conducive to quality. Counseling, assistance, recreation, cultural, and other special programs to help employees are important ingredients of employee well-being. Finally, the organization must determine the level of employee satisfaction and use this information for quality improvement.

5. *Management of Process Quality*. This category examines the systematic processes the company uses to pursue ever-higher quality and company performance. This includes process design, management of process quality for all work units and suppliers, systematic quality improvement, and quality assessment.

Customer needs must be converted into appropriate product and process requirements. The organization must create methods for designing, developing, and validating the products, processes, and services in a timely manner. Process control must be integrated with continuous quality improvement. When a product, process, or service does not meet specifications, the root causes of the problem must be determined and corrected to prevent future problems. Process control methods should be used for continuous improvement.

Documentation to support the quality system must be maintained and shared throughout the organization. In addition, the quality of support services must be assured, assessed, and improved. This includes external suppliers as well as internal support.

6. *Quality and Operational Results*   This category examines the company's quality levels and improvement trends in quality. Current quality levels are reviewed in relation to those of competing firms. Results include not only key product and service features, but also overall company operational performance, business processes and support services, and supplier quality.

7. *Customer Focus and Satisfaction.* The final category examines the company's relationships with customers and its knowledge of customer requirements and of the key quality factors that determine marketplace competitiveness. The company's methods to determine customer satisfaction, current trends and levels of satisfaction are examined and compared to those of its competitors.

Customer problems must be resolved. The scope of complaints must be analyzed to determine the effect on the customer base and used to improve the organization's products and services. Commitment is exemplified through product and service guarantees and warranties. How the company determines customer satisfaction and how its approaches are evaluated and improved are also important. The organization must measure where it stands compared to competitors. They should know if customers have been lost or gained and if market share has changed. The company must also have a scheme to determine future requirements and expectations of customers.

Each major category is assigned a maximum number of points that can be earned during the evaluation process. These points are distributed among several subcategories as shown in Figure 2.4. The scoring system for examination items is based upon three evaluation dimensions: approach, deployment, and results. Approach refers to the methods the company uses to achieve the purposes addressed in each category. Deployment refers to the extent to which the approaches are applied to all relevant areas and activities addressed and implied in each category. Results refers to the outcomes and effects in achieving the purposes addressed and implied in the criteria. Figure 2.5 shows the scoring guidelines that are used.

An Application Guidelines booklet published each year describes in detail the information that must be documented. Like quality itself, the award criteria are being improved each year to reflect the changing process of TQM. The Applications Guidelines booklet can be obtained by contacting the United States Department of Commerce.[9]

Figure 2.4 Baldrige Scoring System

1993 Examination Categories/Items	Point Values

1.0 Leadership — 95

1.1 Senior Executive Leadership 45
1.2 Management for Quality 25
1.3 Public Responsibility and Corporate Citizenship 25

2.0 Information and Analysis — 75

2.1 Scope and Management of Quality and Performance Data and Information 15
2.2 Competitive Comparisons and Benchmarking........................20
2.3 Analysis and Uses of Company-Level Data 40

3.0 Strategic Quality Planning — 60

3.1 Strategic Quality and Company Performance Planning Process 35
3.2 Quality and Performance Plans...25

4.0 Human Resource Development and Management — 150

4.1 Human Resource Planning and Management 20
4.2 Employee Involvement 40
4.3 Employee Education and Training 40
4.4 Employee Performance and Recognition 25
4.5 Employee Well-Being and Satisfaction 25

5.0 Management of Process Quality — 140

5.1 Design and Introduction of Quality Products and Services 40
5.2 Process Management: Product and Service Production and Delivery Processes 35
5.3 Process Management: Business Processes and Support Services 30
5.4 Supplier Quality..20
5.5 Quality Assessment 15

6.0 Quality and Operational Results — 180

6.1 Product and Service Quality Results 70
6.2 Company Operational Results 50
6.3 Business Process and Support Service Results 25
6.4 Supplier Quality Results 35

7.0 Customer Focus and Satisfaction — 300

7.1 Customer Expectations: Current and Future 35
7.2 Customer Relationship Management......................................65
7.3 Commitment to Customers 15
7.4 Customer Satisfaction Determination 30
7.5 Customer Satisfaction Results 85
7.6 Customer Satisfaction Comparison..70

TOTAL POINTS — 1000

Figure 2.5 Baldrige Scoring Guidelines

SCORE	APPROACH/DEPLOYMENT
0%	• anecdotal information; no system evident in information presented
10% to 30%	• beginning of a systematic approach to addressing the primary purposes of the item • significant gaps still exist in deployment that would inhibit progress in achieving the major purposes of the item • early stages of a transition from reacting to problems to preventing problems
40% to 60%	• a sound, systematic approach responsive to the primary purposes of the item • a fact-based improvement process in place in key areas addressed by the item • no major gaps in deployment, though some areas may be in early stages of deployment • approach places more emphasis on problem prevention than on reaction to problems
70%	• a sound systematic approach responsive to the overall purposes of the item • a fact-based improvement process is a key management tool; clear evidence of refinement and improved integration as a result of improvement cycles and analysis • approach is well-deployed, with no significant gaps, although refinement, deployment, and integration may vary among work units or system activities
100%	• a sound, systematic approach, fully responsive to all the requirements of the item • approach is fully deployed without weaknesses or gaps in any areas • very strong refinement and integration—backed by excellent analysis

SCORE	RESULTS
0%	• no data reported or anecdotal data only • data not responsive to major requirements of the item
10% to 30%	• early stages of developing trend data • some improvement trend data or early good performance reported • data are not reported for many to most areas of importance to the item requirements and to the company's key performance-related business factors
40% to 60%	• improvement or good performance trends reported in key areas of importance to the item requirements and to the company's key performance-related business factors • some trends and/or current performance can be evaluated against relevant comparisons, benchmarks, or levels • no significant adverse trends or poor current performance in key areas of importance to the item requirements and to the company's key performance-related business factors
70%	• good to excellent improvement trends in most key areas of importance to the item requirements and to the company's key performance-related business factors or sustained good to excellent performance in those areas • many to most trends and current performance can be evaluated against relevant comparisons, benchmarks, or levels • current performance is good to excellent in most areas of importance to the item requirements and to the company's key performance-related business factors
100%	• excellent improvement trends in most to all key areas of importance to the item requirements and to the company's key performance-related business factors or sustained excellent performance in those areas • most to all trends and current performance can be evaluated against relevant comparisons, benchmarks, or levels • current performance is excellent in most areas of importance to the item requirements and to the company's key performance-related business factors • strong evidence of industry and benchmark leadership demonstrated

According to the guidelines, two companies per year can win a Baldrige Award in each category of manufacturing, small business, and service. Figure 2.6 shows the winners through 1992.

Baldrige Award winners have made stunning achievements within a few years.[10] Customer service response time and defect levels have been reduced by an order of magnitude, productivity has been doubled, and costs have been halved. Improvement has occurred throughout the entire spectrum of the organizations: customer satisfaction, field performance of products, quality of the manufacturing processes, supplier quality, timeliness of customer service, quality of business processes, and employee safety. Most importantly, the employees became experienced at, and got into the habit of, making improvements.

The Baldrige Award criteria form a blueprint for quality improvement in any organization. Thousands of applications are distributed each year, yet only very few completed forms are received. Many companies use the award criteria to evaluate their own quality programs, to set up and implement TQM programs, to communicate better with suppliers and partners, and to educate and train their workers. Using the award criteria as a self-assessment tool provides an objective framework, sets a high standard, and helps compare units that have different systems or organizations. Baldrige Award criteria are also used as the basis for awards within companies and at the local, state, and federal levels.

Figure 2.6 Malcolm Baldrige Award Winner

Year	Manufacturing	Small Business	Service
1988	Motorola, Inc. Westinghouse Commercial Nuclear Fuel Division	Globe Metallurgical, Inc.	
1989	Xerox Corp. Business Products and Systems Milliken & Co.		
1990	Cadillac Motor Car Div. IBM Rochester	Wallace Co., Inc.	Federal Express
1991	Solectron Corp. Zytec Corp.	Marlow Industries	
1992	AT&T Network Systems Texas Instruments	Granite Rock Co.	AT&T Universal Card Services The Ritz-Carlton Hotel Co.

As we have seen, many different philosophies and quality improvement programs exist. Organizations just getting started in quality improvement often have difficulty defining their quality system and setting objectives. The Baldrige Award addresses the full range of quality issues and can help those setting up new systems to get a complete picture of TQM.

The award criteria assist companies with internal communications, communications with suppliers, and communications with other companies seeking to share information. The criteria provide a focus on what to communicate and a framework for comparing strategies, methods, progress, and benchmarks. Finally, the award examination is used for training and education, particularly for management. It represents a summary of major issues that managers must understand and helps draw distinctions between excellence and mediocrity.

ISO 9000

The European free trade agreement, which went into effect at the end of 1992, had a major impact on standardization of quality systems. To standardize requirements for European countries within the Common Market and those wishing to do business with them, a specialized agency for standardization, the International Organization for Standardization (ISO), adopted a series of written quality standards in 1987. The ISO is a powerful body, comprised of representatives from the national standards bodies of 91 nations. The standards are called the ISO 9000 series and have been adopted in the United States by the American National Standards Institute (ANSI) with the endorsement and cooperation of the American Society for Quality Control (ASQC). The standards are recognized by about 100 countries, including Japan. In some foreign markets, companies will not buy from noncertified suppliers. Thus, ISO 9000 registration is becoming a requirement for international competitiveness.

The standards provide basic requirements for quality assurance systems. The standards cover product design and development, manufacturing, testing, final inspection, installation, and service. In product development, the standards require a company to understand customer needs, verify and control the design process to meet requirements, provide employees with correct documentation, assume responsibility for supplier and internal quality, maintain traceability throughout the assembly process, and maintain appropriate records and documentation.

ISO 9000 is not an award like the Baldrige. Companies whose systems are verified to comply with the standards achieve "registration" through a third-party auditor. Unlike the Baldrige criteria, ISO 9000 deals exclusively with quality assurance systems and adherence to procedures; it does not consider activities such as leadership, strategic planning, or customer relationship management. Nevertheless, the rigorous documentation standards help companies uncover problems and improve their processes. At DuPont, for example, ISO 9000 has been credited with helping to increase on-time delivery from 70 to 90 percent, decrease cycle time from 15 days to 1.5 days, increase first-pass yields from 72 to 92 percent, and reduce the number of test procedures by one-third.

REVIEW AND DISCUSSION QUESTIONS

1. Explain the relationship of quality to the five reasons for the lack of competitiveness cited by the MIT Commission. How does TQM address these issues?

2. Prepare a report investigating Japanese "transplants" in the United States. Focus on the differences in management styles between these firms and their traditional American counterparts. What conclusions do you draw?

3. What is wrong with imitating the successes of world-class organizations?

4. Summarize the Deming management philosophy. Why has it been very controversial?

5. Explain the 14 Points in the context of the four categories of Profound Knowledge.

6. How might Deming's concepts of variation be applied to the classroom?

7. Why doesn't the Deming Chain Reaction terminate with "Increased Profits"? Would this contradict the basis of Deming's philosophy?

8. Provide an example of a system with which you are familiar and define its purpose. Examine the interactions within the system and whether the system is managed for optimization.

9. Describe a process with which you are familiar. List some factors that contribute to common cause variation. Cite some examples of special causes of variation in this process.

10. How does the theory of knowledge apply to education? What might this mean for improving the quality of education?

11. Extract three or four key themes in Deming's 14 Points. How might the 14 Points be grouped in a logical fashion?

12. What implications might the 14 Points have for college education? What specific proposals might you suggest as a means of implementing the 14 Points at your school?

13. Summarize Juran's philosophy. How is it similar to and different from Deming's?

14. What is Juran's Quality Trilogy? Is it any different from management approaches in other functional areas of business, such as finance?

15. What implications might Juran's Quality Trilogy have for colleges and universities? Would most faculty and administrators agree that the emphasis has been on quality control rather than planning and improvement?

16. How could you apply Juran's Quality Trilogy to improve your personal approach to study and learning?

17. Summarize the Crosby philosophy. How does it differ from Deming and Juran?

18. Which quality philosophy—Deming, Juran, or Crosby—do you personally feel more comfortable with? Why?

19. Summarize the framework of the Baldrige Award. What are its key philosophical underpinnings?

20. Explain how the philosophies of Deming, Juran, and Crosby relate to the categories in the Baldrige Award. To do this, you might create a matrix with the elements of the philosophies down the rows, and elements of the Baldrige Award across the columns. A checkmark in the matrix would indicate a relationship between the two elements.

21. Prepare a list of specific actions that a high-scoring company in the Baldrige Award process might take in each of the seven categories. How difficult do you think it is for a company to score well in all the categories?

22. What is ISO 9000? How does it differ from the Baldrige Award?

CASES

The Rise and Fall of WonderTech[11]

In the mid-1960s a new electronics company, WonderTech, was founded with a unique high-tech product—a new type of computer. Because of its engineering expertise, WonderTech had a virtual lock on its market. The demand for its products was enormous, and the investors were plentiful. Sales in the first three years were so good that backlogs of orders began to pile up midway through their second year. Even with steadily increasing manufacturing capacity (more factories, more shifts, more advanced technology), the demand grew so fast that delivery times began to slip. Originally WonderTech promised to deliver machines within eight weeks. They intended to return to that standard, but management told investors, "Our computers are so good that some customers are willing to wait fourteen weeks for them. We know it's a problem, and we're working to fix it, but nonetheless they're *still* glad to get the machines, and they love 'em when they get 'em."

The top management knew that they had to add production capacity. After six months of study, they decided to borrow the money to build a new factory. To make sure the growth continued, they pumped much of the incoming revenue directly back into sales and marketing. The company sold its products only through a direct sales force, so they had to hire and train more salespeople. During the company's third year, the sales force doubled.

Despite these efforts, sales started to slump at the end of the third year. At this point, the new factory came on-line. Top management began to panic. The marketing VP was under the fire to turn sales around. He held high-powered sales meetings with a single message: "Sell! Sell! Sell!" He fired the low performers and increased sales incentives, added special discounts, and ran new advertising promotions.

Sales rose again, as did order backlogs. After delivery times began to rise again—first to ten weeks, then to twelve, and eventually to sixteen—the debate over adding capacity started anew. This time management was more cautious. Eventually the approval of a new facility was granted, but no sooner had the papers been signed than a new sales crisis began. The same situation recurred over the next several years. High sales growth occured in spurts, followed by periods of low or no growth. The company prospered modestly, but never came close to fulfilling its original potential. Gradually, top managers began to fear competition and frantically introduced ill-conceived improvements in the product. They continued to push hard on marketing, but sales never returned to its original rate of growth. Eventually the company collapsed.

Discussion Questions

1. What factors led to the demise of WonderTech?
2. Could these factors have been overcome through a better understanding of a system as advocated in Deming's Profound Knowledge?

The Pursuit of ISO 9000 Registration[12]

A major national manufacturer of chemical products has a well-established TQM program. Its most recent effort involved preparing for ISO 9000 registration. The Director of Quality, who had spent some time in the European division, saw the emphasis on ISO in Europe and felt that the firm would be at a significant competitive disadvantage if it did not pursue registration. In the spring of 1992, additional staff was hired in an attempt to register a midwest plant by the end of the first quarter of 1993.

In the purchasing department, the additional work required to document the purchase of raw materials required three additional employees, bringing the number up to 10. All have been intimately involved in the preparation for registration. Many thousands of raw materials are used, and ISO requires that each of their specifications be reviewed, updated, and documented. One of the new employees focuses primarily on training the department's employees in the new procedures. Purchasing agents see many potential benefits. Documentation of specifications will ensure more consistent materials purchases. Training documentation allows the department to tell what training requirements will be needed by new employees.

In manufacturing, ISO appears to be just another quality program. In the past management would be "gung-ho" over the newest program, but then enthusiasm would die. Employees were never told that the program had ended and never saw any benefits. One technician saw no real incentives to participate and felt that management was simply forcing the program on the employees. He felt that employees on different shifts had their own way of performing their work, and that standard operating procedures would never be followed. The technician compared the ISO effort to a previous program on safety. With the safety program, improvements were made at the insistence of the employees. The benefit that the workers derived was quite evident. The benefits to be gained through ISO are not as clear.

Discussion Questions

1. Contrast the attitudes in the purchasing department and manufacturing about the ISO registration process. How might these be explained in terms of organizational behavior theories?
2. How might the company's pursuit of ISO registration be viewed using expectancy theory?
3. What must this company do to be successful in its efforts?

ENDNOTES

1. *Business Week*, 20 April 1987, p. 56.

2. Michael L. Dertouzos, Richard K. Lester, and Robert M. Solow, and the MIT Commission on Industrial Productivity, *Made in America: Regaining the Productive Edge*, Cambridge, Mass.: The MIT Press, 1989.

3. W. Edwards Deming, *Out of the Crisis*, Cambridge, Mass.: MIT Center for Advanced Engineering Study, 1986.

4. April 17, 1979; cited in L. P. Sullivan, "Reducing Variability: A New Approach to Quality," *Quality Progress*, Vol. 17, No. 7, July 1984, pp. 15–21.

5. Mineola, N.Y.: Dover 1929.

6. Reprinted from *Out of the Crisis* by W. Edwards Deming by permission of MIT and W. Edwards Deming. Published by MIT, Center for Advanced Engineering Study, Cambridge, MA 02139. Copyright 1986 by W. Edwards Deming.

7. Philip B. Crosby, *Quality is Free*, New York: McGraw-Hill, 1979, pp. 200–201.

8. Main, *ibid.*

9. Copies of the current year application guidelines can be obtained by writing to the Malcolm Baldrige National Quality Award, National Institute of Standards and Technology, Route 270 and Quince Orchard Road, Administration Building Room A537, Gaithersburg, MD 20899.

10. J.M. Juran, "Strategies for World-Class Quality," *Quality Progress*, March 1991, pp. 81–85.

11. Adapted from Peter Senge, *The Fifth Discipline*, New York: Doubleday, 1990.

12. We thank our colleague, Dr. Reg Bruce and his students, Susan Bennet, Jane Glazer, and Jeff Hempfling, for providing the facts in this case.

CHAPTER 3

Tools and Techniques for Quality Planning and Improvement

Chapter Outline

Tools for Quality Planning
    Quality Function Deployment
    Concurrent Engineering
    The Seven Management and Planning Tools
Tools for Continuous Improvement
    The Deming Cycle
    Tools for Data Collection and Analysis
    Benchmarking
Summary
Review and Discussion Questions
Case

J oseph Juran describes quality management as the "Quality Trilogy": planning, control, and improvement. He says that most managers devote too much attention to control, and too little to planning and improvement—which may be the most important activities for meeting and exceeding customer expectations and gaining competitive advantage. Quality practitioners have adapted a variety of tools from other disciplines such as statistics, operations research, and creative problem solving to aid the planning and improvement processes. This chapter describes and illustrates some of the most useful and popular tools. Since the focus of this book is management, organization, and strategy, this chapter is intended to be only an elementary introduction. The list presented here is by no means exhaustive. The bibliography at the end of the book provides supplementary reading on these and other tools for quality improvement.

The objectives of this chapter are

- to describe how quality function deployment and concurrent engineering can improve the process of designing products and services to achieve better customer satisfaction,
- to show how simple graphical tools can improve management planning,
- to describe and illustrate the Deming Cycle—a simple methodology for continuous improvement, and
- to discuss the application of basic statistical tools for quality problem solving.

The tools we describe can be broadly categorized into two groups: tools for planning and tools for continuous improvement. Planning tools—which include quality function deployment, concurrent engineering, and the "new seven" management and planning tools—are designed to assist managers in planning the quality effort and making efficient use of information. They are often used by cross-functional teams in their quality planning efforts. Tools for continuous improvement—which include the Deming cycle, tools for data analysis, and benchmarking—are means of improving the manufacturing and service systems. The Deming cycle and basic statistical tools are usually found in basic quality training for all employees of an organization and are used by problem-solving teams to attack specific quality problems. Benchmarking is used at all levels of the firm to better understand its processes relative to its competitors' and to make significant improvements in operations.

TOOLS FOR QUALITY PLANNING

Customers' needs and expectations drive the planning process for products and the systems by which they are produced. Marketing plays a key role in identifying customer expectations. Once they are identified, managers must translate them into specific product and service specifications that manufacturing and service delivery processes must meet. In some cases the product or service that customers receive is quite different from what they expect. It is management's responsibility to minimize such gaps. Firms use several tools and approaches to help them focus on their external and internal customers. This section introduces three of these tools.

Quality Function Deployment

Quality function deployment (QFD) is a methodology used to ensure that customers' requirements are met throughout the product design process and in the design and operation of production systems. QFD is both a philosophy and a set of planning and communication tools that focuses on customer requirements in coordinating the design, manufacturing, and marketing of goods.

QFD originated in 1972 at Mitsubishi's Kobe shipyard site. Toyota began to develop the concept shortly thereafter, and it has been used since 1977. The results have been impressive: Between January 1977 and October 1979, for example, Toyota realized a 20 percent reduction in start-up costs on the launch of a new van. By 1982 start-up costs had fallen 38 percent from the 1977 baseline, and by 1984 they were reduced by 61 percent. In addition, development time fell by one-third and quality had improved.

Today QFD is successfully used by manufacturers of electronics, appliances, clothing, and construction equipment, and by firms such as General Motors, Ford, Mazda, Motorola, Xerox, Kodak, IBM, Procter and Gamble, Hewlett-Packard, and AT&T. The 1992 Cadillac was planned and designed entirely with QFD. The concept has been publicized and developed in the U.S. by the American Supplier Institute, Inc., a nonprofit organization and GOAL/QPC, a consulting firm in Massachusetts.

A major benefit of QFD is improved communications and teamwork among all constituencies in the production process—marketing and design, design and manufacturing, and purchasing and suppliers. With QFD, product objectives are more likely to be understood and interpreted correctly during the production process. QFD helps to determine the causes of customer dissatisfaction and is a useful tool for competitive analysis of product quality by top management. Productivity as well as quality improvements result and, most significantly, the time needed for new product development is reduced. QFD allows companies to simulate the effects of new design ideas and concepts. This allows them to bring new products into the market sooner and to gain competitive advantage.

The term *quality function deployment* represents the overall concept that provides a means of translating customer requirements into the appropriate technical requirements for each stage of product development and production. The customers' requirements—expressed in their own terms—are appropriately called *the voice of the customer*. These are the collection of customer needs, including all satisfiers, delighters/exciters, and dissatisfiers—the "whats" that customers want from a product.

For example, a consumer might ask that a dishwashing liquid be "long lasting" and "clean effectively" or that a portable stereo have "good sound quality." Sometimes these requirements are referred to as *customer attributes*. Under QFD all operations of a company are driven by the voice of the customer, rather than by top management edicts or design engineers' opinions.

Technical features are the translation of the voice of the customer into technical language. They are the "hows" that determine the means by which customer attributes are met. For example, a dishwashing detergent loosens grease and soil from dishes. The soil becomes trapped in the suds so dishes can be removed from the water without picking up grease. Eventually the suds become saturated with soil and break down. Thus, a technical feature of a dishwashing liquid would be the weight of greasy soil that the suds generated by a fixed amount of dishwashing liquid can absorb before breaking down. Another might be the size of the soap bubble (which, incidently, has been found to be a key attribute of customers' perception of cleaning effectiveness!). Technical features of a stereo system that affect sound quality include the frequency response, flutter (the wavering in pitch), and the speed accuracy (a cassette tape player should have a speed of 1-7/8 inch/second—inconsistency affects the pitch and tempo of the sound).

A set of matrices is used to relate the voice of the customer to technical features and production planning and control requirements. The basic planning document is called the *customer requirement planning matrix*. Because of its structure (Figure 3.1), it is often referred to as the *House of Quality*. The House of Quality relates customer attributes to technical features to ensure that any engineering decision has a basis in meeting a customer need.

Building the House of Quality requires six basic steps:

1. Identify customer attributes.
2. Identify technical features.
3. Relate the customer attributes to the technical features.
4. Conduct an evaluation of competing products.

Figure 3.1   The House of Quality

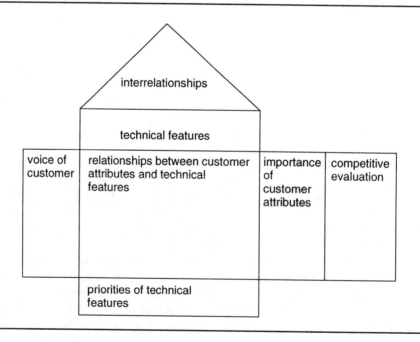

5. Evaluate technical features and develop targets.

6. Determine which technical features to deploy in the production process.

The first step is identifying customer attributes. In applying QFD, it is important to use the customer's own words so as not to have customer needs misinterpreted by designers and engineers. Recall that not all customers are end-users. For a manufacturer, customers might include government regulators, wholesalers, and retailers. Thus, many classes of customer needs may exist.

The second step is listing the technical features that are necessary to meet customer requirements. These technical features are design attributes expressed in the language of the designer and engineer. They form the basis for subsequent design, manufacturing, and service process activities. They must be measurable, because the output will be controlled and compared to objective targets.

The roof of the House of Quality shows the interrelationships between any pair of technical features. Various symbols are used to denote these relationships. A typical scheme is to use the symbol ⊙ to denote a very strong relationship, ○ for a strong relationship, and △ to denote a weak relationship. These notations help determine the effects of changing one product characteristic and enable planners to assess the tradeoffs between characteristics. This process enables designers to focus on features collectively rather than individually.

Next, a relationship matrix between the customer attributes and the technical features is developed. Customer attributes are listed down the left column, and technical features are written across the top. In the matrix itself, a symbol is used to indicate the degree of relationship in a manner similar to that used in the roof of the House. The purpose of the relationship matrix is to show whether the final technical features adequately address the customer attributes. This assessment may be based on expert experience, customer responses, or controlled experiments.

Technical features can affect several customer attributes. The lack of a strong relationship between a customer attribute and any of the technical features suggests that the attributes are not being addressed and that the final product will have difficulty meeting customer needs. Similarly, if a technical feature does not affect any customer attribute, it may be redundant or the designers may have missed an important customer attribute.

The next step is adding market evaluation and key selling points. This step includes rating the importance of each customer attribute and evaluating existing products on each of the attributes. Customer importance ratings represent the areas of greatest interest and highest expectations to the customer. Competitive evaluation helps highlight the absolute strengths and weaknesses of competing products. This step enables designers to seek opportunities for improvement. It also links QFD to a company's strategic vision and allows priorities to be set in the design process. For example, focusing on an attribute that receives a low evaluation on all competitors' products can help to gain a competitive advantage. Such attributes become key selling points and help establish promotion strategies.

Next comes the evaluation of the technical features of competitive products and the development targets. This is usually accomplished through in-house testing and translated into measurable terms. These evaluations are compared with the competitive evaluation of customer attributes to find inconsistencies. If a competing product best satisfies a customer attribute, but the evaluation of the related technical feature indicates otherwise, then either the measures used are faulty or the product has an image difference (either positive toward the competitor or negative toward the product) that affects customer perceptions. Targets for each technical feature are set on the basis of customer importance ratings and existing product strengths and weaknesses.

The final step in building the House of Quality is selecting technical features to be deployed in the remainder of the process. This means identifying the characteristics that have a strong relationship to customer needs, have poor competitive performance, or are strong selling points. These characteristics need to be deployed—or translated into the language of each function—in the design and production process, so that proper actions and controls are taken to maintain the voice of the customer. Characteristics that are not identified as critical do not need such rigorous attention.

A simple example of a House of Quality is shown in Figure 3.2 for the hypothetical case of a quick-service franchise that wishes to improve its hamburger. The voice of the customer consists of four attributes. The hamburger should

- be tasty,
- be healthy,
- be visually appealing, and
- provide good value.

The technical features that can be designed into the product are price, size, calories, sodium content, and fat content. The symbols in the matrix show the relationships between each customer attribute and technical feature. For example, taste bears a strong relationship to sodium content, a moderate relationship to fat content, and a weak relationship to caloric content. In the roof of the house, price and size are seen to be strongly related (as size increases, the price must increase). The competitive evaluation shows that competitors are currently weak on nutrition and value; these can become key selling points in a marketing plan if the franchise can capitalize on them. Finally, at the bottom of the house, are targets for the technical features based on an analysis of customer importance ratings and competitive ratings. The features assigned asterisks will be deployed in subsequent design and production activities.

The House of Quality provides marketing with an important tool to understand customer needs and gives top management strategic direction.

Figure 3.2 House of Quality Example

	Price	Size	Calories	Sodium	Fat	Customer Importance	Competitive Evaluation		
							Us	A	B
Taste			△	⊙	○	4	3	4	5
Nutrition			⊙	○	⊙	4	3	2	3
Visual appeal	△	⊙			△	3	3	5	4
Good value	⊙	○				5	4	3	4
Our priority	5	4	4	4	5				
Competitor A	2	5	3	2	4				
Competitor B	3	4	4	3	3				
Deployment	∗	∗			∗				

Legend: 1 = low, 5 = high

⊙ = very strong relationship
○ = strong relationship
△ = weak relationship

However, it is only the first stage in the QFD process. The voice of the customer must be carried throughout the production process. Three other houses of quality are used to deploy the voice of the customer to component parts characteristics, process planning, and production planning. These are

1. *Technical features deployment matrix*, which translates technical features of the final product into design requirements for critical components.

2. *Process plan and quality control charts*, which translates component features into critical process and product parameters and control points for each.

3. *Operating instructions*, which identifies operations to be performed by plant personnel to assure that important process and product parameters are achieved.

Most of the QFD activities represented by the first two houses of quality are performed by people in the product development and engineering functions. At the next stage, the planning activities begin to involve supervisors and production-line operators. This represents the transition from planning to execution. If a product component parameter is critical and is created or affected during the process, it becomes a control point. This tells the company what to monitor and inspect and forms the basis for a quality control plan for achieving those critical characteristics that are crucial to achieving customer satisfaction. The last house relates the control points to specific requirements for quality assurance activity. This includes specifying control methods, sample sizes, and so on, to achieve the necessary level of quality.

The majority of QFD applications in the United States concentrate on the first, and to some extent the second, house of quality. Lawrence Sullivan, who brought QFD to the West, suggests that the third and fourth houses offer far more significant benefits, especially in the U.S.[1] Japanese managers, engineers, and workers are more naturally cross-functional and tend to promote group effort and consensus thinking. U.S. workers are more vertically oriented and tend to suboptimize for individual and/or departmental achievements. Beginning to emphasize effective cross-functional interactions as supported by QFD will enable U.S. firms to be more competitive with foreign rivals. The third and fourth houses of quality utilize the knowledge of about 80 percent of a company's employees—if they are not used, this potential is wasted.

Concurrent Engineering

A topic closely related to QFD is *concurrent engineering*. This is the concept that all major functions that contribute to getting a product to market have continuing product-development involvement and responsibility from original concept through sales.

The designer's objective is to create a product that meets the desired functional requirements. The manufacturing engineer's objective is to produce the designed product efficiently. The salesperson's goal is to sell the product, and that of finance personnel is to make a profit. Purchasing must ensure that purchased parts meet quality requirements. Packaging and distribution personnel must ensure that the product reaches the customer in good operating condition. Since all these functions have a stake in the product, they must all work together.

Unfortunately, the product development process in many large firms is carried out in a serial fashion with little cooperation among departments. In the early stages of development, design engineers dominate the process. Later the prototype is transferred to manufacturing for production. Finally, marketing and sales personnel are brought in.

This approach has several disadvantages. First, product development time is long. Second, up to 90 percent of manufacturing costs may be committed before manufacturing engineers have any input to the design. Third, the final product may not be the best one for market conditions when it is introduced.

Ford Motor Company was the first U.S. automotive firm to move away from this traditional approach when developing the Taurus/Sable.[2] "Team Taurus" took an approach in which representatives from all the various units— planning, design, engineering, and manufacturing—worked together as a group. Communication was dramatically improved, and many problems were resolved much earlier in the process. For instance, manufacturing suggested changes in design that resulted in higher productivity and better quality.

Comprehensive market surveys were conducted to determine customers' wants and preferences. Ford even asked assembly-line workers for their advice before the car was designed. Workers complained that they had trouble installing doors because the body panels were made up of too many pieces. Designers reduced the number of panels from eight to two. One worker suggested that all bolts should have the same head size so that they would not have to change wrenches constantly. The Taurus/Sable has been one of Ford's biggest success stories and has established new levels of quality for American automakers. Chrysler and General Motors have moved toward similar styles of product development.

Multifunctional teams of 4 to 20 members typically comprise concurrent engineering teams. The functions of such teams include the following:

1. Distinguishing the character of the product in order to determine appropriate design and production methods, and ensuring that the product can be repaired easily.

2. Analyzing product functions so that all design decisions can be made with full knowledge of how the item is supposed to work and so that all team members understand it well enough to contribute.

3. Relating product function to production methods. Computer-aided design tools allow a designer to simulate product performance by varying assumptions within a computer model.

4. Performing a design-for-manufacturability study to determine if the design can be made easier to produce without affecting performance.

5. Designing an assembly sequence that integrates quality control and ensures that each part is designed so that its quality is compatible with the assembly method.

6. Designing a factory system that fully involves workers in the production strategy, operates on minimal inventory, and is integrated with suppliers' methods and capabilities.

One example of an aggressive product-development effort based on concurrent engineering is Cincinnati Milacron. Milacron code-named its effort "Wolfpack" because wolves work in packs and have the instinct to kill. Fifteen teams of managers drawn from different areas of the company are responsible for developing globally competitive machines at significantly lower costs. The Wolfpack concept has cut lead time for new products from 3 years to 18 months and allowed Milacron to regain lost market leadership in several areas.[3]

The New Seven Management and Planning Tools

Many of the problems in implementing the Deming Cycle and Quality Function Deployment are due to the way that American managers have become accustomed to planning and organizing businesses based on Frederick W. Taylor's philosophy.[4]   The barriers to effective planning and quality improvement efforts have been

- strict departmentalization that has separated the planners (staff specialists, such as QA and industrial engineers) from the doers (line and functional managers), thus limiting the abilities of both to make significant improvements;
- relegating planning to a seat-of-the-pants approach, due to the perception that it is either too theoretical to be of practical use or too detailed to be interesting or action-oriented;
- a lack of available tools to make planning available and timely for managers to use.

The seven management and planning tools had their roots in post-World War II operations research developments in the U.S., but were combined and refined by several Japanese companies over the past several decades as part of their planning processes. They were popularized in the United States by the consulting firm GOAL/QPC and have been used by a number of firms since 1984 to improve their quality planning and improvement efforts. They are only new to managers who have not previously seen what powerful aids they can be in improvement processes.

These tools can be used to address problems typically faced by managers who are called upon to structure unstructured ideas, make strategic plans, and organize and control large, complex projects. They have helped to overcome the barriers listed previously and have given managers tools appropriate to their specific needs for planning and implementing quality improvement efforts. Due to space limitations, only a brief discussion of each tool follows. (See books by Brossart, Brassard, and Mizuno[5] for further details and examples.)

Affinity Diagram/KJ Method   This is a technique for gathering and organizing a large number of ideas, opinions, and facts relating to a broad problem or subject area. It enables problem solvers to sift through large volumes of information efficiently and to identify natural patterns or groupings in the information. This method was developed in the 1960s by Kawakita Jiro, a Japanese anthropologist. "KJ" is a trademark registered by the Kawayoshida Research Center.

The technique requires that a group of six to eight people meet to consider a broad issue, such as identifying the elements of poor quality cost for their organization. Responses can be recorded on a flip-chart or on small cards that can be posted and moved around on a board. For example, in determining the elements of quality cost, the group will probably list various elements in a random fashion. Once many ideas have been generated, they can be grouped according to their "affinity," or relationship, to each other. An example is shown in Figure 3.3. This technique helps managers focus on the key issues and their elements rather than an unorganized collection of information.

The Affinity Diagram/KJ Method is intended to be a creative, rather than a logical process. It resembles brainstorming and "story-boarding," a technique developed by Walt Disney to create cartoons and movies.

Interrelationship Digraphs   The purpose of an interrelationship digraph is to take a central idea and map out logical or sequential links among related categories. It shows that every idea can be logically linked with more than one idea at a time, and allows for "lateral" rather than "linear" thinking. This technique often is used after the Affinity Diagram has brought issues and problems into clearer focus. Figure 3.4 shows an example of how failure costs are influenced by other factors.

Like affinity diagrams, this technique also depends on getting together a team of people who own the problem. Some of the same cards or flip-chart lists developed in the Affinity Diagram can be duplicated and used in this technique. New cards or lists of specific items must be added frequently as the issue becomes more focused.

Figure 3.3   Example of an Affinity Diagram

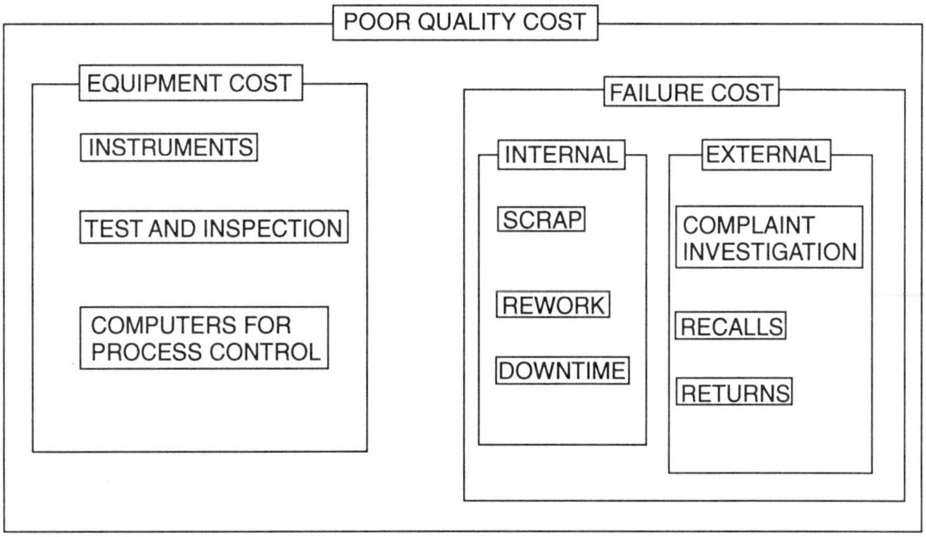

Figure 3.4   Example of an Interrelationship Digraph

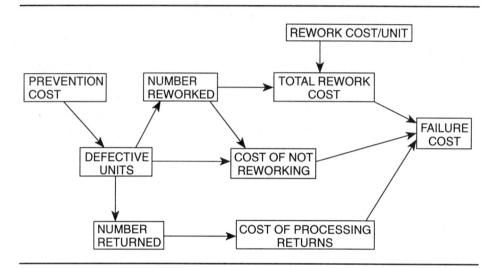

Tree Diagram   A tree diagram maps out the paths and tasks that need to be accomplished to complete a specific project or to reach a specified goal. A planner uses this technique to seek answers to such questions as "What sequence of tasks needs to be completed to address the issue?" or "What are all of the factors that contribute to the existence of the key problem?"

This technique brings the issues and problems disclosed by the Affinity Diagram and the Interrelationship Digraph down to the operational planning stage. A clear statement of the problem or process must be specified. From this general statement, a team can be established to recommend steps required to solve the problem or implement the plan. The "product" produced by this group would be a tree diagram with activities and recommendations for timing the activities. Figure 3.5 shows an example of some of the key elements in establishing a quality cost system.

Matrix Diagrams   These are spreadsheets that graphically display relationships between characteristics, functions, and tasks in such a way as to provide logical connecting points between each item. The House of Quality is an example of one of the many matrix diagrams now used for planning and quality improvement.

Matrix Data Analysis   This process takes data from matrix diagrams and seeks to arrange it quantitatively to display the strength of relationships among variables so that they can be easily viewed and understood. Matrix data analysis is a rigorous, statistically-based "factor analysis" technique. GOAL/QPC feels that this method, although worthwhile for many applications, is too

Figure 3.5 Example of a Tree Diagram

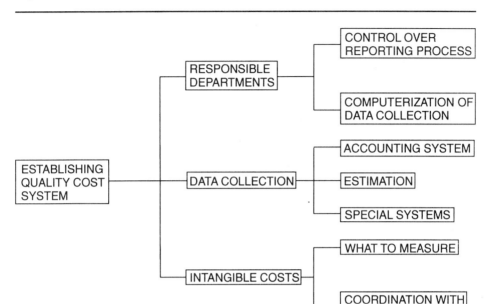

quantitative to be used on a daily basis and has developed an alternative tool called a *prioritization matrix* that is easier to understand and implement. This approach bears a lot of similarity to decision matrices that you may have studied in a quantitative methods course. Interested readers should consult Brassard's book for further details.

Process Decision Program Chart (PDPC)   This is a method for mapping out every conceivable event and contingency that can occur when moving from a problem statement to possible solutions. It is used to plan for each possible chain of events that could occur when a problem or goal is unfamiliar. A PDPC takes each branch of a tree diagram, anticipates possible problems, and provides countermeasures that will prevent the deviation from occurring or be in place if the deviation *does* occur. Figure 3.6 shows one example.

Arrow Diagrams   These have been used by construction planners for years in the form of CPM and PERT project planning techniques. Arrow diagramming has also been taught extensively in quantitative methods, operations management, and other business and engineering courses in the U.S. for a number of years. Unfortunately, its use has been confined to technical experts. By adding it to the "quality toolbox," it has become more widely available to general managers and other nontechnical personnel.

Figure 3.6   Example of a Process Decision Program Chart

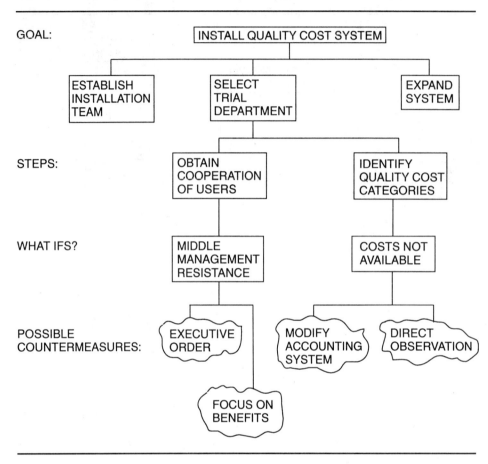

Implementation of process improvements is an essential, but frequently ignored, step. Process improvements often are not implemented because they are too complex to work in practice or are not accepted by those who have the responsibility to carry them out. These seven quality improvement tools assist managers in implementing improvements through active involvement.

TOOLS FOR CONTINUOUS IMPROVEMENT

Managers need systematic approaches to drive continuous improvement programs. One approach that can be learned and applied by everyone in an organization is the Deming cycle.

The Deming Cycle

The Deming cycle is a methodology for improvement, based on the premise that improvement comes from the application of knowledge.[6] Knowledge of engineering, management, or operations may make a process easier, more accurate, faster, less costly, safer, or better-suited to customer needs. Three fundamental questions to consider are

1. What are we trying to accomplish?
2. What changes can we make that will result in improvement?
3. How will we know that a change is an improvement?

This methodology was originally called the Shewhart cycle after Walter Shewhart, its founder, but was renamed for Deming by the Japanese in 1950. The Deming cycle is composed of four stages: *Plan, Do, Study, Act* (Figure 3.7). Sometimes it is called the PDSA cycle.

The Plan stage consists of studying the current situation, gathering data, and planning for improvement. In the Do stage, the plan is implemented on a trial basis in a laboratory, pilot production process, or with a small group of customers. The Study stage is designed to determine if the trial plan is working correctly and to see if any further problems or opportunities can be found. The last stage, Act, is the implementation of the final plan to ensure that the improvements will be standardized and practiced continuously. This leads back to the Plan stage for further diagnosis and improvement.

As Figure 3.7 suggests, this cycle is never ending. That is, it is focused on *continuous improvement*, so the improved standards serve as a springboard for further improvements. This distinguishes it from more traditional problem-solving approaches and is one of the essential elements of the Deming philosophy.

The following example shows how the Deming cycle can be applied in practice: The owners of a luncheonette decided to do something about the long

Figure 3.7 The Deming Cycle

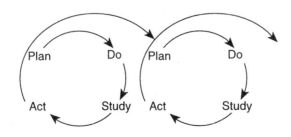

lines that occurred every day in their place of business.[7] After discussions with their employees, several important facts came to light:

- Customers were waiting in line for up to 15 minutes.
- Usually, tables were available.
- Many of their customers were regulars.
- People taking orders and preparing food were getting in each other's way

To measure the improvement that might result from any change, they decided to collect data on the number of customers in line, the number of empty tables, and the delay before customers are served.

In the *Plan* stage, the owners wanted to test a few changes. The changes they decided upon were as follows:

1. Allow customers to fax their orders in ahead of time (rent a fax machine for one month).
2. Construct a preparation table for fax orders in the kitchen where there was ample room.
3. Devote one of their two cash registers to handling fax orders.

Both the length of the line and the number of empty tables would be measured every 15 minutes during the lunch hour by one of the owners. In addition, when the 15-minute line check was done, she would note the last person in line and measure the time until that person was served.

In the *Do* phase, the results of the three measures were observed for three weeks. In the *Study* phase, several improvements were detected. Time in line went down from 15 minutes to an average of 5 minutes. The line length was cut to a peak average of 12 people, and the number of empty tables decreased slightly. In the *Act* phase, a meeting was held with all employees to discuss the results. They decided to purchase the fax machine, prepare phone orders in the kitchen with the fax orders, and use both cash registers to handle walk-up and fax orders.

Tools for Data Collection and Analysis

Seven simple statistically based tools are used extensively to gather and analyze data in the Deming cycle and other problem-solving approaches. Like the seven management and planning tools, these tools—flowcharts, check sheets, histograms, pareto diagrams, cause-and-effect diagrams, scatter diagrams, and control charts—are visual in nature and simple enough for anyone to understand. They provide excellent communication vehicles both vertically and horizontally across organizational boundaries.

Historically, these tools preceded the seven management and planning tools and often are called the "seven QC (quality control) tools." The seven management and planning tools have been referred to as the "new seven."

Flowcharts A flowchart is a picture of a process that shows the sequence of steps performed. Figure 3.8 is an example.

Flowcharts are best developed by the people involved in the process—employees, supervisors, managers, and customers. A facilitator often is used to provide objectivity, to ask the right questions, and to resolve conflicts. The facilitator can guide the discussion through questions such as "What happens next?", "Who makes the decision at this point?", and "What operation is performed here?" Often the group does not agree on the answers to these questions, due to misconceptions about the process or a lack of awareness of the "big picture."

Flowcharts help the people involved in the process to understand it better. For example, employees realize how they fit into a process—i.e., who their suppliers and customers are. By helping to develop a flowchart, workers begin to feel a sense of ownership in the process and become more willing to work on improving it. Using flowcharts to train employees on standard procedures leads to more consistent performance.

Once a flowchart is constructed, it can be used to identify quality problems as well as areas for improvement. Questions such as "How does this operation

Figure 3.8 Example of a flowchart for training new printing press operators

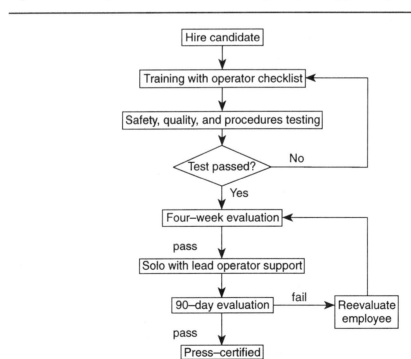

affect the customer?", "Can we improve or eliminate this operation?", or "Should we control a critical quality characteristic at this point?" help to identify such opportunities. Flowcharts help people to visualize simple but important changes that could be made in a process.

Check Sheets   These tools aid in data collection. When designing a process to collect data, one must first ask basic questions such as:

- What question are we trying to answer?
- What type of data will we need to answer the question?
- Where can we find the data?
- Who can provide the data?
- How can we collect the data with minimum effort and minimum chance of error?

Check sheets are data collection forms that facilitate the interpretation of data. Quality-related data are of two general types—attribute and variable. Attribute data are obtained by counting or from some type of visual inspection: the number of invoices that contain errors, the number of parts that conform to specifications, and the number of surface defects on an automobile panel, for example. Variable data are collected by numerical measurement on a continuous scale. Dimensional characteristics such as distance, weight, volume, and time are common examples. Figure 3.9 is an example of an attribute data check sheet, and Figure 3.10 shows a variable data check sheet.

Histograms   Variation in a process always exists and generally displays a pattern that can be captured in a histogram. A histogram is a graphical representation of the variation in a set of data. It shows the frequency or number of observations of a particular value or within a specified group.

Figure 3.9   Example of a Check Sheet for Attributes Data: Airline Complaints

Type	Week 1	Week 2	Week 3	Week 4
Lost baggage	I		II	I
Baggage delay	HHT I	IIII	HHT III	HHT
Missed connection	II	I	III	I
Poor cabin service	III	HHT	III	III
Ticketing error	I			I

Figure 3.10 Example of a Check Sheet for Variables Data

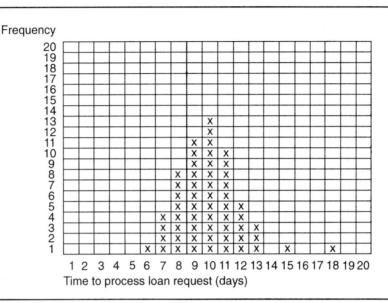

Histograms provide clues about the characteristics of the population from which a sample is taken. Using a histogram, the shape of the distribution can be seen clearly, and inferences can be made about the population. Patterns can be seen that would be difficult to see in an ordinary table of numbers.

The check sheet in Figure 3.10 was designed to provide the visual appeal of a histogram as the data are tallied. It is easy to see how the output of the process varies and what proportion of output falls outside of any specification limits.

Pareto Diagrams   Pareto analysis is a technique for prioritizing types or sources of problems. Pareto analysis separates the "vital few" from the "trivial many" and provides help in selecting directions for improvement. It is often used to analyze the attribute data collected in check sheets. In a Pareto distribution the characteristics are ordered from largest frequency to smallest. For example, if the data in Figure 3.9 is placed in order of decreasing frequency, the result is

Baggage delay	23
Poor cabin service	14
Missed connection	7
Lost baggage	4
Ticketing error	2

Figure 3.11 Example of a Pareto Diagram

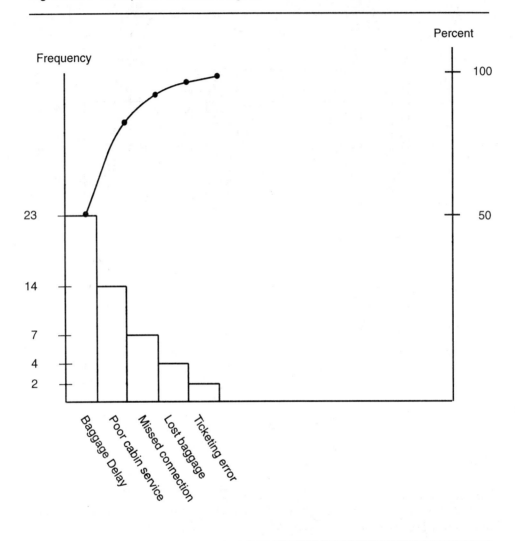

A Pareto diagram is a histogram of these data, as shown in Figure 3.11. A cumulative frequency curve is usually drawn on the histogram, as shown. Such pictures clearly show the relative magnitude of defects and can be used to identify the most promising opportunities for improvement. They can also show the results of improvement projects over time.

Figure 3.12 Example of a Cause-and-effect Diagram

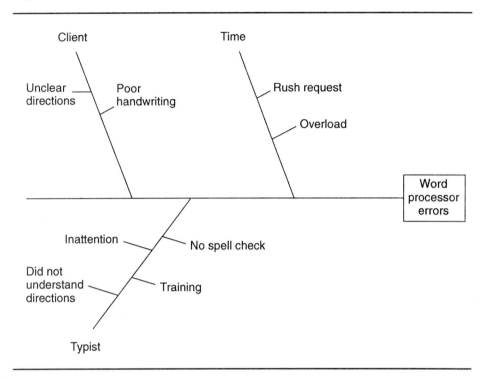

Cause-and-Effect Diagrams The most useful tool for identifying the causes of problems is a cause-and-effect diagram, (also known as a fishbone or Ishikawa diagram, named after the Japanese quality expert who popularized the concept). A cause-and-effect diagram is simply a graphical representation of an outline that presents a chain of causes and effects.

An example is shown in Figure 3.12. At the end of the horizontal line is the problem to be addressed. Each branch pointing into the main stem represents a possible cause. Branches pointing to the causes are contributors to these causes. The diagram is used to identify the most likely causes of a problem so that further data collection and analysis can be carried out.

Cause-and-effect diagrams are usually constructed in a brainstorming setting so that everyone can contribute their ideas. Usually small groups drawn from operations or management work with an experienced facilitator. The facilitator guides the discussion to focus attention on the problem and its causes, on facts, not opinions. This method requires significant interaction among group members. The facilitator must listen carefully to the participants and capture the important ideas.

Figure 3.13 Example of a Scatter Diagram

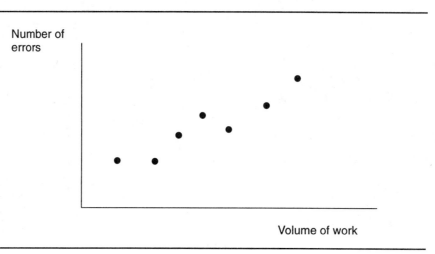

Scatter Diagrams   Scatter diagrams illustrate relationships between variables, such as the percentage of an ingredient in an alloy and the hardness of the alloy, or the number of employee errors and overtime worked (Figure 3.13). Typically the variables represent possible causes and effects obtained from cause-and-effect diagrams.

A general trend of the points going up and to the right indicates that an increase in one variable corresponds to an increase in the other. If the trend is down and to the right, an increase in one variable corresponds to a decrease in the other. If no trend can be seen, then it would appear that the variables are not related. Of course, any correspondence does not necessarily imply that a change in one variable *causes* a change in the other. Both may be the result of something else. However, if there is reason to believe causation, the scattter diagram may provide clues on how to improve the process.

Control Charts   These tools are the backbone of statistical process control (SPC), and were first proposed by Walter Shewhart in 1924. Shewhart was the first to distinguish between common causes and special causes in process variation. He developed the control chart to identify the effects of special causes. Much of the Deming philosophy is based on the use of control charts to understand variation.

A control chart displays the state of control of a process (Figure 3.14). Time is measured on the horizontal axis, and the value of a variable on the vertical

Figure 3.14 Example of a Control Chart

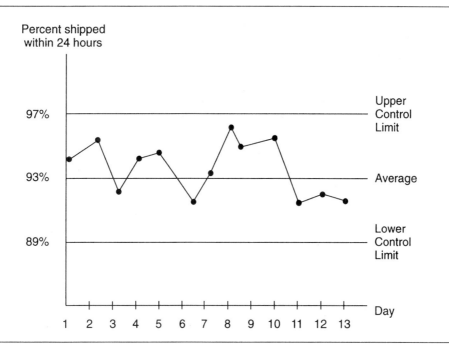

axis. A central horizontal line usually corresponds to the average value of the quality characteristic being measured.

Two other horizontal lines represent the upper and lower control limits, chosen so that there is a high probability that sample values will fall within these limits *if the process is under control*—i.e., affected only by common causes of variation. If points fall outside of the control limits or if unusual patterns such as shifts up or down, trends up or down, cycles, and so forth exist, special causes may be present.

Two fundamental mistakes that can be made concerning variation are

1. treating special causes as common causes, and
2. treating common causes as special causes.

Control charts minimize the risk of making these two types of mistakes. As a problem-solving tool, they allow workers to identify quality problems as they occur and base their conclusions on hard facts.

Rotor Clip Puts a Clamp on Quality Problems[8]

Rotor Clip Company, Inc., a major manufacturer of retaining rings and self-tightening hose clamps, is a believer in the use of simple quality improvement tools. Several years ago, one of its clamps was failing stress testing during final inspections. No reason was clear, so managers and supervisors decided to develop a cause-and-effect diagram to search for a solution. Every employee involved with the part was called to a meeting to discuss the problem. They created the fishbone diagram shown in Figure 3.15. After reviewing all the probable causes, they concluded that the salt temperature of the quenching tank was too close to the martensite line. This was selected for further study, but raising the salt temperature did not alleviate the problem. The group met again and agreed to look at a second possibility—seams in one wire—as a possible cause. Wire samples that failed inspection were examined metallographically and seams were confirmed as the major cause of the defective parts. The material was returned to the supplier and new material yielded parts that passed the final inspection.

A second application involved the use of a Pareto diagram to study rising premium freight charges for shipping retaining rings. They collected three

Figure 3.15 Fishbone diagram for the Rotor Clip clamp problem

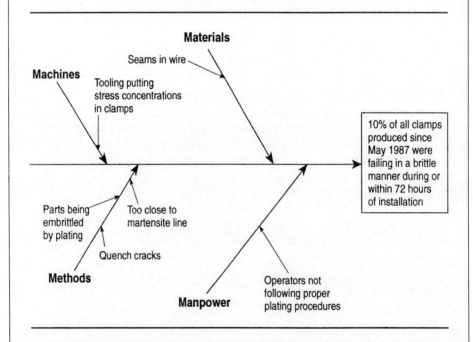

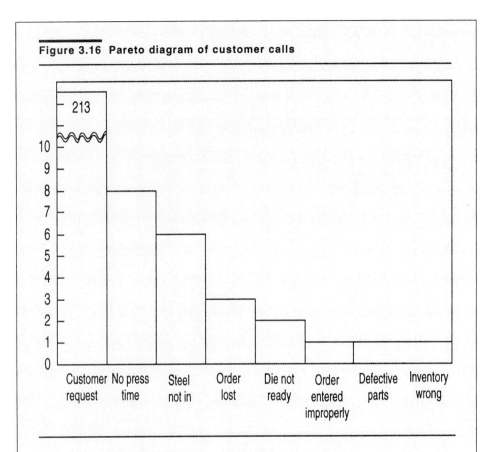

Figure 3.16 Pareto diagram of customer calls

months of data and constructed the Pareto diagram shown in Figure 3.16. The results were startling. The most frequent cause of higher freight charges was customer requests. They made a decision to continue the study and identify which customers consistently expedited their shipments. They worked closely with them to find ways of reducing costs.

A third application was the use of a scatter diagram by the advertising department. Traditionally, it had been difficult to prove the effect of advertising expenditures on the bottom line. Management wanted to learn if the amount of advertising dollars spent correlated with the number of new customers gained in a given year. Advertising dollars spent by quarter were plotted against the number of new customers added for the same period for three consecutive years (Figure 3.17). The positive correlation showed that heavy advertising was related to new customers. The results were fairly consistent from year to year except for the second quarter of 1988. Advertising checked the media schedule and discovered that experimental image ads dominated that particular period. This prompted the advertising department to eliminate image ads from its schedule.

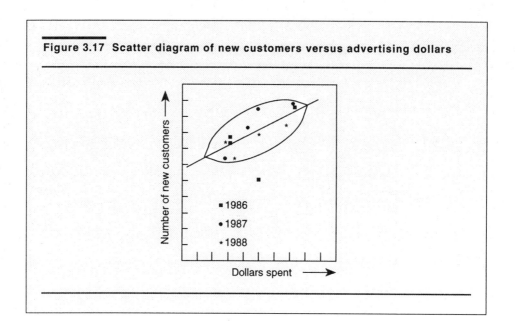

Figure 3.17 Scatter diagram of new customers versus advertising dollars

Benchmarking

Benchmarking is the search for best practices that will lead to superior performance. Benchmarking helps a company learn its strengths and weaknesses—and those of other industrial leaders—and incorporate the best practices into its own operations. Benchmarking was initiated by Xerox, an eventual winner of the Malcolm Baldrige National Quality Award.

Xerox initially studied their direct competitors and discovered that

- their unit manufacturing cost equalled the Japanese selling price in the U.S.,
- the number of production suppliers was nine times that of the best companies,
- assembly line rejects were ten times higher,
- product lead times were twice as long, and
- defects per hundred machines were seven times higher.

These results helped them to understand the amount of change that would be required and to set realistic targets to guide their planning efforts.

Two major types of benchmarking are *competitive* and *generic*. Competitive benchmarking usually focuses on the products and manufacturing of a company's competitors, as Xerox initially did. Generic benchmarking evaluates processes or business functions against the best companies, regardless of their industry. Xerox recognized the potential for improving *all* business processes and realized that better practices in service companies and other types of manufacturing firms could be adapted to their operations. For example, the warehousing and distribution practices of L.L. Bean were adopted by Xerox. Thus, benchmarking should not be aimed solely at direct competitors.

In order to be effective, benchmarking must be applied to all facets of a business. For example, Motorola encourages everyone in the organization to ask "Who is the best person in my own field and how might I use some of their techniques and characteristics to improve my own performance in order to be the best (executive, machine operator, chef, purchasing agent, and so on) in my 'class'"?

The benchmarking process can be described as follows:

1. Determine which functions to benchmark. These should have a significant impact on business performance and key dimensions of competitiveness. If fast response is an important dimension of competitive advantage, then processes that might be benchmarked would include order processing, purchasing, production planning, and product distribution. There should also be an indication that the potential for improvement exists.

2. Identify key performance indicators to measure. These should have a direct link to customer needs and expectations. Typical performance indicators are quality, performance, and delivery.

3. Identify the best-in-class companies. For specific business functions, benchmarking might be limited to the same industry: a bank in one state might benchmark the check-processing operations of a bank in another state. For generic business functions, it is best to look outside one's own industry: a university financial aid office might benchmark a bank's loan operation. Selecting companies requires knowledge of which firms are superior performers in the key areas. Such information can be obtained from published reports and articles, industry experts, trade magazines, professional associations, former employees, or customers and suppliers.

4. Measure the performance of the best-in-class companies and compare the results to your own performance. Such information might be found in published sources or might require site visits and in-depth interviews.

5. Define and take actions to meet or exceed the best performance. This usually requires changing organizational systems. Simply to emulate the best is like shooting at moving target—their processes will continually improve. Therefore, attempts should be made to exceed the performance of the best.

SUMMARY

Quality practitioners have compiled many different tools and techniques to assist quality planning, implementation, and improvement processes. Among these are:

- *Quality function deployment*—a planning technique to ensure that customer requirements are incorporated into the design of products and the systems which produce them
- *Concurrent engineering*—an approach to streamline product development to improve quality and reduce development time, thereby meeting customer needs faster
- *The "New Seven" management and planning tools*—a set of graphical aids to assist in planning and implementation of new projects and ideas which reduce "surprises" later on
- *The Deming cycle*—a simple methodology for continuous improvement that is based on the scientific approach to problem solving
- *The "Seven QC Tools"*—a set of graphically-based tools for collecting, analyzing, and interpreting data to facilitate the solution of quality problems for continuous improvement
- *Benchmarking*—the search for best practices to improve operations in any business function

None of these tools or approaches require rocket science; they are simple, effective, and easy to learn. Moreover, they provide common means of communication among managers, supervisors, and hourly workers so that all can focus their efforts on quality improvement.

REVIEW AND DISCUSSION QUESTIONS

1. Why is good planning important to quality improvement? Why should managers invest in the time to learn many of the tools presented in this chapter?

2. Explain the benefits of the quality function deployment approach. How does it help organizations to design better products and services?

3. Using whatever "market research" techniques you feel are appropriate, define a set of customer attributes for (a) an "excellent" cup of coffee and (b) a college registration process. How might QFD be used to improve these processes? Define a set of "hows" and try to construct the relationship matrix for the house of quality for each of these examples.

4. Most organizations have well-defined mission statements that include a set of goals for the firm and actions that the firm can take. How might QFD be

used to ensure that the actions are consistent with the goals? Find some company's mission statement to illustrate this.

5. What is concurrent engineering? What quality-related advantages does it have?

6. What type of organizational culture would be required to make concurrent engineering successful?

7. Explain the purpose of the seven management and planning tools.

8. How might you use the seven management and planning tools in your daily activities (schoolwork, fraternity or honor society operations, and so on)? Provide specific examples.

9. What is the Deming cycle? How is it used to improve quality?

10. Many books in business describe some sort of problem-solving process. Find two or three descriptions of systematic problem-solving processes. How are they similar to or different from the Deming cycle?

11. Choose some process in which you are involved. Devise a plan to use the Deming cycle to improve it.

12. How might a professor use the Deming cycle to improve his or her teaching performance?

13. Explain the purpose and uses of each of the "seven QC tools."

14. Select a process that you do routinely and draw a flowchart of it. Explain how the flowchart helps you to understand and improve the process.

15. A flowchart for a fast food drive-through window is shown in Figure 3.18. Discuss the important quality characteristics inherent in this process and suggest possible improvements.

16. Design a check sheet to help a high school student who is getting poor grades on a math quiz determine the source of his or her difficulty.

17. Develop cause-and-effect diagrams for
   a. a poor exam grade
   b. no job offers
   c. too many speeding tickets
   d. late for work or school

18. Describe the purpose and role of benchmarking in business organizations. How much effort do you believe companies should spend in benchmarking efforts?

19. Discuss how a college or university might apply benchmarking to improving its operations. You might solicit views from academic administrators and from businesspeople. (You might find some differences of opinion!)

Figure 3-18   Flowchart of a Fast-food Drive-through Process

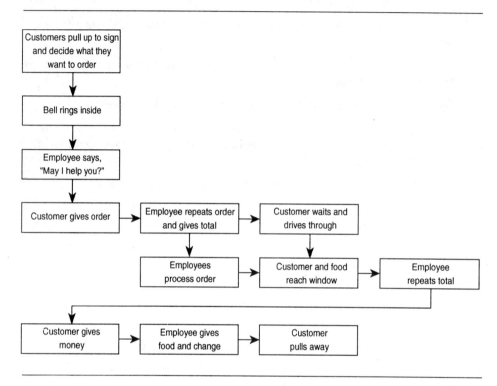

CASE[9]

Welz Business Machines

Welz Business Machines sells and services a variety of copiers, computers, and other office equipment. The company receives many calls daily for service, sales, accounting, and other departments. All calls are handled centrally by customer service representatives and routed to other individuals as appropriate. A number of customers had complained about long waits when calling for service. A market research study found that customers became irritated if the call was not answered within five rings. Scott Welz, the company president, authorized the customer service department manager, Tim, to study this problem and find a method to shorten the call-waiting time. Tim met with the service representatives who answered the calls to attempt to determine the reasons for long waiting times. The following conversation ensued:

TIM: This is a serious problem. How a customer phone inquiry is answered is the first impression the customer receives from us. As you know, this company was founded on efficient and friendly service to all our customers. It's obvious why customers have to wait: You're on the phone with another customer. Can you think of any reasons that might keep you on the phone for an unnecessarily long time?

ROBIN: I've noticed quite often that the person to whom I need to route the call is not present. It takes time to transfer the call and to see if it is answered. If the person is not there, I end up apologizing and transferring the call to another extension.

TIM: You're right, Robin. Sales personnel often are out of the office on sales calls, away on trips to preview new products, or away from their desks for a variety of reasons. What else might cause this problem?

RAVI: I get irritated at customers who spend a great deal of time complaining about a problem that I cannot do anything about except refer to someone else. Of course, I listen and sympathize with them, but this eats up a lot of time.

LaMARR: Some customers call so often, they think we're long lost friends and strike up a personal conversation.

TIM: That's not always a bad thing, you realize.

LaMARR: Sure, but it delays my answering other calls.

NANCY: It's not always the customer's fault. During lunch, we're not all available to answer the phone.

RAVI: Right after we open at 9 A.M., we get a rush of calls. I think that many of the delays are caused by these peak periods.

ROBIN: I've noticed the same thing between 4 and 5 P.M.

TIM: I've had a few comments from department managers who received calls that didn't fall in their areas of responsibility and had to be transferred again.

MARK: But that doesn't cause delays at our end.

NANCY: That's right, Mark, but I just realized that sometimes I simply don't understand what the customer's problem really is. I spend a lot of time trying to get him or her to explain it better. Often, I have to route it to someone because other calls are waiting.

RAVI: Perhaps we need to have more knowledge of our products.

TIM: Well, I think we've covered most of the major reasons why many customers have to wait. It seems to me that we have four major reasons: the phones are short-staffed, the receiving party is not present, the customer dominates the conversation, and you may not understand the customer's problem. Next we need to collect some information about these possible causes. I will set up a data collection sheet that you can use to track some of these things. Mark, would you help me on this?

Over the next two weeks the staff collected data on the frequency of reasons why some callers had to wait. The results are summarized as follows:

	Reason	Total number
A	Operators short-staffed	172
B	Receiving party not present	73
C	Customer dominates conversation	19
D	Lack of operator understanding	61
E	Other reasons	10

Discussion Questions

1. From the conversation between Tim and his staff, draw a cause-and-effect diagram.
2. Perform a Pareto analysis of the data collected.
3. What actions might the company take to improve the situation?

ENDNOTES

1. L.P.Sullivan, "Quality Function Deployment: The Latent Potential of Phases III and IV," in A. Richard Shores, *A TQM Approach to Achieving Manufacturing Excellence*, Milwaukee: ASQC Quality Press, 1990.

2. "How Ford Hit the Bull's Eye With Taurus," *Business Week*, 30 June 1986, 69–70.

3. Mike Boyer, "Milacron Seeks Killer Instinct," *Cincinnati Enquirer*, 31 August 1990, B6.

4. James L. Brossert, *Quality Function Deployment: A Practitioner's Approach*, Milwaukee: ASQC Quality Press/Marcel Dekker, Inc., 1991, Part 2.

5. Michael Brassard, *The Memory Jogger Plus +*, Meuthen, Mass.: GOAL/QPC, 1989; Brossert, *Quality Function Deployment*; Shigeru, Mizuno. *Management for Quality Improvement: The 7 New QC Tools*, Cambridge, Mass.: Productivity Press, 1988.

6. Gerald Langley, Kevin Nolan, and Thomas Nolan, "The Foundation of Improvement," Sixth Annual International Deming User's Group Conference, Cincinnati, Ohio, August, 1992.

7. Langley et al., *op. cit.*

8. Reprinted with permission from QUALITY (April, 1990), a publication of Hitchcock/Chilton Publishing, a Capital Cities/ABC, Inc., Company.

9. This problem was developed from a classic example published in "The Quest for Higher Quality: The Deming Prize and Quality Control," by RICOH of America, Inc.

PART II
Total Quality and Organization Theory

CHAPTER 4

Quality in
Customer-Supplier
Relationships

Chapter Outline

Customer-Supplier Relationships in Total Quality Management
    The Importance of Customers
    The Importance of Suppliers
Principles for Customer-Supplier Relationships
    Practices for Dealing with Customers
    Practices for Dealing with Suppliers
Quality Customer-Supplier Relationships in Action
Customer-Supplier Relations in Organization Theory
Summary
Review and Discussion Questions
Cases

The needs of customers too often are overshadowed by short-term business objectives. Peter Senge of M.I.T. tells a story about a company that embraced total quality management but found its stock price steadily declining. One of the main objectives of their TQM initiative was to reduce new product introduction time. In the effort to meet this objective (on which the managers were measured and rewarded), the new products became increasingly simple and mundane.

Many businesses traditionally have kept suppliers at arms' length, but the quality of output can be no better than the quality of the input. In 1982 IBM purchased some parts from a Japanese manufacturer. According to the specifications, IBM would accept 300 defective parts per million of the product. The response from Japan raised a lot of questions and gave IBM the opportunity to change its perspective on quality and relationships with suppliers. The Japanese commented, "We have a hard time understanding North American business practices. But the 3 defective parts per 10,000 have been included and are wrapped separately. Hope this pleases."[1]

Developing strong and positive relationships with customers and suppliers is a basic principle of total quality management. This chapter will

- demonstrate the importance of customer-supplier relationships to TQM;
- identify the principles and practices of quality customer-supplier relationships;
- give examples of effective partnerships between customers and suppliers; and
- compare the TQM approach to customers and suppliers to conventional organizational theories.

CUSTOMER-SUPPLIER RELATIONSHIPS IN TOTAL QUALITY MANAGEMENT

From the TQM perspective, every company is part of a long chain (actually many long chains) of customers and suppliers.[2] Each company is a customer to its suppliers and a supplier to its customers, so it does not make sense to think of a company as only one or the other (Figure 4.1). One implication of this concept is that your customer's customers are, in a sense, your customers as well. Sometimes a company must focus on both their immediate customers and those next in the chain. Procter and Gamble, for example, works hard to satisfy the needs of both the people who use their products and the retail establishments that sell them, labeling the former "consumers" and the latter "customers."

Companies should try to establish the same kinds of productive relationships with their suppliers that they have with their customers. By developing partnerships, customers and suppliers can build relationships that will help them satisfy their shared customers further along the customer-supplier chain. This is why we have written one chapter on customer-supplier relationships, rather than separate chapters on customers and suppliers.

The idea of creating mutually beneficial relationships with both customers and suppliers is a major departure from the traditional approach to customer and supplier relationships (CSRs). As one book on TQM recently put it, "The historical picture of customer-supplier relationships has been one of self-interested adversaries negotiating against each other to maximize their slice of the pie at the expense of the other."[3] The authors go on to say that the focus

Figure 4.1 The Customer-Supplier Chain

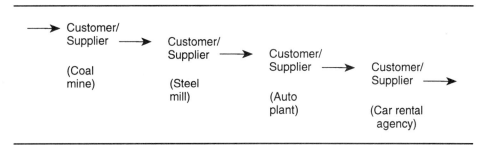

of CSRs under TQM is on expanding the pie rather than on arguing over its division.

The Importance of Customers

It is impossible to overstate the importance of customers to TQM. Customers are at the very center of every TQM activity, and devotion to satisfying them is the first principle of TQM. Customers are recognized as the guarantee of the organization's continued existence. Therefore, a focus on customers, rather than internal issues, is the foundation of the TQM approach to management.

Customer-driven quality is recognized as a core value of the Malcolm Baldrige National Quality Award. The award guidelines state:[4]

> Quality is judged by the customer. All product and service attributes that contribute value to the customer and lead to customer satisfaction and preference must be the foundation for a company's quality system. Value, satisfaction, and preference may be influenced by many factors throughout the customer's overall purchase, ownership, and service experiences.

Thirty percent of the Baldrige criteria is based on customer focus and satisfaction. For many companies, such as AT&T, "The Customer Comes First" is a guiding principle.

The Importance of Suppliers

Suppliers—those companies that provide the organization with goods and services that help them to satisfy the needs of their own customers—are also crucial to successful TQM. A manufacturing company assembling parts made by suppliers illustrates this point: the final product cannot be any better than the parts that comprise it. The importance of suppliers is at least as great when they provide training, software, or other goods or services that do not physically become part of the final product; they will influence its quality nevertheless by shaping the quality of the processes used to produce it.

Suppliers influence the cost as well as the quality of the final product. If a supplier's performance is of consistently high quality, its customer can decrease or eliminate costly incoming inspections that add no value to the product. For these reasons, organizations such as Ford Motor Company and Motorola have increasingly demanded tangible progress in quality from all their suppliers. Companies that do not accept this requirement are dropped from supplier lists.

PRINCIPLES FOR CUSTOMER-SUPPLIER RELATIONSHIPS

Three governing principles describe CSRs under total quality:

- recognition of the strategic importance of customers and suppliers;
- development of win-win relationships between customers and suppliers; and
- establishing relationships based on trust.

First, an organization must recognize that its customers and suppliers are absolutely crucial to its success. Although this may sound obvious, many organizations seem to be driven by the need to observe standard operating procedures and maintain rigid boundaries between jobs, rather than trying to meet customer expectations. Consider the following letter from a hotel desk clerk to the popular newspaper columnist Abigail Van Buren:

> Dear Abby:
> I am a desk clerk at a resort hotel. I would like the public to know that we are not maintenance men. We cannot repair television sets or break into their automobiles when they have locked their keys inside the car. We do not unplug toilets or change light bulbs, and we can't repair the telephone.
> Also, we are not in "housekeeping", so we can't bring them extra washcloths, towels, pillows, blankets, or toilet paper. We are not bellmen either, so please don't ask us to carry luggage or run errands.
> Now I will tell you what front desk clerks ARE paid to do: greet and register incoming guests, and make sure that outgoing guests see the cashier about paying their bill and turning in their key before departing. Thank you.
> Desk Clerk[5]

Although some division of labor is to be expected in any organization, the writer seems ignorant of his or her responsibility for guaranteeing customer satisfaction, preferring to focus on what he or she can't do. As the first and last contact a guest makes with the hotel, front desk personnel probably have the largest impact on guest satisfaction of anyone. It is frightening to imagine how much damage this individual's attitude has done to his or her organization. Of course, the responsibility for this attitude may ultimately rest with the hotel organization that apparently has created a system in which people are more interested in maintaining boundaries than in serving customers.[6]

Fortunately, Abby seems to have grasped the central principle of TQM much better than her correspondent:

> I doubt that you can speak for all hotel and motel desk clerks throughout the world. In the name of good customer relations, you should be prepared to handle all questions and complaints to the satisfaction of the guests so they will want to return to your establishment.[7]

Customers must be at the center of the organizational universe. Satisfying their needs leads to repeat business and positive referrals, as opposed to one-shot business and negative referrals. Suppliers must also be considered crucial to organizational success, because they make it possible to create customer satisfaction. Neither the quality nor the cost of the organization's product can be brought to competitive levels and continuously improved without the contributions of suppliers.

The second principle of customer-supplier relationships is the need to develop mutually beneficial (often called win-win) relationships between customers and suppliers. This was discussed previously as working together to increase the size of the pie, rather than competing over how to divide it. The goal of building partnerships with customers and suppliers can be seen as an extension of the teamwork principle that applies to all TQM activities and as a recognition that the needs of both partners must be satisfied if productive long-term relationships are to be created. W. Edwards Deming has advocated these principles for decades, as is evident in his 14 Points (chapter 2). Joseph Juran has developed a useful framework to distinguish between adversarial and teamwork relationships with suppliers (Table 4.1).[8]

Table 4.1   Juran's Trends in Supplier Relations

Element	Adversary Concept	Teamwork Concept
Number of suppliers	Multiple; often many	Few; often single source
Duration of supply contracts	Annual	Three years or more
Criteria for quality	Conformance to specifications	Fitness for use
Emphasis of surveys	Procedures, data systems	Process capability; quality improvement
Quality planning	Separate	Joint
Pattern of collaboration	Arms length: secrecy; mutual supervision	Mutual visits; disclosures; assistance

The third principle of effective CSRs is that they must be based on trust rather than suspicion. This point is noted in the last row of Table 4.1 and is described by Juran as the "pattern of collaboration." The costs of mistrust are staggering: witness the tremendous number, detail, and rigidity of rules that characterize the U.S. Department of Defense's contracts with its suppliers. The suppliers often incur substantial costs in terms of both money and time due to multiple levels of review and inspection. Although a certain level of rigidity is to be expected in the acquisition of weapons, it is harder to understand when applied to more ordinary items.

Aside from the obvious teamwork implications for relationships based on trust versus suspicion, monitoring supplier or customer behavior does not add any value to the product. If a trusting relationship between customers and suppliers can be developed so that neither must check up on the behavior of the other, the costs of monitoring, such as inspection and auditing, can be avoided. Many Japanese firms do not inspect items purchased from other companies in Japan; they do, however, often inspect those purchased from America. Trust, is not a blind leap into the unknown, it is developed over time "through a pattern of success by all parties to fully and faithfully deliver that which was promised."[9] In other words, trust depends upon trustworthy behavior by both parties in a CSR.

Practices for Dealing with Customers

How can these principles be translated into specific practices? The most basic practices for dealing with customers are (1) to collect information constantly on customer expectations, (2) to disseminate this information widely within the organization, and (3) to use this information to design, produce, and deliver the organization's products and services.

Collect Customer Information   Some of the most popular ways to collect information about customers are surveys, service evaluation cards, focus groups, and listening to what customers say during business transactions, especially when they complain. Some companies, such as Marriott Hotels, have developed elaborate methods for keeping abreast of customer needs. This is not a low-profile activity at Marriot: Chairman Bill Marriott, Jr., himself reads approximately 800 letters from customers and 15,000 guest questionnaires every month![10] The rewards of taking customer information seriously are also apparent at Marriott, where occupancy rates are consistently 10 percent above the industry average. (For an example from manufacturing, see the box on page 110 "Promoting Customer Delight at U.S. Precision Lens.")

Sending employees into customer facilities, another popular practice, provides not only feedback from customers, but also valuable information to employees about the importance of what they do. A manager in a foundry that follows this practice commented:

We take shop floor people and take them out to the customer's plant. We want them to see the final product in place. It gets our employees out in the world to meet the customers. They get to know the customers better and really by doing that, the employees get to have a better, more caring attitude. Because they know more about what's going on.

Having top managers of the company act as customers of their own organizations—renting a room in their own hotel or buying a suit from a retail outlet—is another way to better understand customer needs. This not only gives them a sense of the quality of service, but also makes them more sensitive to how the organizational policies they have created actually affect customers.[11]

Beyond getting a thorough understanding of customer needs, companies also need to assess how well their products and services are meeting customer needs. Some companies have developed innovative ways of obtaining customer feedback.

British Airways has installed video kiosks at Heathrow Airport outside London and Kennedy Airport in New York. When upset, customers can enter the booth and create a video message for BA's management. The videos have proven so informative that, although they were initially viewed only by executives, front-line employees demanded and were given access to them. One important aspect of this method is that it gives people a sense of the emotion associated with customer response to the quality of service ("you lost my *&%$# baggage!"), which cannot easily be conveyed by checking a number from one through five on a customer satisfaction survey, especially when done weeks later.

In trying to understand customer needs, it is important to go beyond what customers say they need and anticipate what will really excite them. It is a well-known principle of innovation that customers will seldom express enthusiasm for a product that is different from anything they have experienced. Thus the original market survey for computers suggested that only a few would be sold, and it took years for 3M to become convinced that Post-It notes would actually be valuable to people in offices. As Kozo Ohsone of Sony puts it, "When you introduce products that have never been invented before, what good is market research?"[12]

The Japanese auto industry is known for trying to understand customer needs so thoroughly that they can incorporate design features that customers would never have asked for, but love once they experience them. Teams of automobile designers visit people at home and observe how they live in order to anticipate their automotive needs. Hideo Sugiura, executive vice president of Honda, comments on his company's efforts to anticipate customer needs: "We should not try to sell things just because the market is there, but rather we should seek to create a new market by accurately understanding the potential needs of customers and society."[13] Lexus, Toyota's luxury car line, has succeeded dramatically in this manner and is consistently at the top of owner satisfaction surveys.

Promoting Customer Delight at U.S. Precision Lens[14]

U.S. Precision Lens (USPL) is the world's largest manufacturer of lens systems for projection televisions. Since 1986 USPL has been a wholly-owned subsidiary of Corning, Inc. The major requirements for success in selling to projection television manufacturers such as Philips and Sony are product quality, delivery, product innovation, and customer service. USPL's goal in each area is "customer delight" through exceeding customer expectations.

USPL understands customer needs through a system it describes as "simple, reliable, and effective"—they ask them what their needs are. Company executives travel frequently to Europe and the Far East to meet with senior members of customer organizations, and customers visit USPL with similar frequency. During these visits, competitors' products are also discussed, so that USPL can set a direction for continuous (they say "relentless") improvement. Planning sessions prior to visits allow input into the data-gathering process from across the organization. Trips are not the exclusive preserve of senior managers; hourly "associates" (employees) also visit customers and share their impressions on their return.

Interestingly, the primary medium of day-to-day communication between USPL and its customers is the fax. This is partly due to the time zone differences between USPL and its customers. The CEO sees every fax message from customers, and USPL's policy is to respond to all faxes within 24 hours. Also, the home telephone numbers of USPL's senior executives are provided to customers, and they use them.

USPL utilizes a survey instrument to procure ratings of its own service quality, as well as that of its competitors, on the dimensions of assurance, responsiveness, reliability, empathy, and "tangibles." In response to feedback through this and other means, USPL has barcoded container labels, vacuum sealed parts, and placed a native speaker in Japan to represent the company.

These and other TQM-oriented practices at USPL have paid tremendous dividends to the company. USPL received the SONY President Award in 1991 as the highest rated supplier for quality and delivery. Philips presented USPL the Supplier Total Quality Award that same year. Electrohome made USPL its supplier of the year for 1990. The ultimate reward for quality, however, is in attracting and maintaining demand for the organization's products. In this category as well USPL is outstanding: The company's market share is approaching 70 percent.

Disseminate Customer Information   After people in the organization have gathered information about customer needs, the next step is to broadcast this information within the organization. After all, if the people in the firm are going to work as a team to meet customer expectations, they must all be "singing from the same hymnbook," as the saying goes. Information does little good if it stays with the person or department that brought it into the organization.

Richard Whiteley, vice-chairman of The Forum Corporation, a customer-satisfaction oriented consulting firm, has a vivid way to describe this need: "Saturate your company with the voice of the customer."[15] Saturation is an attractive way of describing what organizations need to do: If the organization is awash in information about customer needs, it is much harder to downplay customer expectations in favor of administrative convenience or the need to follow procedures.

AT&T, which won two Baldrige Awards in 1992, is one organization trying to maintain a constant customer focus. Jerre Stead, president of Global Business Communications Systems, tells people in his unit: "I say if you're in a meeting, any meeting, for 15 minutes and we're not talking about customers or competitors, raise your hand and ask why. If it goes on for half an hour, leave! Leave the meeting!"[16]

Customer information must be translated into the features of the organization's products and services. This is the bottom line of quality customer-supplier relations from the supplier's point of view: giving the customers what they want. Translating customer needs into product features can be done in a structured manner using Quality Function Deployment (QFD), a technique discussed in chapter 3. QFD allows people to see how aspects of their products and services relate to customer satisfaction, and to make informed decisions about how their products should be improved. The overall process of using information from customers to provide quality products is summarized in Figure 4.2.

Use Customer Information   Binney & Smith, the company that produces Crayola crayons and markers, makes it a point to improve its products by taking advantage of customer feedback. Many of the letters the company receives from parents laud the role that crayons play in the artistic development of their children. Some letters complained that the markers created permanent stains in children's clothes. After two years of research, Binney & Smith responded by developing a new line of washable markers. Marker sales doubled, demonstrating the company's ability to learn and provide what customers are looking for.[17]

More recently Binney & Smith sponsored a contest in which customers could name one of 16 new crayon colors the company created for its Big Box. "Part of our reason for introducing new colors came from consumer suggestions. More than 50 percent said they wanted us to expand and add new colors," according to Brad Dexler, a company spokesman.

Figure 4.2 The Customer-driven Quality Cycle

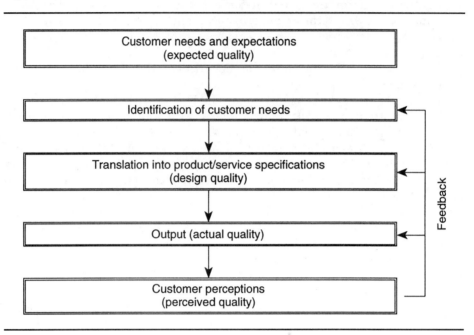

The service aspects of CSRs are often extremely important, even for manufacturing firms, as discussed in chapter 1. One study concluded that 70 percent of customers leave a supplier because of poor quality service, not problems with products per se, and many companies are struggling to bring their service up to the level of their products.[18]

One of the main areas on which companies have focused is telephone service, especially how long it takes to get someone on the phone, and to get one's question answered or order taken. Many companies have worked to make sure that phone calls are answered on the third ring, but to AMP, Inc., the world's largest manufacturer of electronic interconnection systems, three rings is an eternity. Customer calls to AMP are answered within six seconds—that is, on the first ring. Why such an ambitious goal? AMP found that 8 percent of their customers were hanging up before their calls were answered under the three-ring standard. They don't lose many calls now.[19]

Customers in the Fine Arts

Car dealers have customers, bookstores have customers, but how about symphony orchestras and art museums? Traditionally, such organizations have acted as if they were your customer. But fine arts organizations in Cincinnati, spurred both by economic necessity and the proximity and influence of several quality-conscious corporations, have begun to think hard about satisfying customers.[20] Some of the results:

- The Cincinnati Symphony Orchestra has initiated a series of concerts on Thursday nights. Dress is more casual for these concerts, and tickets can be easily exchanged.
- The Taft Museum has doubled the number of events it holds—from 20 to 40 per season.
- The Cincinnati Opera has begun scheduling series of operas linked by a popular theme. For example, "Pretty Women" included *Carmen* and *The Barber of Seville.*

The increased focus on satisfying customers, which has begun to pay off economically, is reflected by statements from leaders in these organizations. Paul A. Stuhlreyer III, managing director of the opera, believes that "the goal should not be an international reputation while losing sight of what [local customers] want...I want to make sure we're still putting 3,000 people into Music Hall for each performance. Then I know we're taking care of the citizens of Cincinnati."

Gretchen Mehring, Cincinnati Art Museum director of public service, puts it: "Our primary focus is the family, especially the children. We're not operating a museum or creating exhibitions to appeal to art experts."

Practices for Dealing with Suppliers[21]

Although the principles of CSRs are the same in dealing with suppliers as they are with customers, the practices are somewhat different. Many of the practices associated with suppliers are followed by the Wallace Company, a 1990 winner of the Malcolm Baldrige National Quality Award, as reported by John W. Wallace, chief executive officer:

> We are . . . asking our suppliers how they ensure quality in their products . . . We have even sponsored two-week long seminars for our suppliers . . . They have got to get their processes well in control to meet our standards and that means we have to know that they are committed to quality products and services . . . I don't have time to be checking another company's products. When

I receive a shipment from a company that really has its processes in control, I know that I don't have to check it. I know that it's okay and can go straight into our receiving unit . . . I know that this may appear to cost a bit more initially but that doesn't bother me because I think it saves me by getting the material right the first time . . . All of the savings in reliability are infinitely more important than a 2 or 3 or 4 percent price difference.[22]

Purchasing decisions based on quality as well as cost.   The first and most obvious practice is that purchasing decisions should be based on the quality of the product and not just its cost.[23] This, however, goes against the grain in most organizations. Generally speaking, the technical people will determine the specifications for a product to be purchased, and then the purchasing department will solicit bids or check prices with several suppliers and negotiate the contract with the one that fills the order. Purchasing personnel have traditionally been rewarded primarily for negotiating low prices, and thus this has been their focus. Supplier firms have often responded to this situation in the obvious way: by doing whatever they need to do (including sacrificing quality) to maintain low prices.

Beyond the compromises this creates for the quality of the final product, there are two other problems with this approach. First, low purchase cost often does not equal low overall cost. If a cheap (in both senses of the word) part causes a large amount of scrap or leads to high warranty costs, it may end up with a higher overall cost, often referred to as life-cycle cost. Second, pressing suppliers for ever-lower prices will minimize their profits. Although this benefits the customer in the short run, in the long run it keeps suppliers operating so close to the bone that they forgo capital investments, maintenance, and other expenses necessary to improve or even maintain their quality.[24]

Reduced number of suppliers   Firms pursuing TQM are also reducing the number of suppliers they work with to the point of having only one supplier for some components. Xerox has reduced its suppliers by about 90 percent—from more than 4,000 to about 450 in 1990.[25] This also goes against the grain of conventional purchasing practices, as it increases the dependence of the organization on the supplier, thus weakening its bargaining position and exposing it to the possibility of an interruption in supply in the case of a labor stoppage or similar problem with the supplier.

Several advantages offset these disadvantages. For one thing, administrative costs are greatly reduced.[26] (Imagine the time to be saved by eliminating the paperwork associated with 90 percent of suppliers!) Also, cutting the number of suppliers reduces the variability in the incoming products, making it much easier to control the quality of outgoing products. This is because there are fewer "special causes" of variation, to use Deming's term.

The type of intensive CSRs that characterize TQM simply cannot be maintained with a large number of suppliers. The significance of partners (like friends or vice presidents) is lost if you have too many of them. For these reasons, many organizations continue to reduce the number of suppliers with which they do business. John Wallace again:

> We are also continuing to dwindle the number of people we're buying from. We have some people that we're single sourcing. The old adage was that you can't do that because they're going to take advantage of you. Number one, we know what the market is. Number two, if you really have a true partnership and you share information, you can work better together; we have that partnership with the Carbide and Dow people and they totally rely upon us. I can tell you that we perform better than anybody on quality. But they are conscious of the cost and the price of material. They know what they are getting and do not try to hang us at all on prices. It's a win-win deal for both companies.[27]

Long-term contracts   Related to the idea of fewer suppliers is the practice of establishing long-term contracts with suppliers (see "Changing Ford's Relationships with Suppliers: Easier Said than Done"). Establishing long-term contracts allows suppliers to make greater commitments to improving the quality of products and provides greater opportunity for joint improvement efforts and the development of teamwork across organizational boundaries.

Developing cooperative relationships   The cornerstone of TQM-style customer-supplier relationships is cooperation. In a sense, practices such as long-term contracts and fewer suppliers create an environment in which

---

Changing Ford's Supplier Relationships: Easier Said Than Done

Ford Motor Company was among the first companies to try to change its relationships with suppliers to be consistent with total quality. In 1983 Ford's purchasing vice president, L.M. Chicoine, sent a statement throughout Ford's purchasing organization to the effect that he would like to see more supplier contracts written for periods of more than one year. After six months he learned that there was virtually no increase in the number of long-term contracts.

Mr. Chicoine found that the reason for this lack of change was a procedure requiring buyers to get authorization from two levels of supervision for any contract greater than one year. Most buyers, not seeing any great rewards to them from negotiating long-term contracts, and seeing very clearly the extra hassle involved in getting two additional levels of approval, simply did not attempt to negotiate long-term contracts. A one-word change was all that was needed. The new policy stated that any contract for less than one year would require two additional levels of authorization, leading to historic changes in the nature of Ford's supplier relationships.[28]

cooperation can flourish. Similar to the operation of teamwork within an organization (see chapter 7), quality customer-supplier relations help both parties to achieve their goals.

One common form that cooperation takes is the early involvement of suppliers in the design of new products.[29] Early involvement allows suppliers to make cost-cutting and quality-improving suggestions about the design while changes are relatively easy and inexpensive to make. When the product design is not revealed to suppliers until late in the process, often out of concern that it will be leaked to competitors, such opportunities are lost. Security concerns can be dealt with through nondisclosure agreements.[30]

Another indication of cooperation is the effort of customers to help suppliers improve quality, which can take many forms. Many TQM-oriented corporations present quality-improvement seminars for their suppliers.[31] Juran recommends joint quality planning between customers and suppliers, featuring the exchange of quality-related information.[32] Although customers traditionally have hammered suppliers to lower their prices, in a cooperative relationship the focus is on helping suppliers to lower their costs, which will ultimately benefit both parties.[33] As John Wallace points out, all of this requires substantial sharing of information:

> You know companies never used to share information. We share our information. You've got to have a pretty good relationship with your customers and suppliers before you can do something like that. But it makes sense given the fact that you're narrowing down the number of companies that are suppliers for you, so that you can build a better relationship—a more trusting relationship.[34]

QUALITY CUSTOMER-SUPPLIER RELATIONSHIPS IN ACTION

Many of the aspects of quality CSRs we have been discussing are illustrated by the relationship between G.E. Appliance and D.J. Inc., both of Louisville, Kentucky.[35] In nine years, D.J. went from being one of 100 G.E. suppliers of plastic parts to being its sole source. D.J. improved its quality by taking advantage of G.E.'s supplier seminars in statistical process control (SPC). The company must have studied hard, as it has not had a single lot of parts rejected by G.E. since 1978. Early involvement in product design is commonplace for these two companies. In one typical case, D.J. recommended a minor change in product design that reduced the cost of a part by more than 5 percent and increased its expected life by 15 percent. This example typifies the advantages enjoyed by companies with quality customer-supplier relationships.

Granite Rock Company of Watsonville, California, a 1992 Malcolm Baldrige Award winner, has also devoted itself to absorbing and making use of information from customers.[36] Bruce Woolpert, who shares with his brother Steve the CEO title at Granite Rock, believes that the role of manager is "to make sure there's a flood of information coming into the company." Where does the flood come from? Granite Rock has its customers rate its performance against its competitors in "report cards," longer surveys, quick-response cards, and focus groups. Information on what customers need and what is being done to satisfy them is distributed throughout the company via team meetings, an annual recognition day, and the appropriately-titled company newsletter, "Rock Talk."

Granite Rock learned that quarry customers wanted to pick up rock very quickly at any time of the day or night. To satisfy this need, the company invested a great deal of money in "Granite Xpress," a system that allows customers to pull up to the quarry, check the computer for their order, and insert a magnetic card to load their own orders. Not only does this system operate 24 hours a day, but it has reduced the time at the quarry for truckers from 30 minutes to 10.

Granite Rock personnel also frequently make trips to benchmark other companies, both in their industry (aggregate and concrete producers) and out of their industry (a gold mine). Perhaps the furthest afield they have roamed is to Domino's Pizza, another company that is concerned about on-time delivery. Domino's told Granite Rock where to get better maps and suggested that they adopt Domino's practice of writing house numbers on maps.

CUSTOMER-SUPPLIER RELATIONS IN ORGANIZATION THEORY

Total quality management can be related to a number of organizational theories. The following sections discuss TQM's relationship with the resource dependence perspective and the theory of integrative bargaining.

The Resource Dependence Perspective

The organizational theory most directly comparable to the TQM view of customer-supplier relations is the Resource Dependence Perspective (RDP) developed by Jeffrey Pfeffer and Gerald Salancik.[37] This perspective—which deals with how organizations manage to get the resources they need from their environment—resembles TQM in some ways, yet differs in others.

The most important similarity between the two perspectives is their mutual emphasis on the idea that the sources of an organization's success lie outside its boundaries. Although the idea that customers ultimately grant the organization its continued existence has become familiar as a fundamental principle of TQM, Pfeffer and Salancik point out that much organization theory focuses on the internal operations of organizations, giving less emphasis to the organization's environment:

> Most current writers give only token consideration to the environmental context of organizations. The environment is there, somewhere outside the

organization, and the idea is mentioned that environments constrain or affect organizations . . . After this, the task of management is considered. Somehow, the things to be managed are usually within the organization, assumed to be under its control, and often have to do with the direction of low-level hired personnel. When authors get down to the task of describing the running of the organization, the relevance of the environment fades.[38]

According to the RDP, the effectiveness of an organization should be understood in terms of how well it meets the demands of external groups and organizations that are concerned with its actions and products. This is similar to the TQM conception of quality as meeting or exceeding customer expectations. There is an interesting difference, however, between the RDP concept of effectiveness and the TQM concept of quality.

TQM has traditionally focused almost exclusively on the organization's customers—i.e., those who purchase the organization's products and provide the wherewithal for the organization's continued survival. The RDP perspective, however, recognizes that organizations must satisfy the demands of not only customers, but also other entities in the environment including various government agencies, interest groups, shareholders, and—to some extent—society as a whole.

A government regulatory agency can make life miserable for an organization it does not believe is following government regulations—e.g., a coal mine with inadequate safety procedures or a restaurant with unsanitary practices. In the extreme case, the government can even shut them down. Interest groups can influence customers to boycott a product for reasons unrelated to the quality of the product itself. Certain brands of California wine were boycotted for years because of the alleged mistreatment of the migrant farm workers who picked their grapes.

Shareholders of public corporations in recent years have become a constituency to be reckoned with. They are making increasing demands on how corporations operate, including not only economic but also social and environmental aspects of performance such as minority hiring and use of recyclable materials.

From this perspective it is clear that although customers are important, groups and organizations other than customers can play a major role in determining an organization's success. TQM advocates can take two avenues in dealing with this issue. The first would be to enlarge the concept of customers to include all those who have a stake in the organization. Following this logic, an organization would not be seen as practicing TQM unless it met the expectations of all of its constituencies, not just its customers in the traditional sense. However, different groups are apt to have very different expectations for the behavior of an organization, thus making it quite difficult to satisfy all parties.

The other avenue would be for TQM advocates to recognize that although providing quality to customers is the overriding focus of an organization's activities, satisfying customers alone will not necessarily guarantee continued success, due to the potential influence of other constituencies. Interestingly, this perspective has recently been incorporated into the Baldrige Award criteria:

> A company's quality system objectives should address corporate responsibility and citizenship. Corporate responsibility refers to basic expectations of the company—business ethics and protection of public health, public safety, and the environment...Plans should seek avenues to avoid problems, to provide forthright company response if problems occur, and to make available information needed to maintain public awareness, safety, trust, and confidence. [This] means not only meeting all local, state, and federal legal and regulatory requirements, but also treating these and related requirements as areas for continuous improvement beyond mere compliance.

Another similarity between TQM and RDP is in their recognition of interdependence between organizations as a fact of organizational life that must be managed effectively.

> In the current dense environment...interdependencies are the problem. The dominant problems of the organization have become managing its exchanges and its relationships with the diverse interests affected by its actions...The increasing density of relationships among diverse interests has led to less willingness to rely on unconstrained market forces. Negotiation, political strategies, the management of the organization's institutional relationships—these have all become more important.[39]

Thus the RDP shares with TQM the idea that managing interdependencies with other organizations is a key to success. The two perspectives diverge again, however, when it comes to how such interdependencies should be managed. Quality customer-supplier relationships are seen from the TQM perspective as consisting of mutually beneficial partnerships. Such an option, however, is not anticipated in the RDP. From this perspective, interdependence should be managed by some combination of gaining as much control as possible over the other organization, minimizing the other party's control over one's own organization, making it difficult for the other organization to monitor and influence one's behavior, and so on.

When compared to the protection of self-interest inherent in the recommendations of the RDP, the TQM win-win doctrine sounds somewhat naive. Yet most organizations practicing TQM and building partnerships with their customers and suppliers have traditionally managed customer-supplier relationships in the manner suggested by the RDP and have been dissatisfied with the results. The partnership efforts are mostly in their early stages, and there is no guarantee that they will ultimately succeed. As of now, however, they are the preferred method of many firms for managing interdependence.

Integrative Bargaining

The idea of building cooperative relationships that benefit both parties to a negotiation is not something that was created by writers or practitioners of TQM. The idea of mutually beneficial relationships and win-win bargaining comes from a long tradition of research and writing on conflict management and negotiation.[40]

The idea behind this research tradition is that both parties will benefit more in the long run if they work together to help each other, rather than each one striving to win each round of negotiation. This tradition has been appropriated by writers on TQM, perhaps because it is consistent with the idea of customer orientation and teamwork. This is another area where TQM doctrine derives in a straightforward manner from existing organizational theory.

SUMMARY

Customers are the focus of companies practicing TQM, and those companies recognize that they cannot satisfy their customers without strong partnerships with their suppliers. The principles for developing quality customer-supplier relationships are

- recognizing the centrality of customers and the importance of suppliers,
- developing win-win relationships, and
- building up and acting on trust.

The practices for implementing these principles in dealing with customers are

- collecting information relentlessly about what customers want,
- distributing this information broadly within the organization, and
- designing one's products and services in accord with customer demands.

Practices for creating effective relationships with suppliers include developing long-term relationships with a limited number of suppliers chosen on the basis of quality, developing cooperative relations characterized by early supplier involvement in product design, and working together to improve quality and reduce costs. TQM principles and practices for customer-supplier relations are related to organizational theories of resource dependence and negotiation.

REVIEW AND DISCUSSION QUESTIONS

1. What can be learned about customer-supplier relationships from the story about IBM and its Japanese supplier?

2. Draw a diagram of a customer-supplier chain that includes at least four organizations. What attributes of quality are required at each link in the

chain? How does quality at the beginning of the chain influence quality at the end?

3. Why are suppliers important to a company's quality efforts?

4. Identify three practices through which companies can better understand their customers' needs.

5. Think of a type of customer that you know reasonably well. Try to identify some unmet needs of this type of customer and to think of some new features of the products and/or services they purchase that would excite them. Why do you think these features are not being offered?

6. Identify a customer-supplier relationship in which you are involved. How does it compare to the principles and practices of TQM relationships? In what specific ways could adopting some of the principles and practices discussed in this chapter improve this relationship?

7. How do the terms used for customers in different industries and occupations (e.g., patients, clients, passengers, students) influence how people in these industries think about their customers?

8. How would TQM and the Resource Dependence Perspective differ in describing the quality and effectiveness of a state university?

9. Can you think of a situation in which customers are not important to the success of an organization?

10. How should an organization go about deciding who its customers are? Identify the customers of a university, a government agency, and a movie producer.

CASES

Pro Fasteners, Incorporated

Pro Fasteners of San Jose, California, has been particularly innovative in building quality customer-supplier relationships.[41] Inspired by such books as Crosby's *Quality Without Tears* and quality-oriented companies such as Nordstrom, President Steve Braccini conceived of a radical new role for his company, which provides industrial hardware and components to the electronics industry.

In the late 1980s, many of Pro's customers were making the kinds of changes we have discussed, such as buying from fewer suppliers and using long-term contracts. They were asking more of the suppliers they kept, including a commitment to keep them stocked with their product, quality guaranteed. Braccini realized that his customers were really saying they didn't want to have to worry about their parts inventory and that Pro Fasteners could do a better job of managing it than they could—and at a lower cost to boot. As

Braccini put it, "Suddenly, the customer could cut his in-house staff. He'd have no purchasing costs, no receiving costs, no quality-assurance costs."

With this vision of being excruciatingly close to the customer came some significant management and organizational challenges for Pro Fastener. They would need to learn to anticipate customer needs. They would have to be on the cutting edge of quality. They would need the computer power to keep track of hundreds of thousands of parts. Most important, they would need committed and adaptive people in the organization to pull this off.

Using teams, among other methods, Pro Fastener has made a great deal of progress in turning the quality vision into reality. One team found a way to ship 100 percent correct parts with 100 percent on-time delivery to Applied Materials, a major customer. Another team responded to customer complaints about setting up credit with a "courtesy account" that can be opened immediately, with no credit check and is good for $100.00. Hundreds of similar changes have transformed the company, particularly its relationships with customers.

The changes did not come easily. Employees often wondered whether Braccini knew what he was doing. His wife and partner was especially concerned about the amount of responsibility that was given to associates. Braccini created an employee quality group called the Continuous Improvement Council (CIC), which eventually decided to kick all of the managers off the quality teams. If a new style of organization was being born, the labor pains were awful.

However, the quality CSRs Pro Fasteners has developed have paid off in a big way. Despite a recession, the company's sales rose 20 percent between 1989 and 1992, and the company won more than 50 quality awards during this period. Overall, as one purchasing agent puts it, "They're the best." What else could you ask for in a supplier?

Discussion Questions

1. How does Pro Fasteners illustrate the principles of customer-supplier relationships discussed in this chapter?
2. If the company had failed in this attempt to change the nature of its business, what would have been the likely causes?
3. What role can information systems play in managing customer-supplier relationships?

Lands' End: The Secrets of Success

Lands' End, a popular and very successful catalogue company, recently shared with customers the secrets of its success. The following are some of the things they had to say:[42]

Here at Lands' End, in the heartland of America, we still believe the customer comes first . . . There are four basic ways we put the customer first. We hope you'll take a few minutes to read about them. Then decide if you'd like to be treated that way yourself.

1. **Make your merchandise as good as you can.** Our goal has always been to make our clothing and accessories as good as they could possibly be. By adding back features others have taken out over the years. By using the finest fabrics available. By inspecting the finished goods by eye to make sure they measure up . . .

2. **Always, always price it fairly . . .** It's our policy to mark up products modestly, just enough to give us a fair profit and to give you a terrific value. Admittedly, we have a few advantages. We're direct merchants with no middlemen taking a bite out of the profits. We don't spring for glitzy, budget-busting advertising...Our main headquarters is in Dodgeville, Wisconsin, surrounded by cornfields (no kidding)...

3. **Make it a snap to shop for, 24 hours a day.** Our store never closes. We're open around the clock every day of the week to accommodate the varied schedules and different time zones of our customers...Should you have detailed questions, we'll hook you up with one of our Specialty Shopper operators. They're our elite corps—the best of the best—able to answer any questions you might have about styling, fit, color matching and more.

4. **Guarantee it. Period.** We strive for perfection, but sometimes a flawed product slips through. The color may be a shade too dark. A button may break. A seam may unravel. In those cases, we beg your tolerance and offer you one final protection. If at any time you are not completely satisfied, return the item for a full refund or exchange. And please, never feel bad about sending something back. We'd rather a truckload of returns than one dissatisfied customer.

Discussion Questions

1. How is Lands' End practicing total quality in its products and services?
2. Would the experience of purchasing a shirt through a catalogue company differ from purchasing the same shirt from a department store? Clearly the experiences would be different. Could they both represent high quality?

ENDNOTES

1. Reported in "Total Quality Management and Competitiveness", by G. Pouskouleli, *Engineering Digest*, December 1991, pp. 14–17. The Japanese response is based on a story in the *Toronto Sun* by S. Ford, April 25, 1983, p.6.

2. This idea has been promoted by Richard J. Schonberger in his book, *Building a Chain of Customers*. New York: Free Press, 1990.

3. Arthur R. Tenner and Irving J. DeToro, *Total Quality Management: Three Steps to Continuous Improvement*. Reading, Mass.: Addison-Wesley, 1992, p.197.

4. 1993 Award Criteria, Malcolm Baldrige National Quality Award. Gaithersburg, Md.: National Institute of Standards and Technology, United States Department of Commerce.

5. As seen in *Dear Abbey* column by Abigail Van Buren. Dist. by Universal Press Syndicate. Reprinted with permission. All rights reserved.

6. We are indebted to David Waldman for this insight.

7. As seen in *Dear Abbey* column by Abigail Van Buren. Dist. by Universal Press Syndicate. Reprinted with permission. All rights reserved.

8. Reprinted with the permission of The Free Press, a Division of Macmillan, Inc., from *Juran on Leadership for Quality: An Executive Handbook* by J.M. Juran. Copyright © 1989 by Juran Institute Inc.

9. John Carlisle, quoted in Tenner and DeToro, *Total Quality Management*.

10. Marriott's approach to gathering information from customers is discussed in detail in *The Customer-Driven Company: Moving from Talk to Action* by Richard C. Whitely. Reading, Mass.: Addison-Wesley, 1991.

11. See Benson P. Shapiro, V. Kasturi Rangan, and John J. Sviokla, "Staple Yourself to an Order," *Harvard Business Review*, July–August 1992, pp. 113–122.

12. Quoted in "When Customer Research is a Lousy Idea" by Willard I. Zangwill. *Wall Street Journal*, March 8, 1993.

13. Whitely, *The Customer-Driven Company*, p.7

14. Based on Houghton Award Application 1992, U.S Precision Lens, Inc.

15. Whitely, *The Customer-Driven Company*, chapter 2.

16. Quoted in "Could AT&T Rule the World?" by David Kirkpatrick. *Fortune*, May 17, 1993.

17. Whitely, *The Customer-Driven Company*.

18. Whitely, *The Customer-Driven Company*.

19. "Complex Quality: AMP Rings Up Service Success," by Dick Schaaf. *The Quality Imperative*, September 1992, pp. 16–26.

20. Based on "Arts groups try to keep the customer satisfied" by Owen Findsen and Cliff Radel. *The Cincinnati Enquirer*, February 7, 1993.

21. These practices are based on *The Deming Route to Quality and Productivity* by William W. Scherkenbach (Rockville, Md.: Mercury Press, 1988) and on

Juran on Leadership for Quality by Joseph M. Juran (New York: Free Press, 1989).

22. Robert C. Hill and Sara M. Friedman, "Managing the Quality Process: Lessons from a Baldrige Award Winner; A Conversation with John W. Wallace, Chief Executive Officer of the Wallace Company." *Academy of Management Executive*, 1992, 6(1), pp. 76–88.

23. This idea has long been championed by Deming. See the discussion of his 14 points in chapter 2.

24. For a discussion of these two points, see David N. Burt, "Managing Suppliers Up to Speed," *Harvard Business Review,* July–August 1989, pp. 127–135.

25. Tenner and DeToro, *Total Quality Management.*

26. Patrick J. McMahon, "Supplier Involvement," chapter 9 in *The Improvement Process* by H. James Harrington (New York: McGraw-Hill, 1987).

27. Hill and Friedman, "Managing the Quality Process."

28. W.W. Scherkenbach, *The Deming Route to Quality and Productivity.* Washington, D.C: CEEP Press, 1986, p.131.

29. This point is discussed by Randall S. Schuler and Drew L. Harris in *Managing Quality: The Primer for Middle Managers.* Reading, Mass.: Addison-Wesley, 1992.

30. McMahon, op. cit.

31. McMahon, op. cit.

32. Juran: *Juran on Leadership for Quality.*

33. Schuler and Harris: *Managing Quality*

34. Hill and Friedman, "Managing the Quality Process."

35. This example is discussed by David N. Burt in "Managing Suppliers Up to Speed," *Harvard Business Review*, July–August 1989, pp. 127–135.

36. The section on Granite Rock is based on "The Changemasters" by John Case, *INC.*, March 1992, pp. 58–70.

37. Jeffrey Pfeffer and Gerald R. Salancik. *The External Control of Organizations: A Resource Dependence Perspective.* New York: Harper & Row, 1978.

38. Ibid., pp. 257–258.

39. Pfeffer and Salancik, *The External Control of Organizations,* p.94.

40. See, for example, David W. Johnson and Frank P. Johnson, *Joining Together: Group Theory and Group Skills.* Englewood Cliffs, N.J.: Prentice-Hall, 1975; Max H. Bazerman and Roy J. Lewicki (eds.), *Negotiating in*

Organizations. Beverly Hills: Sage Publications, 1983; M. Afzalur Rahim, "A strategy for managing conflict in complex organizations," *Human Relations*, vol. 38, no. 1, 1985, pp. 81–89.

41. The material on Pro Fasteners is based on "Quality with Tears" by John Case, *INC.*, June 1992, pp. 82–93.

42. Land's End Direct Merchants. Reprinted with permission.

CHAPTER 5

Designing Organizations
for Quality

Chapter Outline

The Functional Structure
    Problems with the Functional Structure
Redesigning Organizations for Quality
    Internal Customers
    Team-based Organization
    Reduce Hierarchy
    Create Steering Committees
Organizational Design for Quality in Action
    General Electric Bayamón
    Kaizen
Comparison to Theories of Organizational Design
    Structural Contingency Theory
    Institutional Theory
Summary
Review and Discussion Questions
Cases

In 1950 Deming drew the following picture on a blackboard for a handful of Japanese executives:

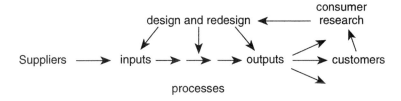

Many people see this as simply a diagram of a typical production system that is linked to customers and suppliers. Visionaries in the practice of TQM see this as a new model of an organization chart.

Many organizations implementing total quality have found it necessary to reconfigure the structures of their organizations. This chapter discusses the changes in organization design necessary to achieve total quality. The chapter will

- describe the functional structure, the most common structure used at the plant or business unit level;

- show how many aspects of the functional structure stand in the way of quality and what changes are necessary to create organization structures that support TQ;

- provide several examples of how firms are making substantial changes in their organizations in order to implement TQ; and

- compare organizational design from a TQ point of view to more conventional perspectives.

THE FUNCTIONAL STRUCTURE

In the functional structure shown in Figure 5.1, the organization is divided into functions such as operations and maintenance, each of which is headed by a manager. The title of such managers is often "director" in small organizations and "vice president" in larger ones. In such organizations communication occurs vertically up or down the chain of command, rather than horizontally across functions.

Functional structures provide organizations with a clear chain of command and allow people to specialize in the aspect of the work for which they are best suited. They also make it easy to evaluate people based on a narrow but clear set of responsibilities. For these reasons functional structures are common in both manufacturing and service organizations at plant and business unit levels.

Problems with the Functional Structure

Despite its popularity, the functional structure is designed primarily for the administrative convenience of the organization, rather than for providing high-quality service to customers. From a TQ point of view, the functional structure has several inadequacies.

The functional structure separates employees from customers.   Few employees in the functional organization have direct contact with customers or even a clear idea of how their work combines with the work of others to satisfy customers. The functional structure tends to insulate employees from learning

Figure 5.1   Functional Structure for a Manufacturing Company

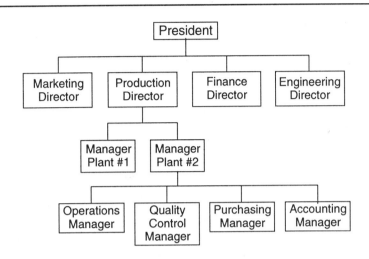

about customer expectations and their degree of satisfaction with the service or product the firm is providing. Being insulated from customers encourages in workers a narrow conception of their responsibilities. This is often expressed in statements such as "It's not my job" or "I just work here." Even when such employees want to help customers, they often have such a limited understanding of how their organizational system works that they are unable to do so. This often results in demotivated workers and poor quality work.

Most of us have experienced this phenomenon when we call a large organization trying to get help and get switched to several different people before (if we're lucky) finding someone willing and able to help us. If our needs as customers relate to the product or service as a whole, but the knowledge and responsibilities of anyone with whom we deal relate only to their function, we are doomed to disappointment.[1]

More seriously, the functional structure promotes the idea that one's boss is the customer whom the employee must satisfy. Of course, this manager is trying to satisfy the *next*-level manager, and so on. If the chain ended at the customer, the structure might work, but this is generally not the case. Managers in functional organizations are usually rewarded for satisfying functional goals, such as meeting design deadlines and limiting manufacturing costs, rather than for providing value to customers.

The focus on vertical reporting relationships to the exclusion of horizontal coordination has led many observers to refer to departments in functional organizations as "chimneys" or "silos." As Myron Tribus describes it, "The enterprise is viewed as a collection of separate, highly specialized individual performers and units...Lateral connections are made by intermediaries close to the top of the provinces."[2]

Paul Allaire, Xerox's chairman and CEO, has presided over a massive restructuring of the corporation. He describes the company's problems with the functional organization and its new approach as follows:

> We were an extremely functional organization. If you were in manufacturing, you strived to make manufacturing as good as possible—and only secondarily to make the businesses that manufacturing affected work well. The same was true for sales, R&D, or any other function...
>
> We [now] want people who can hold two things in their heads at the same time, who can think in terms of their individual organizations but also in terms of the company as a whole. Our architecture won't work if people take a narrow view of their jobs and don't work together.[3]

The functional structure inhibits process improvement. No organizational unit has control over a whole process, although most processes involve a large number of functions. This is because the breakup of the organization into functions is usually unrelated to the processes used to deliver a product to the customer. This structure is likely to create complex, wasteful processes, as people do things in one area that must be redone or undone in another.

For example, some organizations maintain a group of engineers whose sole responsibility is to redesign products so that they can be manufactured effectively. The engineers who design the products in the first place worry only about product performance, not manufacturability. (For another example of problems in coordinating design and manufacturing, see the case "Barriers, What Barriers?" at the end of this chapter). Worse yet, if one function tries to improve its part, it may well make things worse (more wasted time and effort, more cost) for another part of the process. In this environment, continuous process improvement doesn't stand a chance.

Richard Palermo, a vice president for quality and transition at Xerox, explains the problems with functional structures in terms of "Palermo's law," which states: "If a problem has been bothering your company and your customers for years and won't yield, that problem is the result of a cross-functional dispute, where nobody has total control of the whole process." The corollary to Palermo's law? "People who work in different functions hate each other."[4]

Functional organizations often have a separate function for quality, called Quality Control (Figure 5.1) or Quality Assurance. This may send a message to the rest of the organization that there is a group dedicated to quality, so it's not their responsibility. Furthermore, it breaks the feedback loop that informs employees that their work needs to be improved. The QC department is generally responsible for collecting and maintaining quality statistics, which may not seem as valid to the departments actually doing the work.[5]

This arrangement obviously stands in the way of continuous process improvement. Organizations pursuing TQ often retain their quality assurance departments, but these units act more as coaches or facilitators to employees, rather than as the group with primary responsibility for quality.

In summary, the functional organization compromises total quality in several ways: It distances people from customers and insulates them from customer expectations. It promotes complex and wasteful processes and inhibits process improvement. It separates the quality function from the rest of the organization, providing people with an excuse for not worrying about quality. The next section discusses some remedies for the quality problems caused by the functional structure.

REDESIGNING ORGANIZATIONS FOR QUALITY

One of Deming's 14 points is to "break down barriers between departments" because "people in various departments must work as a team."[6] This slogan captures in a nutshell what the TQ philosophy entails for organizational design. People cannot contribute to customer satisfaction and continuous improvement if they are confined to functional prisons where they cannot see customers or hear their voices.

Internal Customers

One way organizations can promote quality and teamwork is to recognize the existence of "internal customers." An internal customer is another person or group within the organization who depends on one's work to get their work done. For example, machine operators in a manufacturing plant are customers of maintenance; if maintenance does not do its job well, the machines will not produce quality products (or perhaps not any products at all).

In a university, professors and students are customers of the audiovisual staff, who provide and maintain overhead projectors and VCRs. In a restaurant, the servers are internal customers of the kitchen staff, because the servers' ability to serve appetizing food in a timely manner to customers depends on the kitchen. In Figure 5.2, Product Design is the internal customer of both Research and Development and Marketing, Manufacturing is the customer of Product Design and Purchasing, and Sales is the customer of Manufacturing. Although not shown in the diagram, all of these departments are customers of staff groups such as human resources and finance.

Richard Schonberger, a noted consultant and writer on manufacturing and quality, has taken the internal customer idea one step further by arguing that organizations should be designed as "chains of customers." That is, customer-supplier links should be forged, one at a time, from the organization's suppliers all the way to its external (real) customers.[7]

Promoting the idea of internal customers does not change the organization's structure so much as it changes the way that people think about the structure. Rather than focusing on satisfying their immediate supervisor (vertical), people begin to think about satisfying the next person in the process (horizontal), who is one step closer to the ultimate customer. In a pizza delivery

Figure 5.2 Internal Customers in a Manufacturing Company

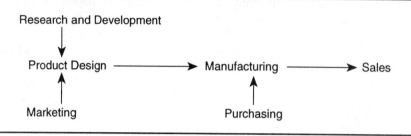

business, the people who deliver the pizzas are internal customers of the people who make them, who in turn are customers of the order-takers. Satisfying internal customers first is the best way to satisfy the external customer. An unusual customer-supplier relationship was uncovered at Oregon State University (see box).

Some managers resist the idea of internal customers, arguing that the only customers people should worry about are the ones who pay the bills. But for those employees who never come near a "real" customer, a focus on internal customers helps them to help those who do. Of course, this only works if the needs expressed by internal customers are in fact closely related to their ability to satisfy actual customers. A certain amount of trust that this is the case is necessary for the system to work.

A good example of creating links between internal customers and their suppliers is provided by an event at AMP Incorporated, a global electronic connector company. Sales engineers visited two of AMP's manufacturing plants and cooked a barbecue lunch for production workers. After lunch, the sales engineers introduced themselves, talked about their customers, and displayed some of the end products, such as power tools, into which the connectors made at the plant are placed. One production associate's reaction was, "I sometimes felt that we made millions of these parts and they simply dumped them in the ocean after we shipped them out. Now I know where most of them go."[8]

Team-based Organization

A more substantial organizational redesign involves structuring the organization into teams, each of which has the responsibility to carry out and improve one of the organization's core processes.[9] (In the pizza delivery example, core processes would include order-taking, pizza-making, and delivery.) Depending on the size of the organization and the nature of the processes, the teams may include everyone who contributes to a given process or only a representative subset. Similarly, the teams may meet continuously on a crash basis until their

Where's the Paperwork?
Quality Improvement at Oregon State[10]

Oregon State University was among the first universities to embrace TQM. In 1990, faced with state budget cuts and trying to improve the quality of its operation, Oregon State began the process of quality improvement. Like many schools, it focused first on improving administrative areas.

The physical plant was among the first areas singled out for quality improvement. Specifically, the group that did repair and remodeling at the university tackled the time it took to complete a work order, which its internal customers identified as the number one problem with the service they were receiving. When the group began to address the problem, they found that the average time to complete a job was 195 days, just over six months.

None of people who actually did the work could believe the entire process took so long, since individually each knew that their work lasted only a few days or weeks. In attempting to understand why it took so long, the group set up a flowchart of the process they used in their work.

They discovered that a woman in another group received their work orders first, and it took 10 days for the paperwork to make its way to the repair and remodeling group. Group members approached the woman and asked what she did with the paperwork during the time she kept it. She did her job and she did it well, exactly as she had been instructed, she told them. What exactly had she been told to do? When the paperwork arrives, put it aside and after 10 days, send it on to the repair and remodeling group!

As it turned out, there had been a time when the group had had trouble getting the material they needed for jobs delivered. Having no success in expediting the flow of material, they simply slowed down the flow of paperwork, so that they would have a head start on the job when the paperwork arrived. Eventually the problems with material delivery were resolved, but no one had remembered to undo the 10-day waiting period. Since the paperwork was held by another functional group, no one in repair and remodeling had a broad enough view of the process to see what was going on.

Sometimes process improvement is hard work. But in this case the repair and remodeling group could get off to a fast start by immediately knocking 10 days off of their time!

new process design is complete, after which they may meet periodically or on an ad hoc basis whenever necessary.

This approach eliminates many of the problems with the functional structure. By bringing together everyone associated with a process, practices that are wasteful or compromise quality become much easier to identify and eliminate. If a team has responsibility for an entire process, they don't have to worry that their improvement efforts will be undermined—intentionally or unintentionally—by the actions of another group.

Using processes as a grouping method can create substantial improvement in organizations by allowing people to see and change procedures they couldn't see or change in the functional structure. As Robert Brookhouse, member of a process organization at Xerox, puts it, "When you create a flow [Xerox's term for process organization], you find where you're wasting time, doing things twice. And because we own the entire process, we can change it."[11]

This is not to suggest that changing to a process-based organization is simple or easy. On the contrary, it takes a lot of thought, because it means essentially taking the organization apart and putting it back together again. As Robert Knorr and Edward Thiede describe it:

> The restructuring should begin by defining each process in terms of its operations, information, and skill needs . . . Process definition also answers key questions about the lines of integration needed among processes and functions, such as who must interact and when? What changes are needed in upstream processes to accommodate the needs of those downstream, and vice versa?[12]

Mark Kelly provides an example of an organizational structure based on teams in *The Adventures of a Self-Managing Team.*[13] The building blocks of the "Clear Lake Plant" organization are process-based teams. Tasks that transcend processes (such as innovation and safety) are handled in task teams made up of members drawn from each of the process teams. This organization is depicted in Figure 5.3. (Compare this to the functional organization in Figure 5.1 to get an idea of the size of the changes we are talking about.)

Reduce Hierarchy

A third type of structural change that often results from a focus on internal customers and the creation of process teams is a reduction in the number of hierarchical layers in the organization. Several levels of middle management are often eliminated. (Of course, if an organization is designed for quality from its inception, those levels are not there in the first place.) This reduction in middle management is also facilitated by advances in information systems that have taken over many of the information summarization and transmission roles formerly played by middle managers.

With the elimination of nonvalue-added activities and the empowerment of front-line workers to improve processes, there is also less supervision and coordination for managers to do. An additional benefit of such "flatter" organiza-

Figure 5.3   Organizational Structure of the Clear Lake Plant

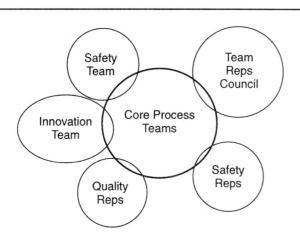

tions is improved communication between top managers and front-line employees.

This is not to say that the flattening of organizational structures is without its drawbacks. People—sometimes many people—lose their jobs. This is not only a significant disruption in the lives of the individuals affected, but also a loss of their experience to the organization. Furthermore, the morale of the people who remain in the organization may suffer. For all of these reasons, organizations should approach flattening with an attitude of caution and concern.

Create Steering Committees

A fourth type of structural change associated with TQ is the creation of a high-level planning group invested with the responsibility for guiding the organization's quality efforts. Such groups—called steering committees, quality councils, or quality improvement teams—are a key part of many firms' quality improvement efforts and an important part of the quality recommendations of both Juran and Crosby.

According to Juran, the role of the quality council is to "launch, coordinate, and institutionalize annual quality improvement."[14] In the Crosby system, the quality improvement team (QIT) sets annual quality objectives for the organization. In general, steering committees act as a focal point for quality in the organization.

Such groups provide a means of demonstrating and increasing the organization's commitment to quality, as well as a mechanism for coordinating the efforts of various organizational units. Although many firms use only top managers in such groups, Portman Equipment Company—an industrial equipment sales, service and rental company—uses people from all types of jobs. Richard Buck, Portman's vice president for quality, argues that the presence of front-line associates in the committee has made a big difference in the decisions the group has made:

> We have general managers, we have some supervisory people, and we have some hourly people. It was our decision in forming a steering committee to break precedence from every company we've studied that used only executives on the steering committee. We opted to break that pattern and listen to the voices of all of our people as we formulate our plans. I think it's one of the better decisions we've made. And looking back on decisions we have made in the steering committee, I think there's good evidence that some of our decisions would not have been the same if we did not have representation from hourly people. I think as managers we tend to learn to think the way managers think...having hourly people gives us a different perspective. We see a broader picture and it's been good for our quality initiative.[15]

ORGANIZATIONAL DESIGN FOR QUALITY IN ACTION

Promoting the concept of internal customers, forming process teams, reducing hierarchy, and creating steering committees all facilitate quality. This section presents examples of organizations that use these ideas to ensure or improve quality in their operations. One example is from Puerto Rico, another from Japan, and a third (in box) from California.

General Electric Bayamón

Located near San Juan, Puerto Rico, G.E. Bayamón produces surge protectors that keep power stations and electric lines from being zapped by lightning. Bayamón is the newest high-performance workplace designed by Philip Jarrosiak, human resources manager for capacitor and power protection operations at GE.[17]

Bayamón's approximately 190 employees are structured into three levels: the plant manager, fifteen "advisers", and the hourly workers. According to Jarrosiak, a traditionally structured plant would have twice as many managers. The hourly workers are divided into teams of about 10 people, each of which has responsibility for a process such as shipping and receiving. Team members represent all parts of a process, so that team decisions take into consideration a wide variety of views and needs. The advisers act as resources for the teams, becoming active only when a team needs help.

To prepare them for such extensive responsibility, workers at Bayamón are given a great deal of training in such areas as machine maintenance, quality control, business practices, and English. The more workers learn, the more they

It's a Jungle in There[16]

With $75 million in revenues, 1200 employees, and 5 million visitors annually, the Zoological Society of San Diego (a.k.a. the San Diego Zoo) is a force to be reckoned with in the animal world. Even during the recession of the early '90s, the zoo (and its Wild Animal Park) managed to increase attendance. Its overall objectives include recreation, education, and conservation.

One of the reasons for the zoo's success may be its reorganization. In the old system, the animals were organized by species (e.g., *phascolarctos cinereus*) and the humans by functions (e.g., *homo sapiens beancounterus*). In fact, the humans were divided into 50 different departments, each of which played a role in the care and feeding of either animals, customers, or both. This led to a somewhat sterile and unrealistic environment for everyone involved. For example, a groundskeeper confessed to occasionally sweeping a cigarette butt from the path under a bush, so it would become the gardener's responsibility instead of his own.

In the new organization, the animals are grouped into bioclimatic zones that mirror their natural habitats. Gorilla Tropics groups the animals normally found in an African rain forest, while Tiger River recreates the environment of a jungle in Asia.

The humans haven't been forgotten in the new zoo design. They are now organized into teams, each of which has responsibility for one of the bioclimatic zones. The team that runs Tiger River includes specialists in mammals and birds, as well as maintenance and construction personnel. Although turf was jealously guarded in the old organization, team members are now learning one another's skills and cooperate in making improvements that transcend the old functional boundaries.

As the teams have taken over responsibility for activities that were previously the prerogatives of management, managers have been freed up to find ways to bring more people to the zoo. (As in any organization with a high level of fixed costs, maintaining a consistently high level of revenues is crucial to its survival.)

Any organization that competes with both Disneyland and Sea World for the southern California entertainment dollar had better act more like a cheetah *(acinonyx jubatus)* than a sitting duck *(anas platyrhynchos)*. With the new team-based system, the San Diego Zoo looks as if it may have found just the organization it needs.

are paid. Workers rotate through the plant's four work areas every six months, so that they bring a broad vision of how the factory operates to their teams.

The design for quality at Bayamón seems to be paying off. In just one year, the plant exceeded the productivity of similar plants by 20 percent and its productivity continues to increase.

Kaizen

Far to the east, many Japanese companies are organized in accordance with *kaizen,* the philosophy of continuous improvement.[18] Underlying *kaizen* is the belief that a great number of small improvements over time will create substantial improvement in organizational performance.

Although Japanese organizations practicing *kaizen* often maintain their functional structure, they superimpose on it a cross-functional management structure charged with continuous improvement of quality, cost, and ability to meet schedules (Figure 5.4). Each year top management articulates goals for improvements of cross-functional activities, which the *kaizen* management structure is designed to attain. Recently such efforts have been broadened in some Japanese organizations to include employee morale.

The relationships among competitive success, cross-functional goals such as quality, and the line organization are explained by Shigeru Aoki, senior managing director at Toyota:

> The ultimate goal of a company is to make profits. Assuming this is self-evident, then the next "superordinate" goals of the company should be such cross-functional goals as quality, cost, and scheduling (quantity and delivery).

Figure 5.4   Kaizen Organizational Structure

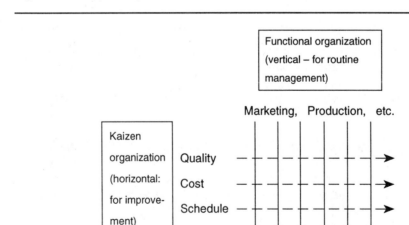

Without achieving these goals, the company will be left behind by the competition because of inferior quality, will find its profits eroded by higher costs, and will be unable to deliver the products in time for customers. If these cross-functional goals are realized, profits will follow. Therefore, we should regard all the other management functions as existing to serve the three superordinate goals...These auxiliary management functions include product planning, design, production, purchasing, and marketing, and they should be regarded as secondary means to achieve QCS [quality, cost, and scheduling].[19]

The committees that devise cross-functional goals at Toyota are composed of heads of departments concerned with a particular goal. The director of quality assurance, for example, heads the cross-functional quality committee. The heads of design and manufacturing also play leading roles in this committee, because their departments are expected to play leading roles in achieving quality goals. It then becomes the job of each function to work toward achieving the goals that the committee has established. In this manner, Toyota and other Japanese companies with similar structures retain the advantages of the functional structure while orienting managers and other associates toward customer-focused, cross-functional goals such as high quality.

COMPARISON TO ORGANIZATIONAL DESIGN THEORY

This section compares the total quality view of organizational design with the viewpoint from organization theory. Topics discussed are structural contingency theory and the institutional theory of organization structure.

Structural Contingency Theory

The structural contingency model, which originated in the 1960s, is the dominant view of organizational design in the management literature. According to this view, the two principal types of organization structures are mechanistic (centralized, many rules, strict division of labor, formal coordination across departments) and organic (decentralized, few rules, loose division of labor, informal coordination across departments).[20] These structures are described in detail in most management and organizational theory textbooks. The structural contingency model holds that there is no "one best way" to organize and that the choice between mechanistic and organic structures should be a function of certain contingencies, most often characteristics of the organization's environment and technology.

The choice between mechanistic and organic structures is usually seen as a function of uncertainty. Organizations face a great deal of uncertainty if their environments are complex and changing and if the technology they use in creating their products is not well understood. The microcomputer industry is a good example of this type of industry. The contingency model says that organizations facing uncertainty should adopt an organic structure. On the other hand, organizations that experience little uncertainty —their environments are simple and stable, and their technology is well understood—are seen as needing a mechanistic structure.

The rationale for these recommendations is that organic organizations are better able to process the information necessary to deal with a complex environment and uncertain technology. They are also more flexible and can adapt to the changing circumstances associated with an unstable environment. However, this information processing and adaptive capacity comes at the expense of efficiency and control. Although mechanistic organizations may not be able to accomplish uncertain tasks or to change rapidly, they are better-suited for accomplishing straightforward tasks in a predictable environment. The mechanistic organization will accomplish such tasks quite reliably, with little danger of employees engaging in costly experiments to see if there is a better way to do the job. The organic organization sacrifices reliability for flexibility.

Clearly a quality-oriented organization practicing continuous improvement cannot afford to freeze its processes by using a mechanistic structure. Most organizations practicing total quality move in the direction of organic structures. The number of levels in their hierarchy decreases, teams are created, and employees are given the authority (and even the responsibility) to develop new and better ways of accomplishing their tasks.

Coordination also tends toward the informal, as people who are interdependent are able to coordinate their work on a personal basis without the interference of a bureaucratic hierarchy. The relatively broader jobs in a TQ company give employees a better sense of how their work contributes to customer satisfaction, whether their customers are internal or external.

John Akers, former CEO of IBM who presided over a substantial reorganization of his company, stated that "Every reorganization solves some problems and creates some problems."[21] Are problems created by the adoption of organic-type TQ organizational designs? It is too early to tell. Few organizations are more than a few years into TQ, so there is not enough of a track record on which to judge. Even fewer, however, have reverted from a TQ-type design to a more mechanistic design, and more organizations all the time are adopting a design that features internal customers, process teams, broad employee responsibilities, and quality steering committees. This indicates that such structures are seen as viable and necessary by an increasing number of managers and organizations.

How can the "one best way" approach of the quality movement be justified in light of organization theory's historical endorsement of a contingency approach to design? It may be that few industries and technologies are simple and stable enough for a mechanistic design to operate effectively. A second possibility is that TQ designs have capacities for producing efficiencies unanticipated in the old mechanistic-organic distinction. Once the improvement of a particular process has reached the point where it is impractical to search for further gains, teams may establish the process as their standard and attempt to recreate it perfectly each time without the involvement of their managers. In other words, efficiencies would be created through different methods than those used in mechanistic firms.

A third possibility is that TQ-oriented firms pay a price in efficiency for their organizational structures, but that the superior quality of their products more than makes up for the higher prices that a lack of efficiency entails. Such firms would be unlikely to compete effectively in markets, such as textiles, where price is the overriding competitive factor.

A final possibility is that firms structured to achieve quality are paying a price for inefficiency that is not offset by their advantages. In this case such structures are not viable in the long run. This possibility does not seem to be the case, based on the limited information currently available.

Institutional Theory

Structural contingency theory, like most organizational design theories, is based on the assumption that organizations choose structures to help them perform better—provide high quality, low costs, and so forth. Institutional theory, on the other hand, holds that organizations try to succeed by creating structures that will be seen as appropriate by important external constituencies—customers, other organizations in the industry, government agencies, and so on.[22]

According to institutional theory, an aspect of organizational structure need not contribute to organizational performance to be worthwhile. If the adoption of a certain structure helps the organization to be seen as legitimate in the eyes of those who have power to determine the organization's fate, then it is worthwhile. For example, many businesses have departments devoted to achieving environmental goals. Whether these departments help achieve these goals is debatable, but the existence of such departments helps to promote the legitimacy of these organizations as being concerned about the environment.

From an institutional theory standpoint, it is important to ask whether quality-oriented organization designs that include steering committees and extensive use of teams are actually intended to promote quality or are merely a means of legitimizing the organization as a progressive, quality-conscious organization. Little evidence has been generated to suggest that such structures demonstrably improve performance, yet they continue to be adopted in huge numbers by organizations in all sectors of the economy.

In some settings, the adoption of quality-oriented structures is motivated primarily by institution concerns. For example, any company that wishes to compete in Europe must be certified as complying with the ISO-9000 quality standards. Suppliers to American automobile producers must also have elaborate quality programs in place. To continue to receive accreditation, hospitals in the U.S. must show progress in implementing continuous quality improvement (CQI).

Thus institutional theory provides another way of thinking about the rapid proliferation of quality-oriented structures in organizations. Although some organizations may be primarily seeking higher performance through the adoption of teams and steering committees, others may be primarily seeking the approval of important constituencies.

SUMMARY

Problems with the functional structure, such as overly complex processes and a narrow focus for individuals, have led many quality-oriented organizations to abandon this structure. New structures feature internal customers, process teams, less hierarchy, and quality steering committees. Although the widespread use of quality-oriented organic structures may be inconsistent with structural contingency theory, more companies are restructuring their organizations for quality. Some companies are adopting quality-oriented structures to appear legitimate in the eyes of important groups in their industry.

REVIEW AND DISCUSSION QUESTIONS

1. What are the advantages and disadvantages of the functional structure?

2. What are the major types of structural change initiated by organizations pursuing total quality?

3. Think back to an experience you have had with poor customer service from an organization. Whom did you blame for it? Do you know anything about the design of the organization involved? Do you think it was the fault of the individual(s) involved or could the problem have resulted from a poorly designed system? Would what you have learned in this chapter change your reaction to receiving poor quality service? How?

4. What are the core processes in a university? a video rental store? a fast food franchise? How could these organizations be redesigned around these processes? What barriers would need to be overcome to accomplish this?

5. Richard Palermo of Xerox was quoted in *Fortune* as saying that "people in different functions hate each other." Allowing for some exaggeration due to dramatic license, do you find this to be true? Talk to several people in a functional organization, and ask them about their feelings for people in other functions. How would you explain the variation in attitudes? If you were assigned to try to solve the problem of bad feelings between departments, how would you begin?

6. Could total quality be effective in a company with a mechanistic structure? How would it work?

7. Do you feel that the institutional theory of structure is a good description of why organizations choose quality-oriented organization designs? Why or why not?

CASES

Barriers? What Barriers?

The general manager of an elevator company had a common problem: He was utterly frustrated with the lack of cooperation between the mechanical engineers who designed new elevators, and the manufacturing engineers who determined how to produce them in the factory. The mechanical engineers would often completely design a new elevator without any consultation from the manufacturing engineers, and then expect the factory to somehow figure out how to build it. (This is known as "throwing it over the wall" to manufacturing.)

Often the new products were difficult or nearly impossible to build, and their quality and cost suffered as a result. The designs were usually sent back to the mechanical engineers (often more than once) for engineering changes to improve their manufacturability. While design and manufacturing played volleyball with the design, customers were forced to wait—often for months—for deliveries.

The general manager knew that if the two sets of engineers would simply communicate early in the design process, many of these problems could be eliminated before they occurred. At his wits' end, he found a large empty room in the facility and had the mechanical and manufacturing engineers working on the next product moved into the room, one group on one side and one on the other. Certainly if all they had to do to communicate was to walk from one side of the room to the other, communication would improve.

The manager relaxed somewhat, feeling that his problem had finally been solved. Upon returning to the new home of the engineers a few weeks later, he was in for a big surprise. The two sets of engineers had finally learned to cooperate! They had cooperated in building a wall of bookcases and file cabinets right down the middle of the room, effectively separating the large room into two separate offices, so they could continue as before.

Discussion Questions

1. What principles of total quality are illustrated or violated in this case?
2. Why do people feel such strong allegiance to their functional departments?
3. What could the general manager have done to improve the communication and the quality of the designs?

The British Post Office

The Post Office in Britain has undertaken a restructuring to improve the quality of service it provides.[23] Under the old organization, delivery of the mail and counter services were both handled through functional departments. At the local level, it was found that Head Postmasters were giving a great deal more attention to delivery, given its day-to-day urgency, than to counter service.

Upon reorganization, three new divisions were created: Royal Mail Letters, Royal Mail Parcels, and Post Office Counters, Ltd. By undertaking a focused set of customers and processes, each of these organizations has been able to reduce overhead and shorten the chain of command. In addition, responsibility for decision making has been placed much closer to the customer, and customers of each of the various post office services have an organization specifically charged with responding to their needs.

The corporate functional departments that remain, such as information technology, charge the divisions for their work. Periodic checks are made to ensure that the quality and costs of their service are comparable to what could be obtained outside the organization. Eventually these departments are expected to become full-fledged profit centers, so that the divisions are not burdened with subpar in-house suppliers.

Discussion Questions

1. Should the application of total quality be any different in a government agency than in a private organization?
2. What internal customer relationships have been created in the new organization?
3. Do you feel that the new organization will promote improved quality?

ENDNOTES

1. An interesting perspective on this problem is provided by Benson P. Shapiro, V. Kasturi Rangan, and John J. Sviokla, in "Staple Yourself to an Order," *Harvard Business Review*, July–August 1992, pp. 113–122.

2. Myron Tribus, Total Quality in Education. Unpublished manuscript. Hayward, Calif.: Exergy, Inc.

3. Quoted from "The CEO as Organizational Architect: An Interview with Xerox's Paul Allaire" by Robert Howard, in *Harvard Business Review*, September–October 1992, pp.106–121.

4. Thomas A. Stewart, "The Search for the Organization of Tomorrow," *Fortune*, May 18, 1992.

5. J.M. Juran, *Juran on Leadership for Quality: An Executive Handbook.* New York: The Free Press, 1989.

6. W.E. Deming, *Out of the Crisis.* Cambridge, Mass.: MIT Center for Advanced Engineering Study, 1986.

7. R.J. Schonberger, *Building a Chain of Customers.* New York: The Free Press, 1990.

8. Jerry G. Bowles, "Leading the World-Class Company," *Fortune*, September 21, 1992.

9. Jeannie Coyle, "Aligning human resource processes with total quality," *Employment Relations Today*, 18 (3), Fall 1991.

10. Based on "TQM—Quality with Reduced Resources," a talk given by Dr. Edwin Coate, vice president for finance and administration, Oregon State University, presented via teleconference by Cuyahoga Community College, September 9, 1992.

11. Stewart, "The Search for the Organization of Tomorrow."

12. Robert O. Knorr, and Edward F. Thiede, Jr., "Making new technologies work," *The Journal of Business Strategy*, 12 (1), pp. 46–49.

13. Mark Kelly, *The Adventures of a Self-Managing Team.* Raleigh, N.C.: Mark Kelly Books, 1990

14. Juran, *Juran on Leadership for Quality.*

15. Interview with Richard Buck.

16. Based on Stewart, "The Search for the Organization of Tomorrow."

17. Based on Stewart, "The Search for the Organization of Tomorrow."

18. M. Imai, *Kaizen: The Key to Japan's Competitive Success,* New York: McGraw Hill, 1986.

19. Imai, *Kaizen*, p.128.

20. This version of the contingency model comes from T. Burns and G.M. Stalker, *The Management of Innovation.* London: Tavistock, 1961.

21. Quoted in D. Hellriegel, J.W. Slocum and R.W. Woodman, *Organizational Behavior* (Fifth Edition). St. Paul, Minn.: West Publishing Company.

22. See J.W. Meyer and B. Rowan, "Institutionalized Organizations: Formal Structure as Myth and Ceremony," *American Journal of Sociology*, 83, pp. 340—363, 1977, or W.R. Scott, "The Adolescence of Institutional Theory," *Administrative Science Quarterly*, 32, pp. 493–511, 1987.

23. Based on R.M. Tabor, "Planning for Postal Services," *Long Range Planning*, 23 (5), 1990, pp. 91–96.

CHAPTER 6

Total Quality and Organizational Change

Capter Outline

The Importance of Change
Cultural Change
    Elements of a Total Quality Culture
    How Organizational Culture is Changed
    Making the New Culture Permanent
    Cultural Change in Action
Continuous Improvement
    Continuous Improvement and the Baldrige Award
    How Continuous Improvement is Practiced
    Continuous Improvement in Action
Reengineering
    Principles of Reengineering
    Reengineering in Action
Quality-oriented Change and Organization Theory
Summary
Review and Discussion Questions
Cases

Lewis Lehr, former CEO of 3M Corporation, once observed, "Our successes of the past are no guarantee of the future. Perhaps our biggest need at 3M is for people who are uncomfortable without change."[1] Organizational change is fundamental to total quality; indeed, there can be no quality without it. Anyone concerned with managing an organization dedicated to quality must understand what types of change are necessary in such an organization and how to manage them. This chapter explores cultural change, continuous improvement, and reengineering—the most important types of organizational change necessitated by TQ. Quality-related change in organization structure and employee responsibilities are discussed in other chapters. This chapter will

- explain the importance of organizational change to TQM,
- identify the types of changes necessary for quality,
- provide examples of firms undertaking these changes, and
- explain how the TQM perspective on organizational change relates to organization theory.

THE IMPORTANCE OF CHANGE

For organizations committed to pursuing total quality, change is a way of life. Organizational change is needed in implementing TQ and constantly thereafter. In the initial stage, an effort must be mounted to begin to change the culture of the organization. Unless a culture based on customer satisfaction, continuous improvement, and teamwork is established, TQ will be little more than "just another one of management's programs." Indeed, this is often the cause of failure of TQ initiatives.

Once TQ is underway in an organization, continuous improvement efforts will relentlessly create changes in product designs, standard operating procedures, and virtually every other aspect of organizations. One important aspect of continuous improvement is reengineering, in which the processes by which the organization operates are reexamined and redesigned to provide higher quality at lower cost.

Why are these changes necessary? The major reason is that customer expectations continuously evolve. Features or services that delight customers one year may be taken for granted the next, and products that customers find acceptable one year may be perceived as substandard the next. Competition continues to raise the standard for quality, and organizations must keep up. (See the box, "Quality Never Goes Out of Style.")

When first published, *USA Today*'s use of color and graphics was exceptional. In short order, however, newspapers copied these features so widely that exclusive use of black and white on the front page began to look old-fashioned. Any organization that focuses on meeting a fixed set of quality goals will quickly find itself trampled into the dust by competitors racing to keep up with customers. As one Xerox executive stated, "Quality is a race without a finish line."

Change is also required because processes tend to become unnecessarily complicated over a period of time, even when they are initially designed in a sensible manner. Each new person working on a process adds a wrinkle or two until, eventually, a monster has been created.

Quality Never Goes Out of Style[2]

In 1853 a young German immigrant named Strauss took a 17,000-mile trip on a clipper ship from New York around South America to San Francisco. He intended to set up shop selling dry goods to people lured to California by the gold rush. By the time he reached San Francisco, however, he had sold all the goods he brought except some canvas for tents.

The miners told him he should have brought pants instead of canvas to sell, because most pants fell apart too quickly while they dug for gold. The enterprising young Strauss immediately took the heavy brown canvas to a tailor and created the world's first pair of jeans. Those "pants of Levi's" (Strauss's first name) were so popular that he quickly sold all of his canvas and switched to a heavy serge fabric made in Nîmes, France ("serge de Nîmes," eventually shortened to "denim"). When the new fabric was treated with indigo dye, it attained its familiar deep blue color.

Levi never liked the term "jeans," so he called his pants "waist-high overalls." In fact, his company did not use the term—derived from the French word "genes" for a type of cotton trousers—until long after his death.

Levi noticed that miners often complained that the weight of gold nuggets was causing their pockets to tear. Always looking for ways to improve the quality of his pants, Levi and tailor Jacob Davis patented in 1873 the innovation of riveting pocket corners to add strength. By the 1930s, Levi's were worn by everyone from cowboys to school children. The rivets, much appreciated by miners, caused the company problems with other customers, which they quickly addressed. In 1937 the company covered the rivets on the rear pockets in response to complaints that they scratched both saddles and school desks. The rivet at the base of the fly was removed by executive order after company president Walter Haas crouched a little too close to a roaring campfire for a little too long and discovered what cowboys had been complaining about.

The popularity of Levi's jeans surged again in the 1950s when actor James Dean (unfortunately no relation to the author) wore them in the movie *Rebel Without a Cause*. Today, Levi's jeans are sold in more than 70 nations. The company says that they are made with "the choicest fabric, the strongest thread, first-class buttons, rivets, and snaps, precise sewing and careful inspection." The jeans carry a "Levi's promise" card guaranteeing customer satisfaction. With this history of continuous improvement in response to customer needs, it's no wonder that, as the company's slogan puts it, "quality never goes out of style."

CULTURAL CHANGE

Culture is the set of beliefs and values shared by the people in an organization. It is what binds them together and helps them make sense of what happens in their company. Cultures can vary dramatically between one company and another. In some firms, raw ambition is taken for granted, while in others subordination of one's own agenda to the good of the organization is expected. Some companies create a status hierarchy reminiscent of the court of Louis XIV, while others downplay status differences.

Culture is a powerful influence on people's behavior; thousands of employees at IBM will never wear anything other than a white shirt, while most people at Apple Computer wouldn't be caught dead in one. Culture has such power because it is shared widely within an organization, and because it operates without being talked about, indeed, often without even being thought of.

Organizations are in some ways like a circle of high school friends who share strong beliefs about which activities, people, and music are okay, and which are not. A new employee who did something that violated the culture might be told, "That's just not how we do things around here." The employee could be forgiven both for the error and for being perplexed at what was wrong, because the rules of culture are often not written down and must be deciphered.

Despite its intangibility, one can learn about an organization's culture in a number of ways. How people dress and how they address one another provide clues. The layout of offices, plant floors, and lounges may also reveal what is important in the organization. For example, do managers but not employees have reserved parking spots? Do offices have doors? Are there any private offices? Culture is expressed in the stories and jokes people tell, in how they spend their time at work, in what they display in their offices, and in a thousand other large and small ways.

From this description, it should be clear why firms deciding to pursue total quality need cultural change. If the TQ effort is inconsistent with the organizational culture, it will be undermined. For example, employees in a company in which status is jealously guarded will feel uncomfortable participating on an equal basis in team meetings with individuals from three different levels of management. People who share the belief that stability is the source of business success will be skeptical about continuous improvement. In situations like these, TQ is like an organ transplanted to a poorly matched donor and will be rejected.

Elements of a Total Quality Culture

The organizational culture needed to support TQ is one that values customers, improvement, and teamwork. In an organization with a TQ-friendly culture, everyone believes that customers are the key to the organization's future and that their needs must come first. If two employees are having a conversation and a customer enters the shop, the conversation ends until the customer is served.

In a culture supportive of TQ, people expect their jobs to change due to improvements dictated by customer needs. They are always looking for better (faster, simpler, less expensive) ways to do things. "Because that's the way we've always done it" is not a valid reason for doing anything. The culture of improvement is exemplified by both Levi Strauss and Gillette (see boxes).

Employees in a quality-oriented culture instinctively act as a team. If someone is away from her desk and her phone rings, another employee will answer it rather than leave a customer hanging. Organizations where a focus on customers, continuous improvement, and teamwork are taken for granted have a good chance of succeeding at total quality. Most organizations do not have such a culture prior to exposure to TQ; some degree of cultural change is necessary.

The existence of a set of cultural values necessary for successful TQ does not mean that all organizations that wish to practice total quality must have the same culture. Many aspects of culture differ greatly from one quality-oriented company to another. Company personnel may prefer to communicate in person or in writing; they may serve smoked salmon and champagne or a bushel of crabs and a keg of beer at the company picnic; they may wear uniforms, grey flannel suits, or jeans. As long as they hold the core values of TQ, quality can find a home in their organization.

How Organizational Culture is Changed

How can a company change its culture to be more consistent with quality? As with most aspects of TQ, it begins with leadership.[3] Leaders must articulate to employees the direction in which they want the company to go. They must set an example by expressing TQ values in their own behavior and by recognizing and rewarding others who do the same. The efforts of the new leadership team in a foundry to establish the values of continuous improvement and teamwork are described in this statement by the quality director, whose efforts had been frustrated under the old regime:[4]

> They brought in a people-oriented environment. They made the environment conducive to change and tried to get to the point where employees felt safe to make change. Before, you did what the boss told you to do and if you didn't you're probably going to get fired. Now we have some coaches in place and facilitators, and they want the ideas from the employees and it's a hell of a lot easier with their input.

A great deal of the effort leaders expend in cultural change is devoted to communication. Employees company-wide must be informed of the new values and practices desired. Any early successes of the new approach must also be publicized. This is not always easy, especially when the company's employees are geographically dispersed. In attempting to change the culture at Southern Pacific Lines, railroad executives held 125 "town meetings" at sites where employees worked, sometimes in groups as small as five to ten.[5]

Gillette Keeps Improving to Hold its Edge[6]

Gillette's dominance of the "wet shaving" market is awe-inspiring. Gillette was the market share leader in 1923 and is the market share leader (with about two-thirds of the U.S. market) today. Its share of the world market is even higher, reaching as high as 80 percent in Latin America. In fact, the word *gillette* means razor blade in some parts of the world. Its global sales continue to expand as joint ventures in China, Russia, and India take off. Faced with numerous competitive challenges over the years, Gillette has always responded with improved products, including the Atra and Sensor.

Success on this scale does not just happen; it is the product of relentless improvements in shaving technology over decades. The CEO shaves half of his face with his product and half with a competitor's to directly compare the closeness of the shave they produce. While the majority of the workforce is clean-shaven, 200 or so come to work each day unshaven (in the case of women employees, with unshaven legs), so that they can test shaving products under controlled conditions.

Donald Chaulk, vice president in charge of the shaving technology lab, explains the basis of the firm's continuous progress: "We test the blade edge, the blade guard, the angle of the blades, the balance of the razor . . . What happens to the chemistry of the skin? What happens to the hair when you pull it? What happens to the follicle? We own the face. We know more about shaving than anybody. I don't think obsession is too strong a word."

In promoting a new culture, leaders must also personally practice behaviors associated with the new culture. This both provides a role model for employees and symbolizes management's sincerity about the new approach. When the Indian soap company, Godrej Soaps, tried to initiate continuous improvement, workers were reluctant to unwrap defective soaps to see how mistakes could be avoided in the future. When informed of this, the managing director said he would go into the plant to unwrap the soaps. As it turned out, he didn't need to do it. When workers heard that the top manager was willing to do this kind of work, they agreed to do it themselves.[7]

None of this should be interpreted to mean that cultural change is easy. On the contrary, it is very difficult, takes several years to complete, and often fails.[8] One reason for the difficulty is resistance by middle management. Managers resist change because it creates more work for them when they often feel overburdened and disrupts the steady flow of work in the organization.[9] Getting on board for a change in culture requires managers to acknowledge that the current approach is somehow lacking, despite any of their previous statements to the contrary. They also may be afraid that they will not be able to perform effectively in the new culture.

Often reward systems get in the way of cultural change and must be adjusted for the new culture to take hold. In many companies, telephone operators are rewarded for the speed with which they process calls, rather than for how completely they satisfy the customers who call. Unless this type of reward system is changed, management's pleas to increase customer satisfaction will fall upon deaf ears. Willingness to make such changes indicates management's commitment to the new culture.

Making the New Culture Permanent

Due to the difficulty of cultural change, leaders must work to ensure not only that change is initiated, but that the new culture becomes a permanent part of the organization. Managers can take a number of paths to this destination:[10]

1. Make involvement in TQ a required part of people's responsibilities. Making it voluntary implies that it is less important than things that are required.

2. Use the existing organization to implement TQ. Special task forces and committees can disband; TQ should be part of the permanent organization.

3. Make sure everyone spends at least one hour a week working on quality issues. Enforcing this rule gets people used to the idea of devoting time to quality and keeps other priorities from crowding out TQ.

4. Change the measurement and information systems.[11] Without appropriate measurements and information systems, quality cannot become part of the fabric of the organization. AT&T Universal Card Services, a 1992 winner of the Baldrige Award, spent $20 million on computer workstations to provide customer support personnel with easy access to detailed card member information.

Cultural Change in Action

Many organizations have attempted to change their cultures to become more responsive to customer needs. Boeing is a good example of a company in a difficult competitive situation that has undertaken this task.[12] Boeing has been a fixture in the aerospace industry since Bill Boeing built his first airplane—a single-engine seaplane—in 1916. Boeing's planes were heavily involved in World War II, with almost 7,000 produced by Boeing and another 13,000 produced by other manufacturers using Boeing designs. In modern times, approximately half the commercial jets in the world have been produced by Boeing; the company contributes substantially to the U.S. balance of trade by exporting planes all over the world.

Not content to rest on its corporate laurels, however, Boeing was among the early leaders of the quality movement in the U.S., implementing quality circles in 1980. (Quality circles are groups of workers who meet for an hour or so each week to work on quality problems and were a forerunner of total quality efforts in many companies.)

Managers at Boeing quickly recognized, however, that the corporate culture would need to be changed if quality efforts were to be successful, and began a process to do so. This process consisted of five steps:

1. Identify norms that currently guide behaviors and attitudes.
2. Identify the behaviors necessary to make the organization successful for tomorrow.
3. Develop a list of new norms that will move the organization forward.
4. Identify the culture gaps—the difference between the desired norms and actual norms.
5. Develop and put in place an action plan to implement the new cultural norms. These new norms will replace the old ones, and this transition will be monitored and enforced.

Boeing backed up this commitment to cultural change with a great deal of training, surveying of employees and customers, and executive commitment. Today the company faces tremendous challenges, including a decline in demand for military aircraft, competition from Airbus Industries (the European airplane consortium) and a very weak global market for jets. Its quality-oriented culture, however, based on customers, continuous improvement, and teamwork, should help it to stay competitive for years to come. As Boeing's John Black reflected:

> This process of continuous improvement, to which we are committed, is not one that can suddenly be grafted onto a company. Every organization must make it their own. Top management leadership MUST be provided, and ALL management must be brought on board. Only when all the people are committed and the process is locked in for the long term, will it achieve the breakthrough that it is capable of providing for us—the key to economic success in the future.

CONTINUOUS IMPROVEMENT

Continuous improvement (*kaizen* in Japanese) to provide quality to customers is essential to total quality. The TQ ideal is *not* to make a big splash by improving a system, only to mindlessly operate in the same "new and improved" manner for years to come. TQ-oriented organizations relentlessly improve their processes, products, and services, as well as their people (through training) day-by-day and month-by-month, over years and even decades.

It is the cumulative effect of hundreds or thousands of small improvements that creates dramatic change in performance. This is not to say that break-throughs do not occur; they certainly do, especially in the early phases of TQ. To use football as a metaphor, the successful practice of TQ is not reflected in the glamour of the occasional "long bomb," it consists of grinding out improvements "one yard at a time."

Consider the chart in Figure 6.1, which shows the result of attempts by a foundry to reduce its production of scrap (products rejected due to poor quality) over three years. Several points about continuous improvement are illustrated by this chart.

- The average amount of scrap declined each year, from approximately 9.5 in the first year to 6.5 in the second year and to 3.5 in the third year.

- Not only the level but also the variation from month to month declined each year. Compare the wild variation in the first year to the relative stability of the third.

- Even when quality efforts had not been undertaken, the company occasionally got lucky and produced good quality. It took the foundry two years to produce a month as good as the first month of the first year. Obviously, the first-year first-month was a fluke, as scrap was 50 percent

Figure 6.1 Scrap Reductions in a Foundry over Three Years

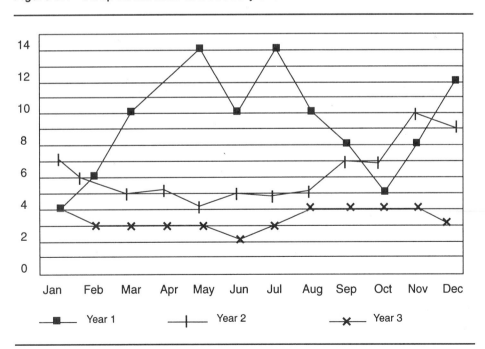

higher the next month! The philosophy of continuous improvement was captured very well by the quality manager who said, "We're nowhere near where we ought to be, but we're getting better. And we're going to be better tomorrow."

Continuous Improvement and the Baldrige Award

Continuous improvement is a core concept in the Malcolm Baldrige National Quality Award criteria. The guidelines state:

> Achieving the highest levels of quality and competitiveness requires a well-defined and well-executed approach to continuous improvement. The term continuous improvement refers to both incremental and "breakthrough" improvement. A focus on improvement needs to be part of all operations and of all work unit activities of a company. Improvements may be of several types: (1) enhancing value to customers...; (2) reducing errors, defects, and waste; (3) improving responsiveness...; (4) improving productivity...; (5) improving the company's performance and leadership position in fulfilling its public responsibilities.[13]

The Baldrige Award seeks evidence of evaluation and improvement cycles in nearly every category of the criteria. The award itself sets an example by continually improving the nature of the award criteria and the application process each year.

How Continuous Improvement is Practiced

The most important ingredient for continuous improvement is one we have already discussed: an appropriate organizational culture. If everyone in the organization understands and believes in the importance of continuous improvement, the rest is a question of technique. If not, no techniques will do the job.

Given the large number of possible areas in an organization that could be improved, setting priorities is crucial, and there are several ways to do this. Many organizations rely on customer input and feedback to help set their priorities.[14] For example, if late deliveries are the most common customer complaint, continuous improvement efforts should be directed at reducing delivery times. Often customers cannot see inside the organization to identify the root causes of problems, so some additional sorting out is generally necessary.

The time-honored tradition of the suggestion system has taken on a new life under TQ to serve this purpose. At Portman Equipment Company, an employee who sees an improvement opportunity fills out a Proposal for Change form, which initiates the formation of a team to attack the issue.[15] At AT&T Universal Card Services, employees contribute an average of 4.6 suggestions per year, half of which are implemented.[16] This rate of suggestions, large compared to most American firms, is still dwarfed by the number of suggestions contributed in some Japanese firms.

The Plan-Do-Study-Act (PDSA) cycle discussed in chapter 3 provides the basic process for continuous improvement. An operation is examined to identify potential areas for improvement. Techniques such as check sheets and Pareto charts are used to prioritize problems. Then steps are taken to improve the operation, and the results of the change are studied. This leads to further action, and the cycle continues indefinitely.

This is somewhat similar to the familiar problem-solving model:

1. specify the problem,
2. identify causes of the problem and determine which are most serious,
3. develop a list of potential solutions,
4. analyze the potential benefit of the solutions and choose one, and
5. implement the solution.

An important difference, however, is that with a continuous improvement mindset, step 5 leads directly back to step 1, unless the operation is now flawless.

Continuous improvement efforts can be directed at a number of different types of improvement. For example, changes could result in work being done more easily, more accurately, faster, at lower cost, more safely, and in a way that provides greater customer satisfaction.[17] Thinking about continuous improvement in this way makes it clear how many opportunities for improvement exist in almost any system. How many operations are there that couldn't be improved on even one of these dimensions?

Persistence is important in pursuing continuous improvement. Not only will small changes in operations take some time to add up to any serious improvement, but they are often disruptive when first implemented. According to the late Japanese manufacturing expert, Shigeo Shingo:[18]

> Since improvement . . . demands new procedures, a certain amount of difficulty will be encountered. . . . Initially, new methods will be difficult. Old procedures, however, are easy just because they are familiar. . . . As long as it is unfamiliar, even an improved procedure will be more difficult and will take more time than the old procedure. . . . Thus, no improvement shows its true worth right away . . . 99 percent of all improvement plans would vanish without a trace if they were to be abandoned after only a brief trial.

Like the cultural change that motivates it, continuous improvement is difficult to sustain. Perhaps the "if it's not broke, don't fix it" mentality is too deeply embedded our culture. In any case, many organizations that wish to embrace continuous improvement have not been able to do so successfully, as indicated by the findings of a recent survey of American manufacturing firms by the National Center for Manufacturing Science (NCMS):

Japan, Germany, and other industrialized nations recognize the continuous improvement process as crucial to world-class manufacturing. But industrial leaders responding to the NCMS survey admit they have a spotty track record in this area. For example, half of those responding say they have no continuous improvement plan in place. . . . Nearly 40 percent of the respondents also indicated that suggestions from continuous improvement team members are not regularly implemented.[19]

Continuous Improvement in Action

An increasing number of companies have begun to convert to the continuous improvement philosophy. One unusual example of this idea in practice is provided by the Walt Disney Company.[20] The opening of Euro Disneyland in 1992 near Marne la Vallée, France, brought to four the number of parks operated around the world by the Walt Disney Company. Disneyland, the original, opened in 1955 in Anaheim, California. Disney World, in Orlando, Florida, opened in 1971 and was expanded in 1982 to include Epcot Center and later MGM Studios Theme Park. Tokyo Disneyland, Disney's first overseas park, opened in 1983.

Disney faced a difficult challenge in bringing its American style of fun to the French people, who are often ambivalent at best about American cultural imperialism. The opening of Euro Disney was not without problems, as Disney faced labor disputes over its personal appearance policies, such as no facial hair, and substantial difficulties with getting construction work done on time and under budget. The company anticipated and tried to defuse any cross-cultural difficulties through an exchange of hundreds of European and American managers.

One major advantage possessed by Disney in establishing its European park was its ability to learn from its past successes, as well as its past mistakes. When the original park was opened in Anaheim, its 185 acres were quickly surrounded by hotels and restaurants that competed with Disney's own. This mistake was repeated neither in Orlando, where Disney bought 28,000 acres (one-third of which is still unused), nor in France.

Disney built six hotels for the opening of Euro Disney, far more than would be immediately needed. Why? The company had dragged its heels in building hotels in Florida, allowing competitors to become established. Almost unbelievably, the plans for Euro Disney (to be completed in 2017) call for an additional 4,000 hotel rooms, a retail and industrial park, and even 8,000 private homes.

When one thinks of continuous improvement, processes that are repeated every hour, day, or week come to mind. However, Disney has applied continuous improvement to the process of park design, which it has practiced only about every 10 years!

REENGINEERING

Reengineering (also known as process redesign) is a type of continuous improvement with the potential to dramatically improve the quality and speed of work and to reduce its cost by fundamentally changing the processes by which work gets done. Reengineering is often used when the improvements needed are so great that incremental changes to operations will not get the job done. Ten percent improvements can be created by tinkering, but 50 percent improvements call for process redesign.

The irony of reengineering is that, once the new process is in place, people often feel that the new way of operating is so much better, they should have thought of it long ago. Another common reaction is "Why did we ever do it like that in the first place?" The answer is often, "That's the way we've always done it." GE Chairman Jack Welch has compared his company to a 100-year-old attic, which has collected a lot of useless junk over the years. Process redesign (called workout in GE jargon) is the process of cleaning all the junk out of the attic.[21]

Often the old ways of doing things were a function of administrative, rather than customer-centered, thinking. In one plant, a product was boxed and wrapped to be sent from one side of the plant to the other, only to be unwrapped and unboxed. Why? Because the two parts of the plant were separate profit centers, and the first had to "sell" the product to the second! If a process is driven by an administrative logic such as cost accounting or functional specialization, it is ripe for reengineering.[22]

The importance of process redesign to quality improvement can be seen in Figure 6.2., based on the work of Professor Asbjorn Aune of Norway.[23] Process is what connects customer expectations to the products or services they receive. It is what ensures (or fails to ensure) that products meet or exceed customer expectations.

Principles of Process Redesign

Waste is the enemy of effective processes. Reducing waste of any kind encompasses both TQ and just-in-time practices and is a central theme in Japanese manufacturing management. Poor processes waste time, money, material, effort, and customer good will. Redesigning processes to reduce waste is, at this point at least, more an art than a science. Every process redesign is unique, but the general principles of redesign include:[24]

1. **Reduce handoffs.** Every time a process is handed from one person or group to another, errors can occur (think of passing the baton in a relay race). Time is often wasted as one group waits for the other to finish or needs to consult with the first group before continuing.

2. **Eliminate steps.** The best way to save time on a step is not to do it at all. If the step does not add value to the product or service or make the

Figure 6.2 The Key Role of Process

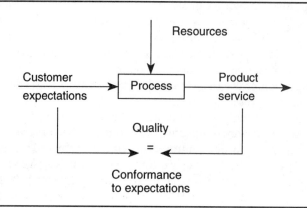

product more attractive to customers, stop doing it. In manufacturing organizations, moving, storing, and inspecting products rarely add value and should be eliminated wherever possible.

3. **Perform steps in parallel rather than in sequence.** Unless one operation cannot be done until another is finished, why not do them both at once? Many organizations operate like two people doing the dishes, where one washes all the dishes that will fit in the drainer, then calls the other to dry them. When the drying is done, the dryer calls the washer back in and leaves again. Stupid? Yes, but that's the way they've always done it.

4. **Involve key people early.** The point of this is to avoid doing things over when key people do not give their input until the process is under way. For years, manufacturing companies have had their engineers design entire products before consulting the manufacturing engineers who will have to build them. The manufacturing engineers would then suggest a number of changes that the designers would reluctantly incorporate into their designs. Many firms recently have changed this process to allow early involvement of manufacturing.[25] This is one of the most common forms of process reengineering and is consistent with the TQ principle, "Do it right the first time!"

Reengineering in Action

The improvements created by reengineering are often amazing and provide impressive testimony to the power of the method. A case in point is the changes made in processing applications at Mutual Benefit Life. In the old days, Mutual Benefit Life (MBL) processed its applications like every other insurance company.[26] An application went through up to 5 departments, 19 people, and 30 steps. Under this system, the hour or so of work associated with an application took between 5 and 25 days to complete!

MBL's president believed that customer service had to be improved and decreed a 60 percent improvement in productivity. The team assigned to produce this improvement realized that this goal could not be achieved by cosmetic changes; a complete process redesign was in order.

The new arrangement trashed the existing system of departments and job descriptions and created the new role of "case manager." Case managers have complete responsibility for applications—from reception to completion—and work quite autonomously. They can operate in this manner due to the support of computer workstations that run an expert system (a program that provides advice based on the knowledge and experience of experts) and other programs. With this support, even a case manager of limited experience can make good decisions. In unusually tough situations, case managers can still call senior underwriters or physicians for advice.

The benefits of the new process are impressive. Applications can now be processed in as few as four hours and on average take only two to five days. Case managers now can process twice as many applications as the previous system, despite the fact that the number of field office positions has been reduced by 100.

QUALITY-ORIENTED CHANGE AND ORGANIZATION THEORY

A large amount of research and writing in organization theory (OT) focuses on organization change. This section compares the TQ perspective on organization change to this literature. Given the amount of work in this area, we can only identify a few of the major ideas in the literature on organization change and show how they relate to total quality. Organizational behavior and organization theory textbooks generally have at least one chapter on organization change, which can be consulted for further details on this research.

The following sections compare TQ to organization theory in terms of the reasons for change, the source of change, the nature of change, the difficulty of change, and how to manage change. Our overall conclusion is that, despite some differences in focus, the research on change conducted by organization theorists is a rich source of information for those embarking on the changes required by total quality.

The reason for change   The reason behind TQ-oriented change is quality improvement for customer satisfaction. This has not been a major focus of the OT literature on change, which has focused primarily on changes intended to improve productivity and/or improve job satisfaction. Of course, many quality-oriented changes may improve productivity or job satisfaction, but that isn't usually their main objective.

The source of change   The source of most change considered in OT is top management. In general, top management responds to changes in the organizational environment, such as increased competitiveness or declining demand. This parallels the cultural change aspect of TQ. In fact, the OT literature on change is most relevant to cultural change, as opposed to continuous improvement or process redesign.

Types of change   The types of changes considered in OT theories partially overlap with TQ-oriented changes. In particular, OT theories that deal with changes in values and norms are relevant to the transformations associated with cultural change in TQ. Other types of change featured in OT theories, such as the introduction of new technology, are not as directly relevant to TQ. (Reengineering, however, often involves the application of some type of information technology.)

Furthermore, the changes discussed in the OT literature tend to differ in two important ways from TQ-oriented change. First, they tend to be limited in scope, usually to one or two departments, and even to only a few aspects of the work of these departments. Second, they tend to be limited in duration, with the idea being to get the change over with and get on with organizational life. This may apply to cultural change (and to some extent to process redesign), but is very different from continuous improvement. Indeed, the management of continuous change over a long period of time has not been addressed often by OT research and presents a clear opportunity for research.

One of the earliest studies of organization change was conducted by Coch and French in a Virginia factory that produced pajamas.[27] In this study, a change in procedure was made in three different ways. In one group, the workers themselves devised the change. In a second group, workers appointed representatives who devised the change. In a third group, the new system was imposed on the workers by management.

The study found that the change was much more successful in the more participative groups; this study is often cited as support for the need for employee participation in organizational change. What is interesting from a TQ perspective is that it is a study of process redesign and, in the participative groups at least, of process redesign initiated by the people actually doing the work. Thus it anticipates by 40 years the kinds of changes that have become commonplace among firms practicing total quality. True to the limits in the thinking at the time, however, the improvement was a one-shot deal. Continuous improvement was an idea whose time had not yet come.

TQ and the OT literature agree on the difficulty of successfully changing organizations and on the fact that "resistance to change" is often the underlying problem. OT research has made significant progress in identifying why organization members resist change and even in identifying various methods for dealing with this problem.[28] Resistance is at least as likely to come from managers as from lower-level employees.

The whole idea of resistance, however, flows from a concept of change mandated by top management. Managers or workers are unlikely to resist a process change that they themselves have devised. For such changes, the literature on resistance to change seems off the mark.

Perhaps the literature on population ecology provides a more helpful perspective on the difficulty of organizational change in the TQ context.[29] From this perspective, worker resistance is not to blame for the difficulty of change. Rather, the structures and systems that management has created are at fault. For example, the hierarchical organization structure of most firms makes it difficult for them to adapt effectively to environmental changes such as the evolution in customer demand. This idea is consistent with Deming's theory that problems are more often related to system imperfections than to worker inability or lack of motivation.

Population ecology theorists generally argue that the difficulty of changing structures, authority, reward systems, and so forth, renders most organizations unsuccessful in their change efforts. Writers on TQ often have commented on the major impediments such structures and systems create, but have gone on to identify ways in which such obstacles can be removed. This difference in prognosis should not mask the fundamental agreement between the ecological OT perspective and TQ on the importance of structural and systemic impediments to change.

From the ecological perspective, change in a set of similar organizations often comes about by ineffective organizations going out of business and being replaced by new ones, rather than by changing from ineffective to effective. Clearly both processes occur. Many organizations that did not provide the quality customers demanded are no longer with us, while others (Xerox is an excellent example) have managed to transform themselves in order to survive. Needless to say, the battle between transformation and extinction continues to be fought every day in many firms throughout the world.

Many of the principles for managing change derived from the OT literature apply directly to total quality change. Some of these principles are as follows:

1. *It is necessary to "unfreeze" people's attitudes and behavior before they can be changed.*[30] This principle, a staple of the OT understanding of change, relates directly to TQ. Before organizations can change in the direction of practicing TQ, people must see why the current approach is inappropriate or incomplete and what problems of competitiveness and customer dissatisfaction this causes. Cultural change in TQ is often the vehicle for unfreezing behavior.

2. *Change can only succeed with effective leadership.* One early proponent of this view was Thomas Bennett.[31] Bennett identified the need for leaders to deal with the emotional aspects of the change for subordinates, the need for clear goals, and the importance of logical problem-solving processes. These and other aspects of the leader's role identified by OT theorists clearly are relevant to TQ.

3. *Change agents must manage interdependence.* Few things in organizations—e.g., jobs or technology—can be changed without affecting other things—structures or processes. Many OT theorists of change recognized this fact and based their theories on the need to identify and manage the interdependence among organizational phenomena.[32] This applies directly to process redesign and is consistent with Deming's emphasis on organizations as systems.

4. *Effective change must involve the people whose jobs are being changed.* This point was noted in reference to the Coch and French study. Although a variety of rationales for the importance of participation have been advanced, its significance for reducing resistance is an article of faith among organization change theorists.[33] This is probably the point of greatest overlap between OT and TQ. The "participation" and "involvement" championed by OT theorists as much as 50 years ago have become so widely accepted in industry that they have evolved into today's concepts of "empowerment" and "self-management."

5. *Refreezing is needed to make gains permanent.* Research in OT has concluded that steps are needed to lock in the changes that have been made.[34] This point has not been lost upon the TQ community, as many organizations are now becoming concerned about maintaining, as opposed to creating, change. Many of the recommendations of the OT literature, especially the need to monitor and revise change efforts continually, are quite relevant to TQ.

SUMMARY

Organizational change is fundamental to total quality. The three most important types of change practiced in TQ are cultural change, continuous improvement, and process redesign. Cultural change, which makes the other two types of change possible, depends on leadership and the creation of systems to make the changes permanent.

Continuous improvement often involves suggestion systems and operates on the principle that major improvements can come from the accumulation of many small changes. Process redesign is a type of continuous improvement in which breakthroughs are made by fundamentally changing the way that work gets done. The organization theory literature on change, despite some differences in focus, provides a number of observations and recommendations that are relevant to managing quality-oriented change.

REVIEW AND DISCUSSION QUESTIONS

1. Briefly describe the three kinds of organizational change practiced in total quality efforts.

2. Think of a type of product or service with which you have been familiar for several years. Name some features once seen as special that are now taken for granted.

3. Describe the culture of an organization you have worked in or are familiar with. What is valued in this culture? Do you think this culture provides fertile ground for total quality? Why or why not?

4. Will an organization's culture be the same throughout or will it vary from department to department? Why?

5. Managers can enforce rules about what people do and say at work. But can they enforce a culture? If yes, how can they do it? If no, what does this say about the limits of managers' ability to ensure quality?

6. How could you apply continuous improvement methods to the job of being a student?

7. Can you think of any company that has been successful for a long time without improving its product? What conditions have made this possible?

8. How could you improve your process for studying for an exam? Getting to class on time? Cleaning your room or apartment?

9. What principles of process redesign are illustrated by the Mutual Benefit Life story? Can you discern other principles not listed in the chapter from this case?

CASES

The Machine That Didn't Change the World[35]

Mike Weaver, president of Weaver Popcorn Company of Van Buren, Indiana, had always believed that if the customer was not happy with an order, the only thing to do was to take it back. "No sale is complete if the customer isn't satisfied," the Reverend Ira E. Weaver, company founder and Mike's grandfather, was fond of saying. What if the order was 280,000 pounds of popcorn (use your imagination), and what if it was in Tokyo, and what if it was worth $70,000? "Let's bring it back," Weaver told Pat Vogel, the company's export manager, when awakened with the bad news around midnight one evening in October 1985.

The refusal of the order by Shintoa Koeki Kaisha Ltd., on the basis of excess impurities, was a hard kernel to swallow for Weaver the man and Weaver the company. Both had regarded the order from Japan as an indication of the company's ability to sell popcorn to anybody, anywhere. How could the company recover its quality image in the face of such an embarrassment?

A few months later, trucks pulled up to the Weaver plant bearing $1 million worth of high-speed optical scanners. The new machines would subject anything passing beneath their electronic eyes to a cold-hearted inspection, dooming to the trash heap any weed seeds, dirt clods, and soybeans trying to pass themselves off as popcorn. Goodbye foreign particles. Goodbye irate customers. Hello quality!

However, continuous improvement seldom occurs in big bangs and rarely can be accomplished simply by buying new technology. These were the quality lessons learned by Weaver in the months and years after the new equipment was installed. Although the machines couldn't solve Weaver's quality problems, they certainly made people more aware of them. Questions were raised about virtually every aspect of the operation, including the raw materials, the tools, and the people.

Things came to a head when, during a quality meeting, Marty Hall from processing informed the group that all the talk about quality was total bull as long as Weaver was accepting popcorn that was way out of spec, for example in moisture content. Aware that the outgoing product cannot be good if the incoming raw materials are not, Hall believed that the quality efforts to date were useless.

This sparked dramatic changes in Weaver's operations. Mike Weaver began to give vastly increased responsibility for quality to people in the plant. The resigning plant manager was replaced by seven team leaders from the plant floor. Employees were brought into the process of hiring, even for managers. Hundreds of minor changes have been made by employees now sensitized to the importance of quality, which has been steadily improving. The lesson? According to Mike Weaver, "With the machines there, everybody began to see that it takes so much more than machines. Nothing has a greater impact on the quality of the corn than these people." As Mike's grandfather might have added, "Amen."

Discussion Questions

1. Would you have made the same decision as Mike Weaver to bring back the popcorn from Japan? Why or why not?
2. Did the optical scanners turn out to be a good idea?
3. Did the fact that Weaver is a family-owned business make a difference in how Mike Weaver thought about quality? Can the same attitude be created in shareholder-owned companies?
4. What elements of the company had to change for the quality of the popcorn to improve?
5. Can quality ever be completely automated so that people don't make any difference?

Reject Rate Reduction at the Reserve Bank of India[36]

The National Clearing Cell (NCC), Madras, is a division of the Reserve Bank of India responsible for check-clearing operations in the Madras area. Check clearing has been computerized since 1987 and involves running checks on a high speed reader sorter system (HSRSS) driven by a mainframe computer. The checks customers cash at their banks that are drawn on other banks are presented to the Clearing Cell, which captures the data on the HSRSS, sorts the checks on the basis of the drawee bank and branch code, and prints out a number of reports including the clearing settlement.

The HSRSS reads the Magnetic Ink Character Recognition (MICR) code on the band at the bottom of the check. The first fields on the MICR line (serial, route, account, transaction codes) are pre-printed, and the amount field is encoded after the customer presents the check to the bank. Checks that are improperly encoded or of poor quality are rejected by the HSRSS; they must be manually sorted and their data manually entered. Banks get back their checks in two lots, one fully sorted by branch and transaction code by the HSRSS, and the other that still must be sorted by branch and transaction code by the bank.

The quality of the entire operation hinges on the reject rate on the HSRSS, and this most important quality parameter was found to be very high, around 10 percent. The banks complained that they were receiving too many rejected checks and were left with a lot of tedious, labor-intensive, and costly work to do after the NCC process was complete. The manual handling of the rejected checks meant possible errors in both data entry and sorting, which often resulted in reconciliation differences among banks. Also, the banks pay a penalty on every item if their reject rate exceeds 3 percent.

The controlling authorities pointed out several times to the manager of NCC, M.R. Srinivasan, that the reject rate was too high and that customers were unhappy that the benefits of shifting to computerized processing had not been realized. Srinivasan explained to his authorities that the high reject rate of checks at Madras was due to the peculiarity of checks presented there and pointed out the high proportion of bank drafts from other places. In short, the blame was shifted elsewhere.

After about a year of this, the manager decided to look inward to try to improve performance and chose one of his shifts-in-charge, Kaza Sudhakar, to do the job. It was felt that the high reject rate was due to poor tuning of the HSRSS equipment. The engineers fine-tuned the equipment and cleaned the entire operations area to eliminate all traces of dust. This reduced the reject rate by only 1 percent. The NCC then issued a series of instructions to the banks to help them improve the encoding of their checks, but this did not help much.

NCC then embarked upon a project to inspect all of the checks presented by the banks and to separate and repair the bad checks. This reduced the reject rate by 2 percent, but at a tremendous time and labor cost. This approach was abandoned, and it was decided to review where the NCC had gone wrong.

The clerks receiving the checks pointed out that the process started at the banks where the checks are encoded. This meant that the solution would have to involve nearly 800 branches of 50 banks in and around Madras! But the potential benefits were great, so the NCC decided to go ahead. Five officers were allotted 10 banks each, with the assignment to train the banks' encoding staff. The first two months of the project produced negligible results, but as more and more banks were trained, the reject rate fell to 4.5 percent!

The banks were advised to continue the training on an ongoing basis, to train every new operator, and to designate an officer to ensure that only quality checks are presented to NCC. The banks were also invited to visit the clearing facilities so they could understand the importance of encoding to the entire clearing operation. Although these steps had resulted in dramatic improvement, the reject rate still exceeded the international standard of 3 percent.

The NCC team once again reviewed the process with people from the banks, who pointed out that most of their checks had five fields preprinted on them; the banks merely encoded the amount field. The banks felt they were paying for the poor quality of the preprinting done by the check printers.

The printers were invited to the NCC and asked to send a proof batch of 100 checks before printing a run, which often numbered in the millions. The NCC promised to run the proof batch on the HSRSS and deliver a report to the printer within half an hour. Some agreed to proof their checks, others did not. Subsequent study showed that banks whose printers had proofed their checks had a reject rate of less than 1 percent! This shifted the balance in favor of checking proof batches, and soon all of the printers were doing so. The overall reject rate for the clearing operation was now around 2 percent, which proudly measured up to any international standard.

The benefits of this improvement were many. NCC manpower devoted to manual entry and sorting could be dramatically reduced and redeployed to other areas in need of personnel. The banks were happy to receive almost all of their checks fully sorted by the HSRSS, and reconciliation differences among the banks were reduced to negligible levels. Banks also could redeploy their manual sorting and reconciliation staff, which had tremendous financial implications for them.

Srinivasan initiated measures to standardize all the procedures that enabled the achievement of low reject rates. The staff was even rotated to see if the standards could be met independent of personnel, and this was accomplished. Regular meetings were arranged with the banks to solicit feedback on the clearing operations and to elicit suggestions for further improvement.

NCC's quality project became truly total in dimension, involving thousands of employees in 800 bank branches in Madras. It had the full support of the top management and the newly-empowered operating staff. One lesson taken from the project was that no operation could be improved just by tuning up the equipment until the people connected with the operation are also tuned up (trained). The improvement has to be continuous, without accepting defeat at any stage. Perhaps the most important lesson is that a project that started aimed solely at better customer service ended up producing substantial cost savings, without a conscious effort in that direction.

Discussion Questions

1. How does the role of technology in improving quality in this case differ from the Weaver Popcorn case?
2. How would you draw the customer-supplier chain (explained in chapter 4) that goes through the clearing operation?
3. How many different approaches to quality improvement were attempted by the National Clearing Cell? Which were the most effective?

ENDNOTES

1. Quoted in E.F. Cudworth, "3M's Commitment to Quality as a Way of Life," *Industrial Engineering,* July 1985.

2. Based on *Everyone Knows His First Name* by Levi Strauss & Company.

3. For a more detailed look at leadership's role in total quality, see chapter 9.

4. Interview with Richard Garula.

5. J.M. Delsanter, "On the right track," *TQM Magazine,* March/April 1992, pp. 17–20.

6. Based on Lawrence Ingrassia, "Gillette Holds Its Edge By Endlessly Searching For A Better Shave," *The Wall Street Journal,* December 10, 1992

7. Kiron Kasbekar and Namita Devidayal, "Improvement is not all smooth sailing," *The Times of India,* January 8, 1993.

8. Dan Ciampa, *Total Quality: A User's Guide to Implementation,* (Reading, Mass.: Addison-Wesley, 1992) cautions about trying to change culture.

9. Several reasons for managerial resistance to change are outlined by J.M. Juran in *Juran on Leadership for Quality,* New York: Free Press, 1989.

10. These suggestions are taken from G.R. Pieters, "Behaving Responsibly," *TQM Magazine,* 2(2), March/April 1992, pp. 25–29.

11. Ciampa, *Total Quality.*

12. Based on John R. Black, "Boeing's Quality Strategy: A Continuing Evolution," *Quest for Competitiveness,* Shetty and Buehler (eds.).

13. 1993 Award Criteria, Malcolm Baldrige National Quality Award.

14. See chapter 4 for a discussion of various ways to get ideas from customers.

15. Interview with Richard Buck, vice president for Quality, Portman Equipment.

16. B.A. Reeve, "What's in it for me?," *UNIverse* (AT&T Newsletter) Special Report, July 1992.

17. Based on chapter 14 in *Continuous Improvement in Operations: A Systematic Approach to Waste Reduction*, Alan Robinson (ed.), Cambridge, Mass.: Productivity Press, 1991.

18. S. Shingo, *The Sayings of Shigeo Shingo: Key Strategies for Plant Improvement,* Cambridge, Mass.: Productivity Press, 1987, p.152.

19. "U.S. Manufacturers Give Themselves a 'C,' Admit They Have Substantial Work to Do," *Focus*, National Center for Manufacturing Sciences, January, 1993, p.4.

20. Based on Cheri Henderson, "Monsieur Mickey," *TQM Magazine*, September/October 1992, pp. 220–224.

21. N. Tichy and R. Charan, "Speed, Simplicity, and Self-Confidence: An Interview with Jack Welch," in J. Gabarro (ed.). *Managing People and Organizations*, Boston: Harvard Business School Publications, 1992.

22. Robinson, *Continuous Improvement.*

23. Reprinted from "Total Quality Management: Time for a Theory?" Paper presented at the EOQ Conference in Prague, 1991, by Asbjorn Aune.

24. These principles are based on Richard C. Whiteley, *The Customer-Driven Company: Moving from Talk to Action,* Reading, Mass.: Addison-Wesley, 1991.

25. See J.W. Dean, Jr. and G.I. Susman, "Organizing for manufacturable design," *Harvard Business Review*, January–February 1989.

26. This example is taken from Michael Hammer, "Reengineering work: Don't automate, obliterate," *Harvard Business Review*, July–August 1990, pp. 104–112.

27. L. Coch and J. P. French, "Overcoming Resistance to Change," *Human Relations*, v. 1, 1948, pp. 512–532.

28. For a summary of this material, see J.P. Kotter and L.A. Schlesinger, "Choosing Strategies for Change," in J.J. Gabarro (ed.), *Managing People and Organizations*. Boston: Harvard Business School Publications, 1992, pp. 395–409.

29. See, for example, H.A. Aldrich, *Organizations and Environments*. Englewood Cliffs, N.J.: Prentice-Hall, 1979.

30. K. Lewin, "Forces behind food habits and methods of change," *Bulletin of the National Research Council* #108, 1947, pp. 35–65. See also E. Schein, "Organizational socialization and the profession of management," *Industrial Management Review*, 1968, pp. 1–16.

31. See Thomas R. Bennett III, *Planning for Change*. Washington, D.C.: Leadership Resources, 1961.

32. See, for example, Harold J. Leavitt, "Applied organization change in industry: Structural, technical, and human approaches," in W.W. Cooper, H.J. Leavitt, and M.W. Shelly (eds.) *New Perspectives in Organizational Research*, New York: Wiley, 1964.

33. For an interesting (and now classic) discussion of this issue, see P.R. Lawrence, "How to Deal with Resistance to Change," *Harvard Business Review*, May–June 1954.

34. See Schein, "Organizational Socialization," *Industrial Management Review*. See also, P.S. Goodman and J.W. Dean, Jr., "Creating Long-Term Change," in P.S. Goodman (ed.), *Change in Organizations*. San Francisco: Jossey-Bass, 1983.

35. Reprinted with permission, *Inc. Magazine,* (May, 1990). Copyright 1990 by Goldhirsh Group, Inc., 38 Commercial Wharf, Boston, MA 02110.

36. This case was written especially for this book by Kaza Sudhakar, Officer, Reserve Bank of India, Madras.

PART III

Total Quality and Organizational Behavior

CHAPTER 7

Quality Teamwork

Chapter Outline

The Importance of Teams in TQM
Types of TQM Teams
    Steering Committees
    Problem-Solving Teams
    Self-Managed Teams
Effective Teamwork
    Criteria For Team Effectiveness
    Team Membership
    Team Processes
    Organizational Support
Teamwork in Action
    A Team with a Transparent Problem
    The Birth of Teamwork at Globe Metallurgical
Comparison to Organizational Behavior Theories
Summary
Review and Discussion Questions
Cases

> No matter what you are trying to do, teams are the most effective way to get the job done.
>
>   —Donald Peterson, former CEO, Ford Motor Company.[1]

Teams are a central facet of Total Quality Management. Although many types of teams exist in organizations pursuing TQM, the concept of teamwork is widespread and a key contributor to TQM success in just about any setting. Chapter 5 introduced teams as an aspect of quality-oriented organizational design. This chapter will

- explain the importance of teams in TQM,
- identify the different types of teams used in TQM,
- explain some of the factors associated with the successful use of teams,
- give examples of effective teams in action, and
- relate the use of teams in TQM to organizational behavior theories.

THE IMPORTANCE OF TEAMS IN TQM

Teams are everywhere in TQM: at the top and bottom of the organization and in every function and department in between. Why are there so many teams? Teamwork enables various parts of the organization to work together in meeting customer needs that can seldom be fulfilled by employees limited to one specialty. The TQM philosophy recognizes the interdependence of various parts of the organization and uses teams as a way to coordinate work.

TQM organizations recognize that the potential contributions of employees are much greater than in the traditional organization, and teams are an attempt to take advantage of this potential. Further, the competitive environment of modern business requires flexible, fast reaction to changes in customer demands or technological capacity. Teams can provide the capacity for rapid response. During the past few years, many companies have gone public with stories of their successful teams. Managers are always looking for ideas that produce results, and teams certainly fall squarely within this category.

TYPES OF TQM TEAMS

TQM uses so many different types of teams that sometimes it is difficult to tell one from another. Essentially, three types of teams are used most often: steering committees, problem-solving teams, and self-managed teams.

Steering Committees

Most organizations practicing total quality have a steering committee, called a quality council by Juran and a quality improvement team by Crosby.[2] Steering committees are responsible for establishing policy for TQM and for guiding the implementation and evolution of TQM throughout the organization. The top manager of the organization is usually on the steering committee, as is the manager with overall responsibility for quality—for example, the Vice President/Director of Total Quality.

The steering committee may meet fairly often when a TQM effort is getting started, but usually meets only monthly or quarterly once things are underway. This group makes key decisions about the quality program—how quality should be measured and what structures and programs should be used to improve quality. The steering committee also periodically reviews the status of

TQM and makes the adjustments necessary to ensure customer satisfaction and continuous improvement. In general, the steering committee has overall responsibility for the progress and success of the TQM effort.

Problem-Solving Teams

The second, and probably most common, type of teams used in TQM are problem-solving teams. As their name implies, problem-solving teams work to improve quality by identifying and solving specific quality-related problems facing the organization. Such teams are sometimes referred to as corrective action teams, or quality circles (see box), although many organizations have created their own names for them. Two basic types of problem-solving teams are departmental and cross-functional.

Departmental problem-solving teams

These teams are limited in membership to employees of a specific department and are limited in scope to problems within that department. Such groups typically meet once a week for one to two hours and progress through a standardized problem-solving methodology. First they identify a set of problems and select one to work on. Then they collect data about the causes of the problem and determine the best approach to solving it. (Often this will entail using many of the techniques described in chapter 3.)

If the solution does not require any major changes in procedures or substantial resources, the group frequently can implement its own solution. If this is not the case, group members will make a presentation to some level of management, requesting approval for their solution and the resources to implement it. These teams typically remain relatively intact as they address a number of problems in succession.

The problems that such teams work on can be quite diverse. A team of hourly workers at U.S. Steel's Gary Works has solved a number of crippling quality problems, helping to reduce the amount of steel rejected by automotive customers by 80 percent.[4] A team of service technicians at an equipment rental company simplified the form used to perform preventive maintenance, saving the company considerable time in the process. A team of people from the "resort" department at Federal Express improved the process of package sorting, which created savings in labor costs and helped to avoid the cost and embarrassment of having to send overnight packages via commercial airlines.[5]

Cross-functional teams

Cross-functional teams are not unique to total quality—they are commonly used in new product development, for example—but are increasingly becoming a mainstay of quality programs. These teams are similar in many ways to the departmental teams just discussed: they receive training in problem-solving, identify and solve problems, and either implement or recommend solutions.

Quality Circles in Japan: Still Unbroken

Quality circles were among the first Japanese management practices used in the U.S. When visiting Japan in the 1970s, American managers noticed groups of workers meeting to address quality problems. The managers recognized this as a practice that could easily be copied and returned home to institute it in their own companies. Quality circles (QCs) took off in the U.S. as the Japanese management mania peaked, and firms like Lockheed and Westinghouse reported early successes with circles. The QC movement boomed in the early 1980s, as most large American companies introduced the practice.

The bloom was soon off the rose, however, as firms found themselves devoting a lot of time and attention to QCs and receiving relatively little in return. There were a number of reasons for the lack of results. Employees were only encouraged to work on quality problems during their meetings (usually about an hour a week) and spent the rest of their week just "doing their job." Supervisors were often not involved in the program and were indifferent, if not downright hostile, to it. Perhaps the biggest problem was that QC's were "just a program," cut off from and often opposed to the way the organization usually worked. Managers preached about the importance of quality work during their QC events, but when crunch time came their attitude was, in the words of one QC member, "If it doesn't smoke, ship it!"

Not surprisingly, companies started to disband their QC programs, which were soon dismissed as just another passing fad. In the context of the current interest in total quality, many managers look back on QCs as essentially a false start on the road to quality. It is interesting in this light to note that many Japanese companies still operate QCs and that they are seen as a critical part of the total quality control (TQC) effort in these companies.[3]

According to the Japanese Union of Scientists and Engineers, 5.5 million workers take part in 750,000 circles. Managers as well as front-line employees are involved, and the circles are considered a normal part of working life, rather than a "program." In fact, QCs often work to achieve the objectives set in the *kaizen* process (see chapter 5), which puts them in the mainstream of TQC activity. Some organizations provide monetary incentives for suggestions provided by circles, and employees in some firms make more than 30 suggestions per year. It appears that the mistake made in the U.S. introduction of quality circles was not in introducing them, but in not taking them seriously.

The differences are that members of cross-functional teams come from several departments or functions, deal with problems that involve a variety of functions, and typically dissolve after the problem is solved. For example, a cross-functional team in a brokerage might deal with problems in handling questions from clients. The issues raised would not be limited to stocks, bonds, or mutual funds, so people from all of these areas would be involved.

Cross-functional teams make a great deal of sense in an organization devoted to process improvement, because most processes do not respect functional boundaries. If a process is to be comprehensively addressed, the team addressing it cannot be limited, by either membership or charter, to only one function. To be effective, cross-functional teams should include people from several departments: those who are feeling the effects of the problem, those who may be causing it, those who can provide remedies, and those who can furnish data.[6]

One cross-functional team made up of nurses, dieticians, and other nursing unit and food services staff addressed the problem of patients receiving their dinners late. This problem was quite aggravating to patients, but if it had been addressed by only the nursing unit, ignorance or apathy in the food services department would most likely have been blamed. Had the problem been addressed by food services, nursing would likely have been blamed. In either case, little would have been accomplished. A cross-functional team was required to unravel the complex scheduling and delivery issues associated with the problem.

Similarly, a cross-functional team at New York Life Insurance Company addressed the problem of returned mail. This was crucial for the company, because if policyholders do not receive their premium notices, New York Life does not get paid (see box).

Self-Managed Teams

The third type of teams used in Total Quality are self-managed teams, also known as self-directed teams, autonomous work groups, or simply teams. Although self-managed teams (SMTs) have been used for decades, their popularity has increased in recent years, due in part to their use in TQM. A recent survey concluded that 26 percent of American companies use teams to some extent, but only a much smaller number use them extensively.[7]

Unlike problem-solving teams, SMTs replace rather than complement the traditional organization of work. In place of a first-level supervisor and a set of employees with narrowly defined jobs is a set of associates (a term increasingly used for employees) with broad responsibilities, including the responsibility to manage themselves. In the absence of a supervisor, SMTs often handle budgeting, scheduling, setting goals, and ordering supplies. Some teams even evaluate one another's performance and hire replacements for departing team members.

A team in an automotive manufacturing plant placed an advertisement in the classified section of their local newspaper that read in part:

Gravedigging in New York[8]

Have you ever sent a letter only to have it returned as "undeliverable" by the post office? How about 7,000 undeliverable pieces of mail every week? This was the problem faced by New York Life Insurance Company. Most of the mail being returned was notices to people that their premiums were due, so a great deal of revenue was being lost. In fact, the company estimated the problem to be costing them as much as $80 million.

The team formed to attack this problem became known as the Gravediggers, because of their relentlessness in "digging up" addresses so that premium notices could be delivered. The 18-member team, whose members were drawn from around the nation, met via teleconference once or twice a week. Following total quality principles, the team began by looking for the root causes of undeliverable mail. Some of the most common were (1) policyholders who forgot to notify New York Life when they moved, and (2) long addresses that did not fit into the window on the mailing envelope.

The Gravediggers instituted a number of corrective measures to deal with the problem. They created units in each of the company's service offices to find addresses and keep company records up to date, they worked out a deal with the post office to forward mail and provide the company with corrected addresses, and they used a more elaborate mail-sorting system with bar codes.

Although they are still working on the problem, the Gravediggers' efforts have already begun to show some results. The volume of returned mail has been reduced by more than 20 percent, and the postal service provided the company with 61,000 correct addresses in a recent nine-month period. In fact, the Gravediggers are already among the most successful teams in the history of New York Life's total quality effort.

Our team is down one good player. Join our group of multiskilled Maintenance Associates who work together to support our assembly teams. . . . We are looking for a versatile person with . . . ability to set up and operate various welding machinery . . . willingness to work on detailed projects for extended time periods, and general overall knowledge of the automobile manufacturing process. . . . You must be a real team player, have excellent interpersonal skills, and be motivated to work in a highly participative environment.[9]

This ad illustrates many of the differences between SMTs and the traditional organization of work for nonmanagerial employees. For example, members of such teams are expected to actually work as a team, rather than just perform their own jobs capably. Their knowledge must be broad rather than narrow, their skills interpersonal as well as technical. In short, members of such teams are more like managers than employees in the traditional sense, hence the term *self-managed* teams.

EFFECTIVE TEAMWORK

Effective teamwork is critical to TQM success. In fact, teams are the main structure of many TQM organizations.[10] If they are not effective, TQM will not be effective: Steering committees will choose poor directions and policies for the organization. Departmental and cross-functional problem-solving teams will choose inappropriate problems or won't be able to solve the problems they identify. Self-managed teams will not be able to fulfill the promise of an empowered, creative workforce.

This section explores what it takes for teams to be effective in a TQM environment. Although the relative importance of these factors will vary from one type of team to another, they generally apply to any type of team found in TQM organizations. As you read this section, consider the ideas in light of your own experiences, rewarding or otherwise, on teams. If you are currently on a team, you may identify some ideas for improvement.

Criteria for Team Effectiveness

Teamwork has been defined as "a group of individuals working together to reach a common goal."[11] There are several criteria for team effectiveness. First, the team must achieve its goals of quality improvement. A steering committee must move the TQM effort ahead, a problem-solving team must identify and solve important problems, a self-managed team must operate and improve a set of production or service processes. This is the basic element of team effectiveness.

Second, teams that improve quality performance quickly are more effective than those that take a long period of time to do so. One of the strengths of teams is their potential for rapid adaptation to changing conditions. A team that takes a long time to accomplish anything is losing the potential benefits of having problems solved sooner and is consuming a greater-than-necessary amount of resources, including the time devoted to team meetings. In short, it is inefficient.

Third, the team must maintain or increase its strength as a unit. Think of the team as representing an asset—a quantity of human capital—beyond that represented by its individual members. This additional human capital is based on the ability to understand and adjust to one another's work styles, the development of an effective set of routines, the growth of trust among team members, and so on. A team that remains intact over a period of time preserves and enhances this human capital. A team that solves an important problem, but has such miserable relations that it dissolves, does not. It may make a contribution to the TQM effort, but it squanders a considerable amount of human capital in the process.

Fourth, the team must preserve or strengthen its relationship with the rest of the organization. With apologies to John Donne, "no team is an island", especially in the TQM environment. A team that accomplishes its goals at the cost of alienating others in the organization violates the TQM spirit of teamwork and compromises its ability to perform successfully in the future, when the collaboration of others may well be needed.

An effective team—whether it be a steering committee, problem-solving team, or self-managed team—must improve quality within a reasonable time frame and strengthen working relationships both inside and outside the team.

Team Membership

Like any system, teams cannot function effectively without high-quality input. The most important elements of team processes are the team members themselves. To be effective, team members must be representative of the departments or functions related to the problem being addressed. For example, a steering committee made up of members from one part of the organization would be insufficiently representative of the organization to be effective. Representation is particularly important for cross-functional teams.

Team members must possess the necessary technical knowledge to solve the problem at hand. This may mean understanding metallurgy for a team in a steel mill or understanding credit approval for a team in a bank. All members need not share the same knowledge, and in fact team members are often selected on the basis of specialized knowledge, but all of the appropriate technical bases must be covered for the team to be effective.

Effective teams must have members with problem-solving skills. These include problem diagnosis and data collection, as well as the ability to use TQM tools such as fishbone diagrams, histograms, and so on. Most organizations provide training in such techniques to people as they form teams.

Finally, teams must also have members with strong interpersonal skills. The critical importance of interpersonal skills is demonstrated by the following passage from a book on self-managed teams:

> We often hear experienced team leaders and members make remarks like this one: "I'll take someone with a good attitude over someone with just technical skills any day. I can train technical skills." With further prodding, we usually discover that they are really talking about interpersonal skills. . . . Because these qualities can be difficult to detect in a casual selection process, they are often overlooked in the pursuit of apparent, more objectively measured technical skills.[12]

What is meant by interpersonal skills? Think of people who are easy to work with in a group. They are good listeners and do not ignore or downgrade someone else's ideas in order to promote their own. They try to understand other people's positions, even when they do not agree with them. They offer help to other group members, rather than waiting to be asked. They are willing and able to communicate their opinions, ideas, and any information that needs to be shared. They can deal with conflict without turning it into a personal issue. Finally, they are willing to share credit for accomplishments with other members of the group, rather than trying to keep the limelight for themselves.[13] If you have worked on a team with people who possess even most of these skills, you are lucky indeed!

Team Processes

Many processes are undertaken within TQM teams, including quality planning, problem selection and diagnosis, communication, data collection, and implementation of solutions. Team processes are not fundamentally different from other processes, such as assembling an electronic device, taking a patient's vital signs, or preparing *coq au vin*. The customers of all these processes can be identified, their elements can be placed in a flowchart, steps that do not add value can be removed, and their quality can be improved continuously.

Most people, however, are not accustomed to thinking of group processes in this manner. This may be why group meetings are often long and boring and why so many people try to escape committee assignments and avoid committee meetings like the plague. A willingness to tolerate poor quality group processes has no place in organizations practicing total quality. This section identifies a few of the processes used in teams and provides some ideas about how teams can use them to operate effectively.

Problem Selection

One of the processes undertaken at least occasionally by most teams and frequently by problem-solving teams is the choice of problems or issues on which to work. This process can be particularly difficult for newly empowered employees, who are more accustomed to being told what to do than they are to establishing their own agenda. New teams are often tempted to select the biggest, most glaring problem in sight that has been haunting them for years. Selecting such problems—called "world hunger" problems in TQM jargon—is usually a mistake.

New teams generally are not skilled enough to solve massive problems, and a failure to address such a visible problem successfully may be difficult for the team to overcome. It makes more sense for a team initially to select a problem of moderate importance and difficulty and to move on to more complex and difficult problems when the team is better established. This approach is more likely to lead to successful solutions, which will build momentum for each team and for the quality effort as a whole.

Another common problem among new teams is that they select problems that are not associated—at least in management's eyes—with important business or quality issues. When given a voice for the first time, many teams ask for things they have been denied in the past, such as a better lunch area or break room. Although managers often consider such behavior an indictment of quality teams, it is in fact an indictment of management itself. It is unrealistic to expect employees to focus on business issues when managers have not taken seriously employee requests for adequate facilities. In fact, it is better for issues such as these to be worked out prior to initiating a team-based quality effort, rather than allowing them to undermine such efforts.

The selection of "trivial" problems by teams may also indicate that management has not done an effective job of sharing information about the business with team members. If they truly understand the nature of the important problems faced by the organization, teams are much more likely to choose worthwhile issues on which to work.

Problem Diagnosis

After problems to be addressed are identified, their causes must be ascertained. Thus a second critical process in TQM groups is problem diagnosis, the process by which the team investigates potential causes of problems to identify potential solutions. Juran refers to this step as the "diagnostic journey" and explains that it consists of three parts:

1. understanding the symptoms (for example, a process out of control),
2. theorizing as to causes (for example, preventive maintenance neglected), and
3. testing the theories (for example, reviewing preventive maintenance records to see if they relate to the problems experienced).

Many teams want to bypass problem diagnosis and begin problem solving as soon as possible, usually because they mistakenly believe that the problem's causes are obvious. Teams that spend more time diagnosing problems have been shown to be much more effective than those that proceed immediately to solutions. Spending time pinning down the sources of problems is consistent with the TQM principle of decision making based on facts and reduces the potential for what are sometimes called "type 3 errors"—solving the wrong problem.

Work Allocation

Another important process is the allocation of work within the team. Many teams approach this process haphazardly, assigning tasks to the next in line or the first person who volunteers. Assigning tasks is one of the keys to team effectiveness and should not be taken so lightly.[14] Each team member has certain skills and will perform well on tasks that use those skills and not so well on tasks that use other skills. The team needs to assign people tasks that will utilize their skills to the greatest extent possible.

Imagine a women's college basketball team that consists of some tall women who are excellent rebounders and inside shooters and some shorter (vertically challenged?) women who are skilled ball handlers and outside shooters. This team will be much more successful if the coach takes the time to assess the skills of each player and assigns them to the position where they can best help the team.

When explained in this context, the point is obvious, but you would be amazed at how many teams have the tall members bring the ball down the floor and pass to the short members underneath the basket! Differences in status within the group can be a problem if team members in higher positions are assigned the more glamorous roles, even when others are more qualified to fulfill them.[15] The status problem is particularly acute in organizations that have very high- and very low-status members, especially when (as in medicine) these differences are institutionalized in society. The vice president of quality at one hospital described a team with this problem:

> We had an emergency room physician who was a disaster. He was very much the old school expert and he was not about to be egalitarian in his approach. This created a lot of problems for that team. In spite of that, we were able to achieve some success with that team but it was, I'm sure, limited. If there was one factor [that hurt us], it was probably his impact on the team.

Communication

Communication is a key process for any team attempting to improve quality. Steering committees communicate priorities to employees. Members of problem-solving teams communicate among themselves and to their internal and external customers. For example, problem-solving teams often have to present their recommendations to management. Self-managed teams have similar communication needs and often must communicate effectively across shifts.

Three times every day in thousands of hospitals, mines, and manufacturing plants, teams of nurses, miners, and machine operators explain to the next shift what has happened in the last eight hours and what needs to be done in the next. The quality of this communication can dramatically affect the performance of the team on the next shift.

The communication process can be improved by carefully assigning people to key communication tasks and by training people in communication. We spend so much time communicating in our daily lives that we sometimes forget that skills such as listening and asking questions are vital to effective communication.

Communication within and across teams can also be enhanced by using a variety of media. Many TQM teams use electronic mail and fax machines, but also benefit from such low-tech media as posters and graphs posted on the walls. As with many team processes, any specific recommendations are less important than the general idea of recognizing communication as a process that consists of a series of steps that can be improved.

Coordination

Another key process is coordinating the team's work with other teams and departments in the organization. Maintaining good relationships outside the team is one criterion of team effectiveness. However, researchers have often found a tendency among teams to turn inward, believing that their own needs, ideas and plans are more valid than those of "outsiders." Ironically, the more cohesive the team becomes, the greater the likelihood of this occurring.[16]

Such a tendency is antithetical to TQM, but is a danger faced by virtually all groups. Teams can try to overcome this problem by keeping their customers in mind and using customer satisfaction as the yardstick against which ideas and plans are measured. Remaining aware of the need to improve team processes should also guard against the tendency to downplay the potential contributions of nonteam members, as outsiders are often the source of ideas for improvement that team members have overlooked.

Finally, good communication should also help to coordinate work with other teams and departments. The likelihood of following a path that works against the needs or plans of other groups will be diminished if teams communicate with other groups early and often. Tools such as quality function deployment and affinity diagrams, discussed in chapter 3, can be used to enhance such communication.

In a sense, quality-oriented process improvement and problem solving are a minefield for the unsuspecting team. Whenever changes are made in an organization, vested interests are challenged. By carefully managing the coordination process, teams will reduce the potential for unnecessary conflict with groups outside the team and will greatly enhance their potential for long-term effectiveness.

In summary, team processes can be improved just like any other process. Several key processes that are candidates for improvement are problem identification and diagnosis, work allocation, communication, and coordination of work with other teams and departments.

Organizational Support

However skillful the team, they will find it hard to be successful unless their efforts are supported by the organization in general, and management in particular. Organizational support is the foundation for effective teamwork. Management must provide the following if a TQM team is to be successful.

First, management must issue a clear charge to the group; that is, a description of what the group is and is not expected to do. Many teams have wasted a great deal of time and energy on issues that they later found they were not authorized to pursue. Management's guidance as to the quality priorities of the organization is crucial, especially in the early stages of a team's work.

Second, human resource management (HRM) systems often must be adjusted. Conventional HRM systems may be barriers to effective teamwork that will undermine TQM if not changed.[17] The need for enhanced training is particularly acute, as team members must be brought up to speed on the various types of skills necessary for effective teamwork.

Performance appraisal and reward systems are also a concern. Many of these systems are designed to reward individual effort or the attainment of functional goals, rather than teamwork. This can greatly undermine teamwork and can be fatal to the team if not addressed. Imagine a class project in which each student was graded on the quality of his or her part, rather than on the quality of the project as a whole and you will have the general idea of the impact of inappropriate reward systems.

Selection processes may also be changed in conjunction with TQM implementation. The members of self-managed teams often take much of the responsibility for hiring people for their team. Human resource professionals should play a consultative role in such efforts, however, to make sure that selection is done in a fair and legal manner.

Third, management must provide the team with the resources necessary to be successful. These include a place and time to meet and the tools to get the job done. Human resources are also important: management should avoid moving people on and off teams frequently, as this can disrupt teamwork and send a message that quality and teamwork are really not a high priority for the organization.

Fourth, when teams make a proposal, management must respond swiftly and constructively. It is not realistic to expect that every quality improvement proposal made by a team will be implemented. For those proposals that cannot be implemented, management owes the team a reasonable explanation as to why it is not feasible and some guidance as to how the proposal might be modified so that it would be acceptable. Few experiences are as demoralizing to quality teams as making an elaborate, reasoned presentation, only to be met with deafening silence from management. This was one of the problems that undermined quality circle programs. It is less of a problem for self-managed teams that generally have broad authority to implement their own solutions.

For those proposals that are accepted, some form of recognition for the team is in order. Often the most effective forms of recognition are symbolic, such as a citation or picture in the company newspaper.

TEAMWORK IN ACTION

This section provides two examples of quality teamwork: one a problem-solving team in a general hospital, and the other an unusual instance of teamwork in a Baldrige Award winner. As you read these minicases, reflect on whether the teams are effectively practicing the team processes we have discussed.

A Team with a Transparent Problem[18]

Have you ever had tests done in a hospital and wondered why it takes so long to get the results back? So did the employees and managers in the radiology department at Sentara Norfolk General Hospital in Norfolk, Virginia. Although everyone associated with the process felt that they were working as fast as they could, performing and reporting the results of an X-ray or CAT scan was taking three days on average (72.5 hours, to be precise). A nine-person team was formed to address the problem, and they vowed to cut the time down to 24 hours.

The first step was to focus the team on the process, rather than on individual performance, and to create a sense of teamwork that would override the differences in status that sometimes hamper the work of medical professionals. Pat Curtis, head of cardiac nursing, was chosen as the team's facilitator, partially for her recognized skills but also because she was from outside radiology and had no formal authority over team members.

Although the team met infrequently, the members had plenty of work to do between meetings, mostly on collecting information. Using techniques associated with Norfolk General's CQI effort (Continuous Quality Improvement, as TQ is often known in health care), the team identified 40 steps in the X-ray process and 50 possible causes of delay, only a few of which were causing most of the problems. Rather than waiting for a grand changeover at the culmination of their work, the team made improvements to the process as they discovered them. This was greatly facilitated by the cross-functional representation and the presence of managers on the team. As one member put it, "Folks who could effect change were part of the decision making."

None of the changes the team made were particularly dramatic. Curtis helped the nursing department to reduce errors such as forgetting to note whether patients would need stretchers or oxygen. X-ray technologists began to walk developed films to the next person in the process, rather than waiting for the internal mail service to move them. Fourteen of the 40 steps were redesigned out of the process.

The results were clearly dramatic. The average time to process an X-ray dropped to 13.8 hours, an 81 percent improvement! This achievement was impressive enough to win the team a Rochester Institute of Technology/USA TODAY Quality Cup for team accomplishment in the not-for-profit category. Physicians in the hospital report that the faster availability of diagnostic information is helping them to improve their own processes, and other companies and government agencies in the Norfolk area are looking to the hospital for help with their own quality improvement challenges.

The team has responded to its success with a renewed commitment to continuous improvement. The introduction of a CD-based digital system to replace tapes for dictating physician comments is expected to cut the time down to 11 hours. The team's new goal? Eight hours. Stay tuned.

The Birth of Teamwork at Globe Metallurgical[19]

Globe Metallurgical, with plants in Beverly, Ohio, and Selma, Alabama, was the first small-company winner of the Malcolm Baldrige National Quality Award. Considering the problems the company has faced, it is lucky to be operating, let alone winning awards. As with many companies, its quality and teamwork principles first crystallized under a great deal of pressure.

On October 8, 1986, Globe's unionized workforce went out on strike over differences with management concerning pay and work rules such as which workers can perform what jobs. In a small town like Beverly, a strike is a very big deal, with lifetime friendships and even family relationships at stake. There was even some violence as suppliers and people working through the strike tried to cross the picket lines.

During the strike, work usually done by union workers was performed by salaried workers and managers on twelve-hour shifts, seven days a week. Although this was no doubt an exhausting routine, it provided an opportunity for people to learn a number of lessons about teamwork and continuous improvement. In the words of Arden Sims, chief executive of Globe:

> The strike was a time of great stress but also a time of great progress. We experimented with everything. . . . Our objective was to find the most efficient way to run the furnaces, with no constraints on how we did it. . . . We were operating in a very fast continuous improvement mode. Every day, people would suggest ways to improve the operation of the furnaces or [other processes]. I kept a pocket notebook, and if I saw something, I'd jot it down and discuss it with the team over coffee or during a meal. I filled a notebook every day.
> . . .
> As we made more and more changes and as we settled into the routine of running the plant, it became evident that we didn't need first-line supervisors. We could produce the product more effectively if everyone just worked together cooperatively—welders, crane operators, furnace operators, forklift drivers, stokers, furnace tappers, and tapper assistants.[20]

What Globe had discovered, without using the name, was self-managed teams. The experiments undertaken during the strike resulted in dramatic improvements in efficiency for the company's operations. Unfortunately for the union employees, many of them never returned to the new-and-improved company, which had learned to operate with many fewer people. It is ironic that the high degree of teamwork exhibited by the management team during the strike was only possible because of a breakdown of teamwork between management and the union, which ultimately led to a substantial reduction in union workers in the company.

COMPARISON TO ORGANIZATIONAL BEHAVIOR THEORIES

Little conflict exists between the use of teams in TQM and theories of organizational behavior, but there are differences in emphasis. Along with social psychology and sociology, organizational behavior (OB) is the source of much of what is known about groups or teams. Since there is no separate tradition of research or thinking about groups within TQM, virtually all of the practices and recommendations ultimately derive from conventional (or unconventional) management theory.

Research knowledge about groups is most heavily emphasized in organizational development (OD), the branch of the organizational sciences that deals with changing and improving organizations. Most team-based practices in TQM come from OD. Some of these practices, such as the nominal group technique, are based on research in organizational behavior or social psychology, others are not.

Teams are actually a subset of the organizational behavior/social psychology concept of groups. All teams are groups, but not all groups are teams. Compare our definition of a team as "people working together to achieve a goal" to the following definition of a group: "A number of persons who communicate with one another often over a span of time, and who are few enough in number that each person may communicate with all the others."[21] Clearly we ask more of our teams than we do of our groups! Organizational behavior has traditionally focused on workgroups, people who work together in the same function. Theory has addressed why some groups are more cohesive or productive than others and whether groups are likely to support or undermine organizational goals.

The specific types of teams used in TQM efforts are also derived from OB research. Self-managed teams are a modern version of semiautonomous work groups, that were championed for use in underground coal mines by researchers from Britain's Tavistock Institute more than 40 years ago.[22] Similarly, cross-functional teams have been discussed within OB for many years as a way to integrate work across interdependent functions.[23]

Much of the knowledge from OB research on groups has not yet been absorbed into TQ thinking in a widespread manner, but probably should be. This includes the research on the relative advantages of homogeneous and heterogeneous groups, which appears to be relevant to effective team-building.

Research has shown that homogenous groups (those in which members are similar in age, race, gender, experience, and so on) are better suited to well-defined, familiar tasks, where the emphasis is on efficient production. Heterogeneous groups, on the other hand, are better at tasks that require creative thinking. This implies that teams used in TQ efforts generally should be quite diverse, due to the heavy emphasis on creativity and fresh thinking in the tasks they face. Based on this research, managers selecting people for teams should make heterogeneity their goal.

SUMMARY

Three types of teams are used in TQM efforts: steering committees, problem-solving teams (both departmental and cross-functional), and self-managed teams. Teams allow organizations to focus on customer needs and to deal with interdependence across functions and processes.

Team effectiveness consists of achieving quality goals in a timely manner and strengthening relationships both within the team and between the team and the rest of the organization. Teams will be effective to the extent that their members have the appropriate technical and interpersonal skills and are able to manage team processes such as problem selection and communication.

Teams cannot be effective without organizational support, especially the provision of resources. Although the use of teams in TQM efforts is broadly consistent with traditional organizational behavior theories, teamwork is more heavily emphasized within TQM.

REVIEW AND DISCUSSION QUESTIONS

1. In the quote that introduces the chapter, Donald Peterson claims that teams are the best way to accomplish any kind of work. Do you agree? Why or why not?

2. What are the similarities and differences among the types of teams used in TQM?

3. Think of a team that you are on, or have been on recently. How does it stack up against the criteria for quality teamwork? What specific steps could be used to improve the performance of your team? How could TQ techniques be used to improve team processes?

4. Identify a problem in some area of your work, school, or home life. What are the symptoms of the problem? What is the obvious cause? Now think harder about the causes of the problem. (Try to spend 10 minutes doing this.) Do other causes come to mind? How would your solution result in better problem diagnosis?

5. How did the team at Norfolk General Hospital illustrate the effective teamwork practices discussed in the text?

6. If self-managed teams can succeed without active intervention from managers, what—if anything—does this imply about the traditional roles of management (to plan, organize, and control) in organizations? Should a new set of roles be identified for such situations?

7. Do you think that the current popularity of teams in organizations is a fad or a fundamental change in the way we manage organizations? Why?

8. Are teams absolutely necessary for total quality to be successful? Sketch out a plan for a total quality effort that does not involve teams.

CASES

A Self-Managed Cheese-Making Team[24]

Monday at 6 A.M., the Green team relieves the Silver team for a 12-hour shift at the R.G. Bush plant of Schreiber Foods. Schreiber is the second-largest producer of cheese in America, and the 53 employees at the Bush plant (near Tempe, Arizona) are responsible for making bulk cheese that is further processed into finished products by other plants. The Bush plant is extremely efficient, producing about a million pounds of cheese each week, due to both advanced production control technology and the use of self-managed teams. In addition to the Green and Silver teams, there are also Red, Blue, maintenance, support, and management teams.

The process that the six-member Green team has just assumed responsibility for includes condensing, evaporating, filling, packing, and palletizing operations. As the shift begins, the designated communicators from the two teams discuss a potential pH problem that was identified overnight. Two team members take their places in the process control room in front of a bank of computer screens, switches, and meters. They check the performance of the process over the past few hours and consult a schedule for preventive maintenance. The other three team members are in the barrel room today and will be performing manual labor: making cardboard barrels, filling them with cheese, and placing them on pallets.

The team members rotate among these tasks, including the communicator job, which is the closest thing to a designated team leader at the plant. Team members have taken over the functions of team advisers, nonteam personnel who guided the teams until they were no longer needed. At this plant, the practice of job rotation is seen as more important than having the most qualified person in a job at all times: Larry is the most technically-qualified person on the team, but today he is filling barrels with cheese.

The team addresses a number of problems during its shift. The computer screen alerts Tim in the control room to a problem with an evaporator. He calls Tony, who escapes from the barrels for a few minutes to find and clean out a clogged check valve. Later, the pH problem reappears; it is now so low that it is out of specification. To make matters worse some burned cheese has been detected. The evaporator must be shut down for cleaning, and the team takes the maintenance team's advice to perform a more extensive cleaning that has to be done soon anyway.

The team wants to get the process back on-line as soon as possible because the evaporator shutdown costs the company money, and the out-of-spec cheese is reflected in the team's incentive payout. After a filter is replaced and the cleaning completed, the process is ready to roll.

While the team works, they are literally surrounded with information. A three-foot-long electronic sign updates them on various aspects of performance including conformance, production, and customer complaints. A bulletin board is crammed with information on raw material consumption, the incentive system, and so on. Wrapped around the control room is a banner that exhorts them to "Do it right the first time."

Green team members communicate constantly. Beyond their daily job communication, they have a monthly team meeting to discuss goals, problems, schedules, and whatever else needs to be covered. There are also corrective action team meetings, communicators' meetings, and incentive meetings. Members understand all of the meetings as the price of empowerment and teamwork, but feel that the sacrifice is better than letting management make all the decisions.

The team recently had its first experience with firing a member, which was particularly hard because he was a friend and a teammate. They had hired him because of his technical ability, despite past problems with attendance. They did everything they could to keep him, but the attendance problems continued, and the team felt he was letting them down.

Ted, the newest member of the Green team, summarizes the team's feeling about self management:

> When I got here, I knew that this was just up my alley. I don't need a boss looking over my shoulder, because I know how to do the work. It never made sense to me to see grown-ups standing around watching other grown-ups do their jobs. I could see it if you were 14 years old. But I'm an adult, and Schreiber respects that.

Discussion Questions

1. Outline what a day at work would be like in a cheese plant that utilized a more conventional organization—no teams, foremen, many job classifications. How would this differ from the day the Green team at Schreiber's Bush plant experienced? What are the advantages and disadvantages of the two arrangements?

2. In the text it was argued that team members should be assigned to the work that they do best. Yet in the Green team case, team members rotated through all jobs regardless of their skills. Do you think this is a good idea? Why or why not?

3. What would a manager's job be like in this kind of plant? Would you want to work as a manager there?

ENDNOTES

1. Quoted in John Hillkirk, "New Award Cites Teams with Dreams," *USA Today*, April 10, 1992.

2. J.M. Juran, *Juran on Leadership for Quality: An Executive Handbook,* New York: Free Press, 1989. P.B. Crosby, *Quality is Free: The Art of Making Quality Certain,* New York: McGraw-Hill, 1979.

3. The information on quality circles in Japan is from B.G. Dale and J. Tidd, "Japanese total quality control: A study of best practice," *Proceeding of the Institution of Mechanical Engineers,* 205(4), pp.221–232.

4. James R. Healey, "U.S. Steel Learns from Experience," *USA Today*, April 10, 1992.

5. Martha T. Moore, "Hourly workers apply training in problem solving" *USA Today*, April 10, 1992.

6. Juran, *Juran on Leadership for Quality.*

7. Wellins, Richard S., Byham, William C., and Wilson, Jeanne M., *Empowered Teams: Creating Self-Directed Work Groups That Improve Quality, Productivity, and Participation,* summary of Chapter 4. Copyright 1991 by Jossey-Bass Inc., Publishers.

8. Based on Jerry G. Bowles, "Leading the World-Class Company," *Fortune*, September 21, 1992.

9. Wellins et al., *Empowered teams*, p. 21.

10. P. Alexander, M. Biro, E.G. Garry, D. Seamon, T. Slaughter, and D. Valerio, "New Organizational Structures and New Quality Systems," in J.P. Kern, J.J. Riley, and L.N. Jones (eds.), *Human Resources Management*, Milwaukee: ASQC Quality Press, 1987, pp. 203–268.

11. A.R. Tenner and I.J. De Toro, *Total Quality Management: Three Steps to Continuous Improvement,* Reading, Mass.: Addison-Wesley, 1992, p.183.

12. Wellins et al., *Empowered teams*, p.147.

13. Partially based on Wellins et al., *Empowered teams*, and H.J. Harrington, *The Improvement Process: How America's Leading Companies Improve Quality*, New York: McGraw-Hill, 1987.

14. This point is based on a model developed by I. Steiner in his book *Group Process and Productivity*, New York: Academic Press, 1972.

15. The problems of differential status in groups are discussed by Alvin Zander in *Making Groups Effective,* San Francisco: Jossey-Bass, 1982.

16. The classic statement of this problem is by Irving Janis in his book *Groupthink*. 2nd Ed. Boston: Houghton-Mifflin, 1982.

17. Wellins et al., *Empowered teams*. See also S.A. Snell and J.W. Dean, Jr., "Integrated Manufacturing and Human Resource Management: A Human Capital Perspective," *Academy of Management Journal*, August 1992, pp. 467–504.

18. Based on Kevin Anderson, "X-ray processing time cut 81%," *USA Today*, April 10, 1992.

19. Based on Bruce Rayner, "Trial-By-Fire Transformation: An Interview with Globe Metallurgical's Arden C. Sims," *Harvard Business Review*, May–June 1992, pp. 117–129.

20. Ibid.

21. G.C. Homans, *The Human Group,* New York: Harcourt, Brace, and World, 1959, p.2.

22. E. Trist and K.W. Bamforth, "Some social and psychological consequences of the long wall method of coal-getting," *Human Relations*, 4(1), 1952, pp. 3–38.

23. For example, J.E. McCann and J.R. Galbraith, "Interdepartmental Relations," in P.C. Nystrom and W.H. Starbuck (eds.), *Handbook of Organizational Design*, vol. 2. *Remodeling Organizations and Their Environments*, New York: Oxford University Press, 1981.

24. Wellins et al., *Empowered teams,* Chapter 4.

CHAPTER 8

Empowerment and Motivation

Chapter Outline

Introduction to Empowerment
The Importance of Empowerment
Principles of Empowerment
    Empower Sincerely and Completely
    Establish Mutual Trust
    Provide Employees with Business Information
    Ensure that Employees are Capable
    Don't Ignore Middle Management
    Change the Reward System
Empowerment in Action
    Semco
    The Ritz-Carlton Hotel Company
Empowerment and Theories of Motivation
    Job Characteristics Theory
    Acquired Needs Theory
    Goal-setting Theory
Summary
Review and Discussion Questions
Case

In 1988 Takeo Miura of Hitachi Corporation made the following statement to a group of senior U.S. business executives:

> We are going to win and the industrial West is going to lose out; there's nothing much you can do about it, because the reasons for your failure are within

yourselves. . . . With your bosses doing the thinking while the workers wield the screwdrivers, you're convinced deep down that this is the right way to run a business. For you, the essence of management is getting the ideas out of the heads of the bosses and into the hands of labor. We are beyond the Taylor model: business, we know, is so complex and difficult that survival for firms . . . depends on the day-to-day mobilization of every ounce of intelligence.[1]

Miura threw down the gauntlet to American business: bring the brainpower of your entire organization to the competition, or prepare to lose permanently. In the years since this challenge was issued, American firms have begun to undertake the process of employee empowerment. This chapter will

- explain what is meant by empowerment,
- explain the importance of empowerment to quality,
- identify the principles of successful empowerment,
- provide examples of firms practicing empowerment, and
- link empowerment to theories of motivation.

INTRODUCTION TO EMPOWERMENT

Empowerment means giving someone power. Managers in many companies have found that giving people throughout the organization the power to make a difference contributes greatly to providing quality products and services to their customers.

Empowerment is a natural extension of employee involvement concepts such as worker participation in decision making. In some companies empowerment is used as the umbrella term for increasing employee involvement in decision making. Empowerment is more than another term for involvement, however. It represents a high degree of involvement in which employees make decisions themselves and are responsible for their outcomes. This is a more radical change than having employees merely participate in managers' decisions, even when they are given some influence (see Figure 8.1).

For empowerment to occur, managers must undertake two major initiatives:[2]

Figure 8.1   Continuum of Employee Involvement Practices

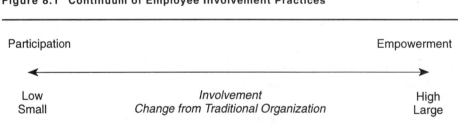

Participation		Empowerment
Low	*Involvement*	High
Small	*Change from Traditional Organization*	Large

- identify and change organizational conditions that make people powerless, and
- increase people's confidence that their efforts to accomplish something important will be successful.

The need to do both of these implies that organizational systems often create powerless employees and that these systems must be changed first. Examples of systems in need of change are those that specify who can (and cannot) make certain types of decisions and systems of standard operating procedures (and who can override them). Even when systems are changed to permit empowerment, individuals who have lived under those systems are not readily able to operate in an empowered manner. The other need in empowering people is to deal with the psychological after-effects of powerlessness by convincing people that they are in fact able to "make a difference."

Empowerment is an application of the teamwork principle of total quality, embodying "vertical" teamwork between managerial and nonmanagerial personnel. If employees are given important responsibilities—and the authority that goes along with them—it is more realistic to describe their relationship with management as teamwork than it would be in a hierarchical system. After all, people can hardly be seen as team members if they only execute decisions made by others.

The need to empower the entire workforce in order for quality to succeed has long been recognized, even if it is only recently coming into practice. Juran wrote that "ideally, quality control should be delegated to the workforce to the maximum extent possible."[3] Empowerment resembles Juran's concept of "self-control." For employees to practice self-control, they must know their unit's goals and their actual performance and have a means for changing performance if the goals are not being met.[4] Although it is a difficult struggle, organizations are increasingly meeting these conditions.

A recent survey found that more than 40 percent of the largest U.S. corporations are moderate to high users of employee involvement practices such as empowerment.[5] Manufacturing, especially in the chemical and electronics industries, has tended to empower employees more than service organizations, although the financial services industry has taken a leading role.

Empowerment has even played a role in such business successes as the Ford Taurus program.[6] Employee ideas were responsible for reducing the number of different welding guns on the assembly line from three to one and for developing a standard screw size for use in the car's interior plastic moldings. Although these changes may not sound very dramatic, a Ford executive estimated that such ideas often are worth more than $300,000 each.

The objective of empowerment is "to tap the creative and intellectual energy of everybody in the company, not just those in the executive suite...to provide everyone with the responsibility and the resources to display real leadership within their own individual spheres of competence."[7] In the quote that introduced this chapter, Takeo Miura took American managers to task for ignoring the creative and intellectual energies of the workforce.

The traditional treatment of employees by American managers led W. Edwards Deming to plead with managers to drive out fear—defined as "feeling threatened by possible repercussions as a result of speaking up about work-related concerns."[8] Today managers in quality-oriented companies, hampered by decades of policies encouraging employees to keep their ideas to themselves, struggle to find ways to encourage employees to take responsibility for their work.

THE IMPORTANCE OF EMPOWERMENT

Empowerment is important primarily because it improves organizational performance. Everyone in an organization is an asset, albeit an asset whose value is not automatically realized. If money is put into a closet instead of a bank, it will not gain interest. Employees who are put into jobs that are like being in a closet (in the dark, isolated) similarly will not provide value to the organization.

Giving employees responsibility for their own work has led to improvements in quality, productivity, motivation, customer service, and morale, as well as in the speed of decision making.[9] The benefits of empowerment have become obvious to many managers, such as Art Wegner, president of Pratt & Whitney, a producer of jet engines:

> If I try to make a lot of decisions with the goal of reducing costs by 30 percent, I'm not likely to understand all the issues very well. But if you get everybody— all those people in the organization—asking themselves, "How am I going to get 30 percent of the costs out of there?"—the power of that is unbelievable.[10]

Although empowerment is relevant for all aspects of organizational performance, it plays a special role in quality improvement. Total quality requires people to make real changes in the way work is done and relies upon in-depth understanding of the current system. Only employees involved in the system day-to-day possess such an understanding, which is why so many managers see employee involvement as an integral part of total quality. As one survey concluded, "Employee involvement...may be viewed as creating the organizational context needed to support quality improvement processes."[11]

The importance of empowerment to total quality is underlined by its inclusion as a core value in the Malcolm Baldrige National Quality Award. The guidelines state:

> Improving company performance requires improvements at all levels within a company. This, in turn, depends upon the skills and dedication of the entire workforce. Companies need to invest in the development of the workforce and to seek new avenues to involve employees in problem solving and decision making.[12]

Empowerment Spurs Team to Success

"I'm not trying to win games. I'm trying to build character, which is something that will carry them much further than basketball. If you build character, and they have some pride in themselves, then they will win basketball games." Who would say a thing like that, some basketball version of Knute Rockne? The coach of a losing team, trying to rationalize his poor record? How about John Lucas, coach of the NBA's San Antonio Spurs?

Lucas is a recovered cocaine addict, who applies what he has learned from his experience to both basketball and life. "I've had to relinquish control to save my life. I'm just giving them the same thing. I have no trouble accepting what they do." "They" is the Spurs basketball team, and "what they do" is take a lot of responsibility for running the team.

The Spurs were pretty desperate for some help when Lucas was hired. The previous coach left with a losing record, and high-priced superstar David Robinson just wasn't giving the team its money's worth. Lucas formed a council of three players to guide the team, consisting of Robinson, Sean Elliott, and Dale Ellis, with Robinson as "chief executive officer." (Robinson, a graduate of the U.S. Naval Academy, is also nicknamed "the Admiral." He certainly has an impressive list of titles for such a young man!) The council, rather than the coach, decides how to deal with players that break team rules.

Lucas's most unusual coaching tactic is to turn some timeout huddles over to the players. He can occasionally be seen standing away from the group with his arms folded. He is not unconcerned, he says that he just wants the players to feel "ownership" for the team and its success. And so far at least, it seems to be working. As David Robinson puts it, "I think the best motivation is that part-ownership motivation. You're playing for yourself."

But the bottom line for a coach is the team's win-loss record, and the empowerment experiment seems to be working here as well, as the Spurs have gone from also-rans to serious contenders in their division. And as long as the Spurs keep winning, Lucas will get away with saying things like, "Basketball is a simple game. For complicated people [like Robinson], it's not a complicated game. The challenge for David is to continue to grow as a person."[13]

Beyond its impact on quality and other aspects of organizational performance, empowerment also leads to greater levels of satisfaction among the workforce.[14] This plays a special role in TQ, insofar as Deming speaks of the right of employees to enjoy their work and claims that there should be more joy in the workplace.

Although enhancing people's enjoyment of their work is a worthwhile goal in itself, empowered employees give faster and friendlier service to customers as well.[15] This is not much of a surprise, as we have all been victimized at some point by surly employees who decided to take their organizational powerlessness out on us. Employee satisfaction is related to customer satisfaction.

Companies, such as Disney, that excel at customer service have long been aware of this relationship. Disney cast members, as those who work at Disneyland and Disneyworld are called, are treated with special care. For example, before the opening of the Star Tours attraction, it was previewed by cast members and their families for four nights. The cast members who tried it received free dinners. Social events for cast members are also held, including Minnie's Moonlight Madness, an after-hours treasure hunt.[16]

It's not just "being nice" to employees that leads them to provide better customer service. The continuous improvement of organizational processes removes many hassles that produce disgruntled employees, who in turn produce dissatisfied customers. As Hal Rosenbluth, president of Rosenbluth Travel puts it, "By maintaining an enjoyable, bureaucracy-free work environment, one that encourages innovative thinking . . . and honest communication, people are freed to concentrate solely on the needs of the clients."[17] The relationship between empowerment and quality is summarized in Figure 8.2.

PRINCIPLES OF EMPOWERMENT

Although many organizations have undertaken the journey toward empowerment, many have become lost along the way. Empowerment may sound easy, but there is a lot more to it than telling employees they are (poof!) empowered, like the Fairy Godmother's transformation of Cinderella before the ball. A number of principles are involved in successfully giving power to employees.

1. Empower Sincerely and Completely

It should go without saying that empowerment must be done sincerely. It cannot be done superficially. To gain its benefits, managers must empower for its improvement value, not for its public relations value. As Dan Ciampa, a consultant with expertise in empowerment puts it:

> Simply bringing employees together once a month and exhorting them to work harder to achieve the business's objectives is not enough. A process is needed that enables them to make significant improvements in their own work area

Figure 8.2 How Empowerment Leads to Quality

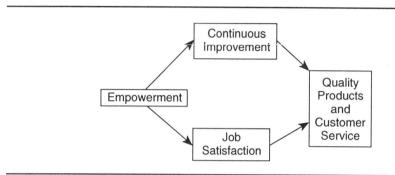

that help meet the business imperatives in a way that will satisfy the needs of the individual employee.[18]

Furthermore, nothing could be worse for employees than to be told they are responsible for something, only to be jerked back at the first sign of trouble or uncertainty. Managers must think long and hard before making the commitment to empowerment—once done, it can't be done halfway. Semi-empowerment just doesn't work.

This does not mean that there should be no limits. On the contrary, managers must be clear on exactly what responsibility and authority rests with employees. Questions such as "What procedures can we change?" and "How much money can we commit?" must be answered ahead of time. Finally, managers must be willing to wait for results, as miracles do not happen overnight.[19]

2. Establish Mutual Trust

As Juran has put it, "The managers must trust the workforce enough to be willing to make the delegation, and the workforce must have enough confidence in the managers to be willing to accept the responsibility."[20] Trust is not created just by saying you trust someone; it must be backed up by actions. For management, this means granting employees access to information such as their personnel files and resources such as the quality improvement budget.[21]

In one plant utilizing self-managed teams, trust was symbolized by giving each new employee a key to the plant, a highly unusual practice.[22] The ultimate issue for many employees, however, is job security. They must trust that management will not take advantage of productivity increases to cut the workforce, in effect working themselves out of a job. Firms embarking upon employee involvement activities often make explicit commitments to this effect to employees.[23]

3. Provide Employees with Business Information

For empowerment to succeed, it must focus on making the organization more competitive.[24] Empowerment can contribute to organizational performance only if employees have access to the necessary information about the business and its performance. Information about the employees' department or other subunit is particularly necessary, as this is the level of performance that they can affect. Sharing business information with employees relates directly to quality, customer service, and competitiveness.[25]

In the absence of appropriate information, empowered employees may squander their power on problems that are not very important. As Peter Senge has put it, "Empowering the individual where there is a relatively low level of alignment [between organizational and employee goals] worsens the chaos and makes managing . . . even more difficult."[26]

The criticism of misplaced goals was often leveled at earlier employee-involvement efforts, such as quality circles. Although managers formerly blamed employees for having the wrong priorities, sophisticated managers today recognize that they are responsible for providing employees with the information necessary to develop educated priorities.

4. Ensure that Employees Are Capable

"You can't empower incompetence," says one manager. If employees are going to take on important organizational responsibilities, they must be prepared to do so. To operate in an empowered, TQ environment, employees must possess not only technical skills (including statistics) but also interpersonal and problem-solving skills. Unfortunately, many people entering the workforce today lack even the most basic skills in reading and math, let alone these relatively advanced skills.[27]

Employee capability can be ensured through selection and training processes. Unless the human resource processes are adapted to provide capable employees, empowerment cannot succeed, and management's worst nightmares will be realized. Unfortunately, many employees are not trained in these areas, which helps explain the mixed results many organizations have had with empowerment.[28]

A Corning Glass plant in Erwin, New York, exemplifies this principle.[29] The union agreed to replace 21 different jobs with one "specialist" job. Employees were placed in teams and given broad authority over production scheduling and the division of labor. Did a bright new day dawn at Erwin? Not exactly. Conflict and confusion went up, and productivity went down. Plant manager Gary Vogt concluded: "We took steps to empower people, but the desired outcomes were not reached because we had not prepared them." An elaborate training program was created, and workers now become certified for the various tasks in the operation through testing. The promise of empowerment is now being fulfilled, and quality and productivity have increased.

Empowerment at AT&T Universal Card Services

AT&T Universal Card Services (UCS), a 1992 winner of the Malcolm Baldrige National Quality Award, has had the luxury of building an organization based on quality and empowerment from the ground up. Launched in March 1990, the Universal Card is the second-biggest in the industry and is still growing.

More than 100 quality measurements are taken daily from various portions of the business. These measurements are displayed on TV monitors and walls all over the company. They are also followed closely by UCS employees, who get a bonus equal to 12 percent of their daily salary for every day UCS meets its quality targets. On average, associates earn about $2,200 a year from these bonuses.

UCS employees can take advantage of numerous training opportunities, ranging from traditional classes to computer-based instruction. Hourly employees undergo about 84 hours of training per year beyond the 8-week orientation for new customer-service employees.

With this level of training and motivation for quality as a backdrop, UCS phone associates are empowered to do whatever is necessary when cardmembers call for help, regardless of company rules. One time an associate received a collect call from a tourist in Paris who had become stranded when his card had been "eaten by the ATM" on a Saturday afternoon. The cardmember was desperate, as he was scheduled to leave the next day and was broke. While the cardmember stayed on the line, the associate contacted the American embassy in Paris and arranged for a limo to take the traveler to the only bank still open in the city, where the associate had authorized an emergency cash advance. It is in situations such as these that motivation, training, and empowerment come together to produce customer satisfaction, if not outright "delight."

Rosenbluth Travel, on the other hand, has made substantial investments in providing the kind of employees needed for an empowered, quality-oriented workforce.[30] Extensive research has led to tests that predict the likely success of applicants for such positions as corporate reservationist, based on personality type and skill repertoire. When individuals are hired, they attend a two-day orientation session at corporate headquarters, where they are immersed in the company's philosophies and values and begin to understand the company's concept of customer service. (This point is illustrated by the corporate officers serving the new associates afternoon tea on the second day.) This is just the beginning of training, however. Reservationists must successfully complete up to 320 hours of classroom instruction, which focuses on the mechanics of reservations and how to provide quality service.

5. Don't Ignore Middle Management

A well-known principle of organization theory popularized by Deming is that organizations are systems. When changing one part of an organization, it is necessary to consider the effects of the change on other parts of the system. Thus, managers must consider how empowering lower-level employees will affect middle managers. If the needs and expectations of middle managers are ignored, empowerment will be confusing at best and disastrous at worst. One manager described the situation with middle managers in his company like this:

> We pretty much promoted people because of their technical knowledge, not their management skills. Therefore we have a group of people in supervisory positions who aren't people-oriented; they don't know how to get the ideas and the solutions and better ways of doing things out of their people. And they are not receptive to employee-involvement programs, they are not receptive to too much change in their lives, they feel comfortable in this doing role rather than a coaching or facilitator's role. So therefore we have to train these people to think differently and manage their departments from a management point of view rather than a doer's point of view. . . . It's the middle management transition from the old style of management to today's new style of management that's the problem, that stops companies from getting where they need to be as fast as they need to get there.

Among the roles for middle managers in organizations with empowered workforces are[31]

- maintaining focus on the organization's values,
- managing solutions to system-level problems—those that involve many functions and departments, and
- acting as teachers and coaches.

It's tempting to think of middle managers faced with empowerment efforts as dinosaurs, rapidly becoming extinct because the world has changed too quickly for them. However, remember that most middle managers are a product of their organizations and have attained their level of success in an environment that rewarded different things than are needed from managers now. Given a new set of instructions from top management, backed up by new performance appraisal criteria, many (but far from all) managers will be able to make the necessary transition.

6. Change the reward system

Rarely can substantial organizational change be created without changing the reward system. The reward system includes all of the rewards that employees receive, as well as the criteria for distributing these rewards. An organization is to its reward system like a boat is to its anchor: unless the reward system is changed, the organization may drift a little bit in one direction or another, but it won't get very far.

It is hard to specify exactly what kind of reward systems will be needed to complement empowerment. Some of the practices common to organizations utilizing employee involvement include pay-for-skills, in which employees' pay increases as they learn new job-relevant skills, and profit-sharing, in which employees receive bonuses related to the profits of their organization.[32] Nor should intrinsic rewards be overlooked: a picture in the company newsletter or an evening of celebration upon a major accomplishment may be of tremendous value to employees who have seldom received any recognition at all in the past.

EMPOWERMENT IN ACTION

Semco

Semco is a machinery manufacturer in Brazil, with sales of over $30 million per year.[33] Semco's president, Ricardo Semler, practices three-pronged empowerment with his 800-person workforce: sharing power, sharing information, and sharing profits. Semler believes that empowerment saved the company from failure in the 1980s, so it is not surprising that he is a firm believer in the connection between empowerment and organizational performance.

The company is divided into units, called cells, of 150 people or less; when a unit reaches this size, it is subdivided. The eleven layers of management that the firm had in the 1970s have been reduced to three. Important decisions at Semco are made by self-managed cross-functional teams, which set their own working hours, strategies, and even salaries. Great care is taken to make sure that these decisions are based on the best information available, by making timely and accurate financial and performance data available to the teams at all times.

To reward its associates for the unusual amount of responsibility they assume for running the company, and to keep them focused on the overall performance of the firm, bonuses are distributed based on corporate profits. The teams have responsibility for allocating the bonuses, and usually do it on an equal basis. In general, Semco appears to have firmly embraced the principles of empowerment.

The Ritz-Carlton Hotel Company

"Ladies and gentlemen serving ladies and gentlemen." That's how Horst Schulze, president of Ritz-Carlton, describes customer service in his company.[34] Although in some companies the emphasis on customers might seem to diminish the importance of employees, Ritz-Carlton has found a way to treat both groups with dignity and respect. Its efforts in this direction were recently rewarded with a Malcolm Baldrige National Quality Award.

Living out the ideal of respect for both customers and employees requires some subtle compromises. Many guests, whose schedules are very demanding, want breakfast delivered to their rooms within 30 minutes after it is ordered. However, chefs work at different paces, and not all menu items can be prepared within this time. The solution was to offer only certain items with a half-hour guarantee and to provide time ranges for others, so that different chefs can work in their preferred manner. In this way both customers and chefs are satisfied.

One way Ritz-Carlton empowers employees is by giving them authority to commit company funds when needed to satisfy customers. The company is experimenting with giving front-desk employees authorization to spend up to $2,000 and sales managers $5,000 to ensure customer satisfaction. Schulze dramatizes the importance of employees when he introduces himself to them: "My name is Horst Schulze. I'm president of this company; I'm very important. [Pause.] But so are you. Absolutely. Equally important." Employees' feeling of importance may be responsible for a turnover rate that is less than half the industry average.

Ritz-Carlton relies heavily on employees' suggestions for quality improvement. Their goal is to have twice as many employee complaints as customer complaints—the rationale being to resolve problems before customers experience them. Sometimes managers have to take a deep breath before implementing employee suggestions. Schulze himself received a proposal from a room service waiter to spend $50,000 to implement a recycling program. The company's commitment to empowerment was sufficient to make the investment, which has really paid off: weekly garbage pickups have been reduced by two days, and Ritz-Carlton now sells its cardboard and paper, rather than paying someone to take it away. The changes save $80,000 a year, so the initial investment was quickly paid back.

EMPOWERMENT AND THEORIES OF MOTIVATION

The TQM approach to the management of employees in general, and empowerment in particular, is quite consistent with organizational behavior (OB) theory. In fact, most of TQM thinking about empowerment and motivation is derived, directly or indirectly, from OB theory. Managers' willingness to accept these ideas and put them into practice, however, has been greatly increased by the incorporation of these ideas into the total quality package.

A few examples should serve to make our point. The idea that quality problems are usually attributable to management-created systems rather than employee motivation was proposed by organizational psychologist Chris Argyris.[35] Rensis Likert described an organizational system he called "System IV," which featured empowered work groups and cross-functional teams. Douglas McGregor developed the well-known "Theory Y" approach to managing employees, which is based on the assumption that people wish to do a good job and emphasizes that people in organizations should make decisions for themselves. These are the fundamental principles of the TQ approach to managing people, but they were developed decades ago by theorists concerned with reconciling the psychological needs of people and the economic needs of businesses.

The TQM philosophy is also consistent with several more recent theories of work motivation. This means that implementing TQ should result in increased employee motivation, because the kinds of changes that TQ represents are among those that theories say will result in increased effort on the job. Specifically, the following sections discuss the TQ approach in terms of job characteristics theory, acquired need theory, and goal setting theory. The theories themselves are not described in detail, as they are covered in OB and management textbooks. Here they are compared to total quality practices.

Job Characteristics Theory

The job characteristics theory (JCT) states that people will be more motivated to work and more satisfied with their jobs to the extent that their jobs possess certain core characteristics: skill variety, task identity (doing a meaningful unit of work), task significance, autonomy, and feedback. If jobs do not have such characteristics—that is, involve few skills and give workers little control over what they do—most employees are likely to be unmotivated and dissatisfied.[36]

In general, we would expect TQ to increase the motivating potential of jobs through increases in the foregoing task characteristics. In fact, TQ practices resemble some of the steps recommended by job design experts for making jobs more motivating. For example, getting people involved in problem solving and other quality improvement activities should increase both the variety of skills they use in their jobs and their perception of doing a meaningful unit of work. Empowerment should increase the degree of autonomy people feel they have in doing their work. Focusing their efforts on increasing customer satisfaction should increase people's perception of the significance of their roles in the organization.

Three factors have been identified that will influence the way people react to jobs that have high levels of the task characteristics: knowledge and skill, growth-need strength, and satisfaction with contextual factors.[37] Knowledge of how to do one's job should be enhanced by the training that often accompanies TQ and empowerment. Growth-need strength, on the other hand, is rooted in people's personalities and is unlikely to be affected by TQ. Satisfaction with contextual factors (company policies, working conditions) may increase with implementation of TQ, as various groups in the organization make improvements to satisfy internal customers. This means that TQ is likely not only to increase the levels of task characteristics that people find motivating, but also to change two of the three factors that influence how people react to these characteristics, in such a way that they are more likely to find such jobs motivating.

Acquired Needs Theory

Another perspective on employee motivation states that people are motivated by work that fulfills their needs. Specifically, the need for achievement, the need for affiliation, and the need for power have been the subjects of extensive research.[38] People who have a strong need for achievement will work hard to reach a high standard of excellence. The need for affiliation refers to the desire to have close relationships with other people, for example as part of a team. The need for power is the desire to have influence over one's environment and the people in it.

How will the implementation of TQ, including empowerment practices, influence people who are motivated by these needs? As research has not addressed this question, we can only speculate. The need most likely to be fulfilled by participation in TQ is the need for affiliation. The most obvious way this would occur is through the formation of self-managed or cross-functional teams. TQ promotes close relationships between people in the same or different subunits, and even in different organizations in the customer-supplier chain.

The connection between TQ and the need for achievement is a bit murkier. Effective utilization of TQ should allow organizations to achieve higher levels of performance in such areas as quality and customer satisfaction, but these achievements are likely to come through team, rather than individual, efforts. Thus the opportunity to participate in such efforts is likely to motivate people with high achievement motivation only if they can see the relationship between their own work and team performance and feel a sense of achievement on that basis.

TQ and empowerment are likely to be motivating for employees with a high need for power. In fact, employees with a high need for power are likely to be quite frustrated with traditional organizations that give them little influence. Empowerment, if it follows the principles described in this chapter, should go a long way toward reducing this frustration and provide newfound motivation for individuals with a high need for power.

However, empowerment can be a double-edged sword. Middle managers whose subordinates are being empowered may feel that their own needs for power are less fulfilled under TQM. This need not occur, as empowerment of lower-level employees should be accompanied by finding new and fulfilling roles for middle managers. Many organizations will not be able to accomplish this, however, and even if they do, a certain number of middle managers with a high need for power will miss the old "command and control" type of organization.

Goal-setting Theory

The central insight of goal-setting theory is that people whose goals are clear will work more quickly, perform better, and generally be more motivated than people who lack clear goals. A great deal of research has been performed on goal-setting theory and generally supports the theory's predictions. According to the theory, goals will be motivating to people when they are specific and difficult, and people accept them as their own.[39]

How does goal-setting theory relate to total quality in general and empowerment in particular? This connection has not been the subject of research, but we can offer some conjecture about it. One likely link between empowerment and goal-setting is the goal-acceptance aspect of the theory. Although there has been some debate about this among scholars, it seems that people who set their own goals (as in empowerment) are likely to be more motivated by them than are people whose goals are set by others (as in the traditional organization). People who set their own goals may also find that their goals are clearer (to them, at least).

The principle that goals should be specific and difficult can be related to total quality and empowerment. In general, the principle of continuous improvement leads to fairly difficult goals. In traditional management, when an acceptable level of performance is reached, people simply try to maintain it. Under TQ, an acceptable performance level would be a stepping-stone to further improvements. Therefore, the difficulty of goals would be enhanced by TQ.

One wonders whether this compromises the long-run specificity of goals. Continuous improvement is a noble ideal, likely to spur heroic efforts in many cases. When, if ever, is the goal reached? Can workers be motivated by a goal of eternal improvement or must milestones be placed along the way to maintain motivation and enthusiasm? Perhaps as organizations gain more experience with TQ, such questions will be answered. Given the increasing importance of continuous improvement for competitiveness, organizations will need to find ways to motivate employees for sustained improvement in order to be economically viable in the twenty-first century.

SUMMARY

Empowerment—giving people real authority in their work—is being practiced by an increasing number of organizations. Empowerment improves quality by allowing people to use their resources to address quality problems and by changing conditions that lead to poor customer service. Empowerment is not simple, but can be successful if a number of principles are followed. These principles include developing trust between managers and employees and sharing business information widely within the organization.

Companies as diverse as Semco of Brazil and the Ritz-Carlton hotel chain have found that empowerment provides important competitive advantages.

The doctrine of empowerment evolved from behavioral science concepts and is consistent with several organizational behavior theories, including job characteristics theory, acquired needs theory, and goal-setting theory.

REVIEW AND DISCUSSION QUESTIONS

1. What is employee empowerment? What do you see as the most important barriers to employee empowerment?

2. Have you ever experienced fear in the workplace? What impact did it have on your performance? Is a little bit of fear a good thing for motivating performance?

3. Are there circumstances in which employee empowerment would hurt rather than improve quality? Why would this occur?

4. What sort of performance appraisal process would be appropriate for empowered workers in a total quality company?

5. Which of the principles of empowerment do you think is most important? Why?

6. Have you ever received exceptional service from an empowered employee? What happened? How did you react to it?

7. In what ways do Semco and Ritz-Carlton exemplify the principles of empowerment?

8. Which theory of motivation do you see as most consistent with empowerment? Why?

9. Philip Atkinson[40] tells the story of a government agency that fired up its employees to do great things with a wilderness training experience. One young man, upon his return to work, noticed some parking spaces owned by the organization in a busy part of the city. The spaces were always free and could be rented for a substantial sum. The young man made a proposal to do so, but it was rejected out of hand. Undeterred, he rented the spaces himself, only to find that there was no mechanism to deposit the checks into corporate accounts. Eventually, the young man left the company to work for one in which people's ideas were taken more seriously, and initiative was valued. How does this story illustrate the principles of empowerment discussed in this chapter?

CASES

The Case of the Stranded Traveler

One of the authors recently traveled to Texas to attend a meeting. Before leaving home, he made a reservation to be picked up by a shuttle company (one with operations in several cities) and taken to his hotel, about one-half hour from the airport. The company's promotional materials strongly recommended securing reservations, as this would ensure "priority service." He was instructed to call the shuttle service once inside the terminal. He was told on the phone where to wait, what the sign on the van would say, and that it would pick him up within about 10 minutes. He was happy to hear that the van would be arriving soon, because it was raining and unseasonably cool, even for February, and it had been a long flight.

After 20 minutes, although many of the company's vans had passed by, the van with the correct destination sign still had not arrived. One of the company's drivers pulled over and asked the traveler which van he was waiting for. The driver radioed the dispatcher, who told him that the correct van would be there momentarily.

After another 15 minutes, another of the company's vans pulled over, but it was still not the right one. The woman driving this van asked the traveler which van he was waiting for and, after hearing the story, also radioed the dispatcher. She requested and received permission to change her route to take the traveler to his hotel.

The traveler relaxed in the back seat of the van, believing that his experience with "priority service" was almost over. As it became increasingly clear that the van was not leaving the airport, but was circulating among the terminals, the traveler asked the driver what was going on. She said that drivers were not allowed to leave the airport with fewer than three passengers. She had requested permission to drive the traveler immediately to his hotel to make up for the inconvenience he had suffered, but the request was denied. The driver apologized and said she would take him directly to the hotel if it were up to her.

After another 10 minutes or so cruising the terminals, a couple boarded the van. The driver requested permission to leave the airport, and this time permission was granted. Fortunately, one of the passengers knew a good route to the hotel, because the driver was not very familiar with this destination.

As the traveler got out of the van, the driver continued to apologize for the poor service he had received from the company and gave him the name of a manager to call to complain. Like most people in this situation, the traveler did not call the manager, but quietly resolved never to use this company's services when visiting this or any other airport.

Discussion Questions

1. In what ways did the shuttle company fail to provide quality service?
2. Were the dispatcher's decisions appropriate?
3. How would you change the company's policies to improve quality?
4. What are the lessons about empowerment from this case?

ENDNOTES

1. Quoted in David Ulrich and Dale Lake, "Organizational capability: Creating competitive advantage," *Academy of Management Executive*, 5(1), 1991, pp. 77–92.

2. J.A. Conger and R.N. Kanungo, "The Empowerment Process: Integrating Theory and Practice," *Academy of Management Review*, 13 (3), 1988, pp. 471–482.

3. J.M. Juran, *Juran on Leadership for Quality: An Executive Handbook*, New York: The Free Press, 1989, p.264.

4. Juran, *Juran on Leadership for Quality*, pp. 147–148.

5. E.E. Lawler, S.A. Mohrman, and G.E. Ledford, *Employee Involvement and Total Quality Management,* San Francisco: Jossey-Bass, 1992.

6. Richard C. Whiteley, *The Customer-Driven Company: Moving from Talk to Action,* Reading, Mass.: Addison-Wesley, 1991.

7. M.J. Kiernan, "The new strategic architecture: Learning to compete in the twenty-first century," *Academy of Management Executive*, 7 (1), 1993, p. 14.

8. Kathleen D. Ryan and Daniel K. Oestreich, *Driving Fear out of the Workplace*, San Francisco: Jossey-Bass, 1991.

9. Lawler, Mohrman, and Ledford, *Employee Involvement;* Dan Ciampa, *Total Quality: A User's Guide for Implementation,* Reading, Mass.: Addison-Wesley, 1992.

10. Quoted in Whiteley, *The Customer-Driven Company,* p. 180.

11. Lawler, Mohrman, and Ledford, *Employee Involvement*, p. 105.

12. Malcolm Baldrige National Quality Award, 1993 Award Criteria, p. 3.

13. Based on Bob Ford, "Lucas is winning at coaching, life," *The Cincinnati Enquirer*, February 21, 1993.

14. Lawler, Mohrman, and Ledford, *Employee Involvement,* p. 60.

15. Lawler, Mohrman, and Ledford, *Employee Involvement,* p. 60.

16. Brad Stratton, "How Disneyland Works," *Quality Progress*, July 1991, pp. 17–30.

17. Hal F. Rosenbluth, "Have Quality, Will Travel," *The TQM Magazine*, November/December 1992, pp. 267–270.

18. Dan Ciampa, *Total Quality: A User's Guide for Implementation,* Reading, MA, Addison-Wesley, 1991.

19. Lawler, Mohrman, and Ledford, *Employee Involvement*, p. 51.

20. Juran, *Juran on Leadership for Quality*, p. 277.

21. A.R. Tenner and I.J. DeToro, *Total Quality Management: Three Steps to Continuous Improvement,* Reading, Mass.: Addison-Wesley, 1992.

22. Mark Kelly, *The Adventures of a Self-Managing Team,* Raleigh, N.C.: Mark Kelly Books, 1990.

23. Lawler, Mohrman, and Ledford, *Employee Involvement,* p. 47.

24. Ciampa, *Total Quality.*

25. Lawler, Mohrman, and Ledford, *Employee Involvement,* p. 60.

26. Peter M. Senge, *The Fifth Discipline: The Art and Practice of the Learning Organization,* New York: Doubleday Currency, 1990.

27. See *America's Choice: High Skills or Low Wages!*, National Center on Education and the Economy's Commission on the Skills of the American Workforce. National Center on Education and the Economy, 1990.

28. Lawler, Mohrman, and Ledford, *Employee Involvement,* p. 16.

29. Based on Ronald Henkoff, "Companies that train best," *Fortune*, March 22, 1993, pp. 62-75.

30. Rosenbluth, "Have Quality, Will Travel," *The TQM Mazagine,* 2(5), pp. 267–270.

31. Based on Jack Johnson and Jack T. Mollen, "Ten tasks for managers in the empowered workplace," *Journal for Quality and Participation*, December 1992, pp. 18–20.

32. Lawler, Mohrman, and Ledford, *Employee Involvement,* p. 20.

33. The information on Semco is from Matthew J. Kiernan, "The new strategic architecture: Learning to compete in the twenty-first century," *Academy of Management Executive*, 7 (1), pp. 7–21. See also R. Semler, "Managing Without Managers," J.J. Gabarro (ed.), *Managing People and Organizations*, Boston: Harvard Business School, 1992.

34. Based on Cheri Henderson, "Putting on the Ritz," *The TQM Magazine*, November/December 1992, pp. 292–296.

35. This discussion of organizational behavior theory's contribution to TQM thinking is based on J.J. Riley, "Human Resource Development: An Over-

view," in J.P. Kern, J.J. Riley, and L.N. Jones (eds.), *Human Resources Management*, Milwaukee: ASQC Quality Press, 1987.

36. Job Characteristics Theory is described in J.R. Hackman and G.R. Oldham, *Work Redesign*, Reading, Mass.: Addison-Wesley Publishing Company, 1980.

37. Hackman and Oldham, *Work Redesign*.

38. D.C. McClelland, *Assessing Human Motivation*, Morristown, N.J.: General Learning Press, 1971. See also D.C.McClelland and R.E. Boyatzis, "Leadership motive pattern and long-term success in management," *Journal of Applied Psychology*, 1982, pp. 67, 737–743.

39. Edwin Locke, "Toward a Theory of Task Performance and Incentives," *Organizational Behavior and Human Performance*, Fall 1968, pp. 157–189. For a more recent treatment of goal-setting, see Mark E. Tubbs and Steven E. Ekeberg, "The Role of Intentions in Work Motivation: Implications for Goal-Setting Theory and Research," *Academy of Management Review*, January 1991, pp. 180–199.

40. Philip Atkinson, "Leadership, total quality, and cultural change," *Management Services*, 35 (6), 1991, pp. 16–19.

CHAPTER 9

Quality Leadership

Chapter Outline

Introduction
    The Importance of Leadership to Quality
The Roles of a Quality Leader
    Establish a Vision
    Live the Values
    Lead Continuous Improvement
Quality Leadership in Action
    Leadership at Motorola: Beyond Six Sigma?
    Crosby's Quality Nightmare
TQM and Leadership Theory
    Consideration and Initiating Structure
    Roles of Managers
    Transformational Leadership Theory
    Management and Leadership
Summary
Review and Discussion Questions
Case

M otorola's former CEO, Bob Galvin, made a habit of making quality the first item on the agenda of executive staff meetings—and leaving the meeting before discussion of financials. His actions spoke louder than words: if quality was taken care of, financial performance would follow. His leadership guided Motorola to become one of the first winners of the Malcolm Baldrige National Quality Award.

Leadership is fundamental to management and organizational behavior and is on just about everyone's short list of prerequisites for organizational success. Thus it is not surprising that leadership plays a crucial role in the total quality organization. Virtually every article and book written about quality emphasizes leadership. "Teach and institute leadership" is one of W.E. Deming's Fourteen Points. Leadership is the first category in the Malcolm Baldrige National Quality Award and is recognized as the "driver" of successful quality systems. Indeed, leadership is seen by many quality experts as the *sine qua non* (if you don't have it, you have nothing) of TQM. As two quality experts put it, "Without management leadership, quality and productivity will result only as fortunate accidents."[1] This chapter will

- discuss the importance of leadership for quality,
- describe the role of leaders in pursuing total quality,
- provide some examples of leaders who have inspired their organizations to attain very high quality in businesses as disparate as raising chickens in Maryland and making noodle soup in Japan, and
- compare the TQ view of leadership to several prominent leadership theories.

THE ROLES OF A QUALITY LEADER

Why is leadership so important to quality? Leaders establish plans and goals for the organization. If the plans and goals do not include quality or, worse yet, are antithetical to quality, the quality effort will die. Leaders help to shape the culture of the organization through key decisions and symbolic actions. If they help to shape a culture that puts convenience or short-term benefits over quality, it will die. Leaders distribute resources. If resources are showered on programs that cut short-term costs while quality is starved for resources, it will die. This list could go on. Virtually everything that an organization needs to succeed in meeting its customers' expectations—goals, plans, culture, resources—can either be helped or hurt by leaders. With this in mind, let us examine in more detail the roles that managers play in a total quality company.

Many writers and managers have tried to define what a manager must do as an effective quality leader. Edwin L. Artzt is Chairman of Procter and Gamble, one of the nation's oldest and most successful companies and one of the earliest to emphasize quality. He believes:

> To lead quality—and I'm talking about leaders at every level in an organization—means providing the clear strategic choices, the guiding principles, and the disciplined application to continually improve and reinvent ourselves . . . and to do that with a focus on the good of the whole.[2]

The guidelines for the Malcolm Baldrige National Quality Award also dwell heavily on leadership. Here is what the Baldrige examiners look for:

A company's senior leaders must create clear and visible quality values and high expectations. Reinforcement of the values and expectations requires their substantial personal commitment and involvement. The leaders must take part in the creation of strategies, systems, and methods for achieving excellence. The systems and methods need to guide all activities and decisions of the company and encourage participation and creativity by all employees. Through their regular personal involvement in visible activities . . . the senior leaders serve as role models reinforcing the values and encouraging leadership in all levels of management.[3]

A final overview of the concept of quality leadership comes from Dan Ciampa, president and chief executive officer of Rath & Strong, a consulting group specializing in total quality:

The mandate is to inspire, to invoke commitment, to enable employees to form a different concept of the organization in which they believe deeply, and to change without being threatened.[4]

Underlying the concept of quality leadership in general, and these three quotes in particular, are some clear imperatives for managers who aspire to quality leadership. First, they must establish a vision. Second, they must live the values. Third, they must lead the improvement efforts. Let's examine each of these in turn.

Establish a Vision

A vision is a vivid concept of what an organization could be. It is a striking depiction of possibilities, of potential. It is a dream, both in the sense of being desirable and in the sense of being a long way from the current reality, but it is not an "impossible dream." To be quality leaders, managers must establish a vision for and in their organization. "Establishing" a vision implies both the intellectual and emotional work of conceiving the vision and the interpersonal and managerial work of communicating the vision to the organization and leading employees to embrace it.

Quality-oriented visions have inspired some of the most dramatic corporate success stories in business history. IBM was founded on the idea of exceptional customer service and fair treatment of employees. Federal Express sought what at the time was seen as almost inconceivable speed and reliability in the package delivery market. Apple Computers wanted to make computing accessible to the masses.[5] These visions were creative, captivating, and most of all achievable. (For an example of a quality-oriented vision at Perdue Farms, see the box.)

Jane Carroll, president of The Forum Corporation, Europe/Asia, emphasizes the visionary role of leadership for quality, which she calls focus. She believes that most managers do not understand the need for a quality vision and their personal involvement in establishing it:

The Tough Man Behind the Tender Chicken[7]

Most people on the East Coast have heard of Perdue Farms and its stern leader Frank Perdue, who has convinced a generation of consumers that "It takes a tough man to produce a tender chicken." Although there is little doubt that Frank Perdue is tough on competitors, much of the success of the company comes from his listening carefully to what customers want and finding a way for his organization to give it to them.

The most important quality attributes chicken shoppers look for are a yellowish color, a high meat-to-bone ratio, an absence of pinfeathers, and freshness. In every one of these attributes, Perdue leads its competitors by their own rankings. Sometimes Frank Perdue has to take unorthodox steps to provide quality to customers. For example, to give his birds a yellowish cast, he added marigold petals to their diets. He also invested in a turbine engine to blow-dry his chickens, so that more of the pinfeathers would be eliminated. This was an investment in quality that didn't cut costs one bit, nor did it expand capacity. But it did increase their quality, as perceived by consumers.

Perdue gets the quality message out to his customers by appearing in the company's commercials, for example comparing the yellowness of his chicken to one from his competitors. His down-home accent and manner-isms have convinced many a consumer to try his chicken, and the quality of the product has convinced them to stay with it. His example in investing funds and creating innovative solutions to increase quality sets the tone for the entire Perdue organization and typifies what leadership for quality is all about.

In our experience, very few CEOs have a real sense of what their role is in the quality improvement process. It goes far beyond simply being a cheerleader and handing out an occasional award. Top management has to provide the proper focus for the organization. This is not something that can be delegated.[6]

Putting together a vision is hard work, but quality leaders do not have to do it alone. They can draw upon the talents and imagination of all the members of their organizations in developing their vision. In fact, in many organizations, people are walking around with "mini-visions" of their own, that sound like "if only we could [do something they have been told can't be done], things would be so much better around here." The raw material for a vision may be all around leaders in the organization. The first step may be simply listening for it. Leaders who are open to the ideas of people throughout the organization will be much better prepared to develop a vision that people will accept.

In the current competitive environment, if a given organization is not pursuing a customer-oriented vision, competing organizations probably are and are planning to use their vision to win over the competition's customers (or are already doing so). This is why a quality vision is such a crucial first step in quality leadership. An organization with no vision about how to create long-term customer loyalty has little chance of survival. (Unless, of course, it's a monopoly.)

The second part of establishing a vision is instilling it in all the members of the organization. This will be a lot easier if many people were involved in the first part of the process, and the leader doesn't act like Moses coming down the mountain with the stone tablets. When Corning Glass instituted a quality vision, Chairman Jamie Houghton introduced it to employees at all levels in countries all over the world. Communication is vitally important. A leader who is able to present the vision in an intriguing way has an advantage in trying to capture the imagination of the people in the organization, according to Francis Adamson, manager of quality engineering/TQM at Heinz U.S.A.:

> The ability to fascinate is one of the most powerful tools of the charismatic leader. Leaders can use it to weave a fabric of commitment throughout the organization. This is the empowering function of the leader: allowing everyone to buy into the vision.[8]

Live the Values

Pursuing the quality vision commits the organization to living by a set of values such as devotion to customers, continuous improvement, and teamwork. A manager who hopes the organization will embrace and live by these values must live them to the utmost. As Procter and Gamble Chairman and CEO Edwin Artzt puts it, "Leaders of the best companies profoundly believe in, and promote, the core values of customer-focused quality."[9]

When dramatic organizational changes are taking place, people in organizations are very sensitive to any sign of hypocrisy. A leader can undermine 100 hours of speeches with one decision that reveals his or her commitment to quality values to be superficial. This is not just a symbolic issue: Harvard's David Garvin found in a study of the air conditioner industry that the quality of a firm's products was strongly related to the quality values expressed by management.[10]

Managers' actions can symbolize their commitment to quality-oriented values in many concrete ways. For example, they can attend training programs on various aspects of quality, instead of just sending others. They can practice continuous improvement in processes that they control, such as strategic planning and capital budgeting. Perhaps most importantly, they can provide adequate funding for quality efforts, so that TQM will not be the "poor cousin" to other business issues.[11]

Virtually every management team that has staged a major quality turn-around has recognized this need to "walk," not just "talk," quality. In looking back on the return to financial success from near-bankruptcy of his company, Harley-Davidson's Ron Hutchinson has stated:

> We realized that, if we really wanted to communicate to our people a change in the company's direction and approach, what we needed to do as senior managers was demonstrate that we were going to live by a new set of rules.

Lead Continuous Improvement

Beyond establishing a vision for the organization and expressing quality values through their decisions and actions, quality-oriented leaders must lead the continuous process improvement efforts that are the meat and potatoes of total quality management. All of the vision and values in the world are worthless if the organization is not continuously making strides to improve its performance in the eyes of customers. Visions of world-class quality and competitiveness can only be achieved if an organization keeps finding ways to do things a little better and a little faster. Leaders must be at the center of these efforts.

Managers are sometimes reluctant to take an active role in the organization's improvement efforts for fear of dominating or undercutting their newly empowered workers. Like many aspects of management, this is a question of balance, but it is a mistake for managers to remain uninvolved in process improvement efforts. Harry Levinson and Chuck DeHont, quality leaders at Sierra Semiconductor, have thought about this dilemma and concluded:

> It is often perceived, incorrectly, that management should never specify how problems should be solved, that to do so would be considered improper delegation. What is actually true is that managers who set no rules for how problems should be solved have abdicated their leadership roles.[12]

There are a number of ways for managers to lead continuous improvement, and which ones make the most sense will depend on the specific organization. One option already mentioned is for leaders to lead by example, by working continuously to improve the processes that they control. For some of these processes, organizational members are among the customers, which gives management the opportunity to model for them the behaviors associated with obtaining and acting upon customer input.[13] If management were to streamline the capital budgeting procedure by speeding up the process and eliminating nonvalue-added activities, it would provide a powerful example for people to emulate.

A second way that managers can lead process improvement is to help organization members prioritize processes to work on. Here managers can take advantage of their knowledge of the "big picture" and suggest avenues of improvement that are likely to have big payoffs in terms of quality improvement and customer satisfaction. This point was underscored by a recent statement by Gerhard Schulmeyer, president and CEO of Asea Brown Boveri, a multinational company headquartered in Germany:

> It doesn't help simply to encourage everybody to work harder. The issue is to take a fresh look at the problems and *concentrate our efforts on core processes that have the largest leverage in improving our position in the market.*[14]

Of course, managers leading process improvement bear some responsibility for educating all their associates as to how the various processes within the company fit together. If this is done effectively, organization members will be able eventually to set their own priorities for process improvement.

Managers can also lead this effort by removing barriers to success in process improvement.[15] Barriers may consist of a nettlesome standard operating procedure or a recalcitrant manager in a key position. Without leadership from management, such barriers may undermine efforts at process improvement. Of course, in dealing with such barriers managers must continue to operate in a manner consistent with quality values. For example, managers who balk at changes must be treated with respect and their reservations considered seriously, even if they are eventually overruled.

One final way for managers to lead process improvement is to keep track of improvement efforts, to encourage them, and to provide recognition when key milestones are reached. One top manager of our acquaintance makes it a practice *always* to be present for such recognition ceremonies. If he cannot attend, the ceremony is rescheduled. By doing this, the manager is accomplishing several things at once: he is showing his sincere interest in the process, he is providing reinforcement for those people working to make key changes, and he is letting his subordinates know that it is not acceptable to make excuses for missing quality-related functions. (For an additional and unusual example of leadership for continuous improvement, see the box on *Tampopo*.)

Tampopo: The Quest for the Perfect Noodle Soup[16]

Like many aspects of organizations, the nature of leadership is changed dramatically by TQM. Moving beyond a command and control mentality, leaders in a TQM organization help their associates to provide better products and services to customers. This style of leadership is personified by Goro, a truck driver and noodle expert who in the film *Tampopo* helps Tampopo in her quest to create the perfect noodle soup. An unlikely blend of western and samurai movie clichés, *Tampopo* is at the same time a parody and a virtual roadmap for continuous quality improvement.

Goro and his friend Guntu meet Tampopo when they stop in at the Lai Lai noodle stand for a quick bite. When Goro tells a drunken customer that

Tampopo's noodles are mediocre, he gets taken outside and beaten up, a fate that (metaphorically at least) awaits many leaders who publicly state that the status quo is not good enough. But Tampopo is wise enough to accept Goro's judgment on the poor quality of her noodles and asks for his help.

One of Goro's first suggestions is to study her customers as they enter the shop, so that she can adjust her service to their needs. Tampopo soon begins to recognize that quality noodle soup involves a lot more than just cooking. She closes her shop until further notice and devotes herself to elevating the quality of her noodle business. In a scene reminiscent of *Rocky,* Tampopo (now in a sweat suit) runs through the park, with Goro following on a bicycle. She then practices lifting pots of boiling water, working to reduce her soup production time below three minutes.

The next step is to learn from the competition. The nearby shop Goro and Tampopo visit first is full, demonstrating that customers are there if only Tampopo is good enough. In the second shop, the cooks talk to each other too much and forget people's orders. In the third, the cook's motions are elegant, with no wasted motion. In the fourth, a busy place by a rail station, the cook must keep track of many orders at once. Tampopo shows her progress by rattling off all the orders that have been given. At the fifth shop, the broth is so good that Goro and Tampopo stoop to spying to try to duplicate the recipe. By the sixth, the owners see what is going on and kick them out, but Tampopo tells them they have nothing worth stealing: their dough sat out too long, their pork is overcooked, and their soup tasteless.

Although this noodle benchmarking tour has greatly improved the quality of Tampopo's soup, she recognizes that it is not yet good enough. Help then comes from an unlikely source, an old friend of Goro's living in a hobo camp where everyone is a gastronome. He takes them to yet more restaurants, including one where they rescue a man from choking. The man lends them his chauffeur, who against all odds is also a noodle expert, and takes them to even more restaurants. (The quest for quality can be exhausting, and in this case pretty rough on the waistline.) In the shop with the best-tasting noodles, Tampopo has to trick the proprietor into divulging his process: "These noodles are not as good as usual, perhaps you did not let them sit long enough." "I left them overnight, as usual," he growls, and so on until Tampopo has the entire recipe.

At this point, Goro and Tampopo's other advisors urge her to reopen her shop, now renamed after her. The drunken customer from her old shop turns out to be a contractor and decorator, who remodels the shop for efficiency and attractiveness. Tampopo herself also gets remodeled, as she drops her dumpy old outfit for a new chef's uniform. The transformation is remarkable.

Still the quest for improvement continues. The experts tell Tampopo that her soup "lacks profundity" and suggest adding spring onions. Although the other elements are nearly perfect, there is nothing to distinguish it, no unexpected element to delight customers and exceed their expectations. With the spring onions added, she tries again. The experts drink her soup to the bottom. Success! Soon customers are swarming to her new shop, and Goro and the others drift away, as Tampopo no longer needs them. A cycle of quality leadership is complete, and Goro rides off into the sunset.

QUALITY LEADERSHIP IN ACTION

Leadership at Motorola: Beyond Six Sigma?[17]

Motorola Incorporated is an $11 billion corporation in the top 50 of the Fortune 500, with over 100,000 employees worldwide. Motorola's major businesses include cellular telephones, pagers, and semiconductors. It is among the top companies in the U.S. electronics industry, as well as among the top exporters in the United States.

At a management meeting in 1979, a Motorola executive stood up and said, "Our quality stinks!" Thus began a revolution in quality that continues today. In 1980 a corporate quality office was established, and in 1981 Motorola University, an educational organization providing the opportunity for continuous learning to all Motorolans, was instituted.

By the mid-1980s, Total Customer Satisfaction had become Motorola's fundamental objective. In 1987, on behalf of Motorola's top management, Robert Galvin committed the Motorola Corporation to a quality goal of 10-times improvement by 1989, 100-times improvement by 1991, and Six Sigma capability by 1992. Six Sigma capability means a defect rate of only 3.4 parts per million (ppm) in each of the company's processes, manufacturing and administrative alike. To appreciate the importance of Six Sigma, 99.9 percent quality (a little better than two sigma) means that 15,000 newborn babies would be dropped by doctors and nurses every year; Six Sigma means that three babies would be dropped every 100 years!

Motorola's quality achievements to date are well known. Perhaps the most celebrated is its being among the first recipients of the Malcolm Baldrige National Quality Award. Motorola has also won awards in Japan, Malaysia, Europe, and Israel. The company has largely met the 10-times and 100-times improvement goals, and several facilities have even exceeded the Six Sigma goal. Motorola estimates that it has saved as much as $2.2 billion since the beginning of its quality initiative, a dramatic illustration of the "cost of quality" beginning of its quality initiative, a dramatic illustration of the "cost of quality" principle. (The company believes over $1 billion in nonmanufacturing costs is still available to be saved.)

On average, however, Motorola's operations are at about 5.4 Sigma capability, or 40 ppm, somewhat short of the Six Sigma goal. Motorola's leaders have recommitted the company to meeting and even going beyond Six Sigma, based on the assumptions that customer expectations continue to rise and the competition never rests. Specifically, the company plans to change its metrics from parts per million to parts per billion(!), to pursue a goal of 10-times defect reduction every two years and to develop customer-driven measures of satisfaction. Furthermore, the company's leaders are stressing cycle time reduction, particularly in new product development, and have established a cycle-time reduction goal of 10-times improvement in five years. Quality leadership involves setting challenging objectives, and Motorola's top managers clearly have fulfilled this role.

Crosby's Quality Nightmare

An example of what is *not* needed in a quality leader is provided by Philip Crosby in *Quality Is Free.*[18] Crosby goes to visit his old pal Ernest Dinsmore, manager of the Flagship Hotel, to see how a real hotel is run "from the inside." Crosby's arrival at the hotel is a comedy of errors: He dashes inside through a cloudburst as the doorman watches safely from the door. He has to wait several hours for his room to be made up, then has to climb the stairs because the elevator is broken and, to top things off, his car is towed from the front of the hotel.

Dinsmore dismisses these problems as "growing pains" and takes Crosby on a tour of the guts of the hotel. The maids are gathered in one room arguing because, due to a shortage of vacuum cleaners, those on the upper floors cannot vacuum until those on the lower floors are finished. Dinsmore decrees, Solomon-like, that henceforth the rooms will be vacuumed only every other day, first the bottom floors, then the top. This way there will be enough vacuum cleaners to go around. Another dispute, this time among the bellmen, is also handled by Dinsmore. The tips, which seem to be getting lower all the time, will all be given to the bell captain, who will distribute them according to the effort he feels people are exerting. When Crosby remarks on the number of room service trays laying in the hallway, Dinsmore tells him that guests don't mind, because it reminds them that room service is available.

After this madness, the hotel restaurant appears to Crosby an oasis of quality and efficient service. They are promptly seated, drinks quickly appear, and the promises of an attractive menu are fulfilled as wonderful presentations emerge from the kitchen. This oasis turns out to be a mirage, because Dinsmore wants to "improve" the operation. Although most hotels lose money on their restaurants, this one was making about 10 percent net profit. It was obvious to Dinsmore that by raising prices and cutting back on the help, it could be turned into a real money machine.

At their farewell meeting, Dinsmore discusses the difficulty of finding people willing to do quality work and complains about the falling standards of today's workers. A few months later, Crosby learns that the Flagship has been closed and Dinsmore has been offered a position running a chain of motels. He hopes Crosby can be his guest at one of them sometime soon. Crosby says he "can hardly wait."

TQM AND LEADERSHIP THEORY

There are a great number of theories of leadership, and we can only discuss the relationship of TQM to a few of them. This section outlines some of theories that seem to relate most closely to TQM and compares them to the TQM view of leadership.

Consideration and Initiating Structure

In a series of studies done several decades ago at Ohio State University, researchers tried to identify the behaviors associated with effective leadership. These studies concluded that many of these behaviors could be captured by two dimensions: consideration and initiating structure.

Consideration (also known as socioemotional orientation) means taking care of subordinates, explaining things to them, being approachable, and generally being concerned about their welfare. Initiating structure (also known as task orientation) means getting people organized, including setting goals and instituting and enforcing deadlines and standard operating procedures. Research has indicated that, although different situations will require different leadership behaviors, most organizational units over a period of time will require both types of leadership in order to be successful.[19]

One apparent difference between this classic view of leadership and the TQM view is that the former emphasizes leadership at the work group level, whereas the latter deals with the more global level of organizations or major subunits. Writers on TQM leadership have focused less on lower-level leaders, due perhaps to the emphasis on self-management at those levels.

Despite these differences, consideration and initiating structure are not irrelevant for organizations pursuing TQM. Such organizations recognize the importance of employees for the success of their quality efforts and for their performance in general. Thus leaders will certainly need to be considerate of employee needs. The section on Rosenbluth in chapter 8 illustrated how consideration of employees minimizes their frustration and allows them to focus on customer service and continuous improvement. In a TQM environment, consideration would not be done in a paternalistic manner, emphasizing the power of leaders over subordinates. On the contrary, people would be treated as respected associates.

Initiating structure will also be appropriate in the TQM environment, but perhaps will be accomplished differently than in the traditional organizational setting. Traditionally, leaders were responsible for the whole gamut of activities associated with initiating structure—setting goals, establishing deadlines, enforcing rules, and so on. In organizations striving for empowerment, many of these activities will be taken over by employees.

The discussion of leadership for TQM suggests that quality leadership consists more of setting a direction for people through establishing a vision and identifying values. By leading continuous improvement efforts, leaders will establish priorities for activities throughout the organization. Such activities will provide the necessary context for employees to initiate structure for themselves.

The Roles of Managers

One well-known model, advanced by Henry Mintzberg, categorizes the work of managers into ten roles. Although this is a model of managerial roles, rather than leadership per se, it is useful to explore how roles may change as managers attempt to practice total quality leadership.

There are interpersonal roles (figurehead, leader, and liaison), informational roles (monitor, disseminator, spokesperson), and decisional roles (entrepreneur, disturbance handler, resource allocator, and negotiator).[20] Each of these roles is likely to be played by managers practicing total quality, although the relative importance of the roles, and the ways in which they are played, may differ from more traditional organizations.

The figurehead role, which involves the ceremonial or symbolic tasks of managers, is certainly played in TQ organizations. A manager presiding at a recognition ceremony for a team's quality accomplishments would be fulfilling this role. The leadership role would obviously be important for TQ-oriented managers, but the directing and controlling aspects of this role would be downplayed. The liaison role—dealing with customers, suppliers, and others—would still be played, but it would also be fulfilled to an increasing extent by employees, as an outgrowth of their empowerment.

The informational roles of management would continue to be played, but nonmanagerial personnel would be more involved in these activities, rather than looking to managers as the source of all information. Employees involved in benchmarking, for example, would play an important part in monitoring and disseminating information. While top managers would retain an important role as spokespersons, this role also would be increasingly shared with people throughout the organization. By now, probably hundreds if not thousands of nonmanagerial personnel have stepped up to the microphone to share their teams' accomplishments with the world.

Many of the behaviors leaders use to initiate and support a TQM program are characterized by the entrepreneurial role, one of the decisional roles. In this role, managers try to improve their organization by identifying problems and instituting processes to solve them. The disturbance-handler role—in which leaders resolve conflicts among subunits—should be diminished, at least in the long run, as people take on a more holistic view of the organizational mission.

The resource-allocator role continues to be key, as TQM will not succeed unless leaders are unswerving in their commitment of resources to continuous improvement and customer satisfaction. Finally, the negotiator role will still be played, but will be different, as companies try to create long-term, win-win arrangements with suppliers, unions and customers.

The Mintzberg model attempts to describe the behavior of managers, not to prescribe what they should do. It also attempts to capture the broad scope of managerial activities across many type of organizations. For this reason it is difficult to compare it directly to the more limited, but explicitly prescriptive, content of the TQM leadership model. Nevertheless, the comparison is instructive in linking this discussion to the mainstream management literature on leadership: Managers in TQ settings will play some roles (entrepreneurial) more than other managers, other roles (disturbance handler) less often, and others (leader) differently.

Transformational Leadership Theory

Another model that can be compared to the TQM approach is Transformational Leadership Theory.[21] According to this model, leaders who wish to have a major impact on their organizations must take a long-term perspective, work to stimulate their organizations intellectually, invest in training to develop individuals and groups, take some risks, promote a shared vision and values, and focus on customers and employees as individuals.

The Transformational Leadership model dovetails with leadership for TQM. Many of its aspects (emphasis on vision and focus on customers and employees as individuals) are right out of the TQM playbook, while others are generally consistent with TQM.

It would be tempting to say that all managers in TQM organizations should be transformational leaders, but this is unrealistic and probably unwise. It is not realistic because few, if any, organizations have such a concentration of transformational leaders. It is not wise because such a concentration would likely breed more chaos than quality. An organization pursuing TQM needs both those who establish visions and those who are effective at the day-to-day tasks needed to achieve them.[22] These "transactional leaders" play an important role in promoting total quality.

Management and Leadership

A recent treatment of leadership by John Kotter compares the concept of leadership to the concept of management.[23] According to this view, management is needed to create order amid complexity, and leadership is needed to stimulate the organizational change necessary to keep up with a changing environment. This view avoids the simplistic ideas that management is somehow trivial, generally unnecessary, and should be replaced by leadership, and that the same person cannot practice both management and leadership.

Kotter differentiates leadership from management by contrasting the activities central to each. While management begins with planning and budgeting, leadership begins with setting a direction. Direction-setting involves creating a vision of the future, as well as a set of approaches for achieving the vision. To promote goal achievement, management practices organizing and staffing, while leadership works on aligning people—communicating the vision and developing commitment to it. Management achieves plans through controlling and problem solving, whereas leadership achieves its vision through motivating and inspiring.

Kotter's view of leadership—similar to transformational theory—dovetails with our depiction of quality leadership. Both focus on developing and communicating a vision. Kotter's view of inspiring resembles our discussion of giving people values to embrace and then making sure that the leader is practicing them.

The idea of aligning people is consistent with the idea of empowerment, because it gives people a goal, then leaves them to move in that direction. Our description of the role of leaders in continuous improvement is more hands-on than Kotter's description, perhaps suggesting that some management behaviors will continue to be important to leaders in total quality organizations.

SUMMARY

Quality leadership is clearly important for a company trying to practice total quality. Much of what managers can do to promote TQM can be summarized by three processes: establishing a vision, living the values, and leading improvement. David Kearns's leadership of Xerox (see the case) and Frank Perdue's leadership of Perdue Farms demonstrate that these processes are not just abstractions, but actually capture the behavior of real leaders whose companies have experienced considerable success with quality. These leadership processes overlap with several theories of leadership, particularly Transformational Leadership Theory.

REVIEW AND DISCUSSION QUESTIONS

1. What three processes must leaders undertake to promote total quality in their organizations?

2. Take a few minutes and try to conceive of a total quality vision for an organization with which you are familiar. Suppose you choose your university. What would your vision be? Think of all the customers of the university. Now think of what would make them ecstatic about the service the university is providing for them. As a customer, what would delight you? Would this also delight your current or future employer? How about the taxpayers (if you are in a public university or college) or the school's benefactors?

3. In what specific ways did Ernest Dinsmore fail to fulfill the roles of a quality leader? What advice would you give him on how to start improving the quality of the service in his new hotel?

4. Most of the talk on leadership for quality focuses on top managers. What can middle and first-level managers do to promote quality in their organizations? How does this differ from the role of top management?

5. John Young, president and CEO of Hewlett-Packard, has summarized the role of the CEO in quality improvement in the following recommendations.[24]

   a. Dramatize the importance of quality to the organization.
   b. Establish agreed-upon measures of quality.
   c. Set challenging and motivating goals.
   d. Give people the resources and information needed to do the job.

   e. Reward results.
   f. Keep an attitude that high quality is not only desirable, but possible.

   How do these recommendations differ from those given in this chapter? Are they really different or do they capture the same ideas in different words?

6. William Scherkenbach, a quality expert and Deming disciple, states:[25]

   If management is to improve their organization, they must change the process. This means that they cannot accept conference room promises, but must work directly with their people on the process, the how and the why. During this period of transition, everyone must be willing to learn. . . . No one is too senior to be involved in the how.

   Do you agree or disagree? Why?

7. What aspects of an organization's culture or structure could keep managers from leading effectively?

8. Sir John Harvey-Jones, head of Britain's Imperial Chemical Industries from 1982 to 1987, once commented "The task of leadership is really to make the status quo more dangerous than launching into the unknown."[26] Do you think this statement represents a good approach to total quality leadership? Why or why not?

CASE

David Kearns and the Transformation of Xerox

David Kearns, former chairman and CEO of Xerox, provides an excellent example of leadership for quality.[27] Xerox's problems in the early 1980s were legion and typical of American manufacturers facing serious foreign competition for the first time. Xerox discovered to its horror that Japanese companies were able to sell copiers in the U.S. for roughly what it cost Xerox to build them.

Its former lion's share of the copier market had dwindled to a paltry 8 percent. Even at the time, Xerox was hardly complacent: productivity was increasing by as much as 7 or 8 percent every year. Kearns calculated that gains closer to 18 percent a year were needed to catch Xerox's competitors.

About this time, Kearns read Philip Crosby's *Quality is Free* and invited Crosby to address Xerox's management. Kearns's pleas for change initially were resisted by a management team who said they were already doing everything they could. This led Kearns to tell his managers that trying to change Xerox was like "pushing a wet noodle." It was time for more drastic action.

In 1983 the top management team at Xerox designed a new approach to quality that was dubbed "Leadership through Quality." The central principle of the new approach was that quality would be defined as customer satisfaction, not internal standards. If customers were not satisfied, quality had not been attained. A second principle was to focus on processes, not just outcomes. In the past, poor outcomes were an occasion to blame someone and to hammer into them the importance of doing better. This was replaced with an approach that focused on examining the process that had created the outcome and improving it.

In order to operate according to these principles, a number of specific practices were undertaken. Xerox is perhaps best-known for its extensive use of benchmarking—a process of comparing your operations to the best practices of other companies. The company's approach is to benchmark against the best, in whatever industry it is found. Xerox has benchmarked its billing processes against American Express and its distribution processes against L.L. Bean.

To demonstrate their commitment to these principles, Kearns and his management team were the first to undergo the newly devised quality training. They then became the teachers for the next level of management, and training flowed throughout the organization in this manner. In a move that represented a major departure from tradition, each senior manager was made responsible for taking calls from customers one day a month. Xerox managers still interrupt their meetings to take such calls.

Although Kearns's efforts were crucial to this process, he believes that leadership must (and in this case did) come from other sources as well, including the Amalgamated Clothing & Textile Workers, the union representing Xerox's production employees:

> We've also learned that it's important to have union leaders as deeply committed to the quality process as management. A strong and enlightened union leadership shared management's vision and understood that changes had to be made if there was to be a future for all Xerox employees. We shared each other's trust.[28]

Xerox's competitive resurgence was dramatic. Market share, revenues, and profits all have recovered substantially. In 1989 Xerox became one of the first winners of both the American and Canadian National Quality Award. Kearns believes that "Xerox is probably the first American company in an industry targeted by the Japanese to regain market share without the aid of tariffs or government help."[29] Despite the recovery and the awards, however, Kearns has not abandoned the principle of continuous improvement:

> We take great satisfaction in winning these awards, but the fact is that we're far from finished with our drive to improve. We have learned that the pursuit of quality is a race with no finish line. We see an upward and neverending spiral of increased competition and heightened customer expectations.[30]

David Kearns was succeeded as Xerox's Chairman in 1991 by Paul Allaire. Kearns is now working within the U.S. Department of Education to bring the quality perspective to America's schools.

Discussion Questions

1. How did David Kearns fulfill the roles of a quality leader at Xerox? How did his approach differ from Frank Perdue's?
2. Is Kearns's approach broadly applicable, or would different approaches be needed in other settings?
3. Kearns began a practice of having senior managers personally take phone calls from customers with problems. Call the president of an organization of which you are a customer and report a quality or service problem you are experiencing. Will the president take the call? Will the president or someone else return your call? (If you get to talk to someone, congratulate them on their responsiveness, and be as constructive as possible in describing your problem.)

ENDNOTES

1. Harry J. Levinson and Chuck DeHont, "Leading to Quality," *Quality Progress*, May 1992, pp.55–60.

2. Quoted in Jerry G. Bowles, "Leading the World-Class Company," *Fortune*, September 21, 1992.

3. 1992 Award Criteria, Malcolm Baldrige National Quality Award, p.2.

4. Dan Ciampa, *Total Quality: A User's Guide for Implementation,* Reading, Mass.: Addison-Wesley Publishing Company, 1992. p. 115.

5. These examples are from A.R.Tenner and I.J. DeToro, *Total Quality Management.* Reading, Mass: Addison-Wesley, 1992.

6. Quoted in Bowles, "Leading the World-Class Company."

7. This box is partially based on information from Bradley T. Gale, "Quality Comes First When Hatching Power Brands," *Planning Review*, July/August 1992, pp. 4–9, 48.

8. F.B. Adamson, "Cultivating a charismatic quality leader," *Quality Progress*, July 1989, pp.56–57.

9. Quoted in Bowles, "Leading the World-Class Company."

10. D. Garvin, "Quality problems, policies, and attitudes in the United States and Japan: An exploratory study," *Academy of Management Journal*, 1986, 29 (4), pp. 653–673.

11. These and other means of demonstrating commitment to TQM values were suggested by Tenner and DeToro, *Total Quality Management*.

12. Levinson and DeHont, "Leading to Quality," p. 56.

13. See P.Richards, "Right-side-up organization," *Quality Progress*, October 1991, pp. 95–96.

14. Quoted in Bowles, "Leading the World-Class Company."

15. This idea is discussed in Howard S. Gitlow and Shelly J. Gitlow, *The Deming Guide to Quality and Competitive Position*, Englewood Cliffs, N.J.: Prentice-Hall, 1987.

16. Based on James C. Spee, "What the Film *Tampopo* Teaches about Total Quality Management." *Tampopo* is directed by Juzo Itami and stars Nobuko Miyamoto and Tsutomu Yamazaki, 1987 Itami Productions. Available on Republic Pictures Home Video in Japanese with English subtitles.

17. Based on George Fisher, Gary L. Tooker, and Christopher B. Galvin, "Six Sigma: 1992 and Beyond," (a letter to Motorola employees by the company leadership) and Ed Bales, "Quality at Motorola and its Application to Education," talk given at the National Meeting of the Academy of Management, Las Vegas, August 11, 1992.

18. Philip B. Crosby, *Quality Is Free*, New York: McGraw-Hill, 1979.

19. R. House and M. Baetz, "Leadership: Some Generalizations and New Research Directions," in B.M. Staw (ed.), *Research in Organizational Behavior*, Greenwich, Conn.: JAI Press, 1979, p. 359.

20. Henry Mintzberg, *The Nature of Managerial Work,* New York: Harper & Row, 1973.

21. B.M. Bass, *Leadership and Performance Beyond Expectations,* New York: Free Press, 1985. This discussion is based on David A. Waldman, "A Theoretical Consideration of Leadership and Total Quality Management," *Leadership Quarterly*, 1993, v. 4, pp. 65–79. See also J. Conger and R. Kanungo, "Toward a Behavioral Theory of Charismatic Leadership in Organizational Settings," *Academy of Management Review*, October 1987, pp. 637–647.

22. Philip Atkinson, "Leadership, Total Quality and Cultural Change," *Management Services*, June 1991, pp. 16–19.

23. J.P. Kotter, "What Leaders Really Do," in J.J. Gabarro (ed.), *Managing People and Organizations*, Boston: Harvard Business School Press, 1992, pp. 102-114.

24. John A. Young, "The Quality Focus at Hewlett-Packard," *The Journal of Business Strategy*, Vol. 5, no. 3, 1985, pp. 6-9.

25. William W. Scherkenbach, *The Deming Route to Quality and Productivity*, Washington, D.C.: CEEPress Books, George Washington University, 1986, p. 139.

26. Quoted in Sir John Harvey-Jones, Harvard Business School Case 9-490-013, p. 8.

27. This section is based on David Kearns, "Leadership through Quality," *Academy of Management Executive*, 1990, 4 (2), pp. 86–89; "A CEO's Odyssey Toward World-Class Manufacturing," *Chief Executive*, September 1990; and Alan C. Fenwick, "Five Easy Lessons," *Quality Progress*, December 1991.

28. Kearns, Leadership through Quality, p.88.

29. Kearns, Leadership through Quality, p.88.

30. Kearns, Leadership through Quality, p.88.

PART IV

Total Quality and Strategic Management

CHAPTER 10

Total Quality and Competitive Advantage

Chapter Outline

Sources of Competitive Advantage
    Cost Leadership
    Differentiation
    The Importance of Quality to Competitive Advantage
Quality and Differentiation Strategies
    Competing on Superior Product Design
    Competing on Service
    Competing on Flexibility and Variety
    Competing on Innovation
    Competing on Time
Competitive Performance of Baldrige Winners
Summary
Review and Discussion Questions
Case

Competitive advantage denotes a firm's ability to achieve market superiority over its competitors. In the long run, a sustainable competitive advantage provides above-average performance. A strong competitive advantage has six characteristics:[1]

1. It is driven by customer wants and needs. A company provides value to its customers that competitors do not.

2. It makes a significant contribution to the success of the business.

3. It matches the organization's unique resources with the opportunities in the environment. No two companies have the same resources; a good strategy uses them effectively.

4. It is durable and lasting and difficult for competitors to copy. A superior research and development department, for example, can consistently develop new products or processes to remain ahead of competitors.

5. It provides a basis for further improvement.

6. It provides direction and motivation to the entire organization.

As each of these characteristics relates to quality, quality can be an important means of gaining competitive advantage. This chapter focuses on how total quality contributes to competitive advantage. This chapter will

- discuss the role of quality in cost leadership and differentiation, the two principal sources of competitive advantage;
- relate quality to the achievement of higher profitability; and
- describe the importance of quality in meeting customer expectations in product design, service, flexibility and variety, innovation, and rapid response.

SOURCES OF COMPETITIVE ADVANTAGE

The literature on competitive strategy suggests that a firm can possess two basic types of competitive advantage: low cost and differentiation.[2]

Cost Leadership

Many firms gain competitive advantage by establishing themselves as the low-cost leader in an industry. These firms produce high volumes of mature products and achieve their competitive advantage through low prices. Such firms often enter markets that were established by other firms. They emphasize achieving economies of scale and finding cost advantages from all sources. Low cost can result from high productivity and high capacity utilization. More importantly, improvements in quality lead to improvements in productivity, which in turn lead to lower costs. Thus a strategy of continuous improvement is essential to achieve a low-cost competitive advantage.

Lower costs result from innovations in product design and process technology that reduce the costs of production and from efficiencies gained through meticulous attention to operations. This approach has been exploited by many Japanese firms. Japanese companies adopted many product innovations and process technologies that were developed in the United States. They refined the designs and manufacturing processes to produce high-quality products at low costs, resulting in higher market shares.

To achieve cost leadership for high-volume products, companies use a variety of approaches:[3]

- Early manufacturing involvement in the design of the product, both for make-versus-buy decisions and for assurance that the production processes can achieve required tolerances.
- Product design to take advantage of automated equipment by minimizing the number of parts, eliminating fasteners, making parts symmetric whenever possible, avoiding rigid and stiff parts, and using one-sided assembly designs.
- Limited product models and customization in distribution centers rather than in the factory.
- A manufacturing system designed for a fixed sequence of operations. Every effort is made to ensure zero defects at the time of shipment. Work-in-process inventory is reduced as much as possible, and multiskilled, focused teams of employees are used.

A cost leader can achieve above-average performance if it can command prices at or near the industry average. However, it cannot do so with an inferior product. The product must be perceived as comparable with competitors or the firm will be forced to discount prices well below competitors' prices to gain sales. This can cancel any benefits that result from cost advantage.

You Can't Fool All of the People All of the Time

The problems with focusing on costs at the expense of quality are illustrated by the case of the Schlitz Brewing Company.[4] In the early 1970s, Schlitz, the second largest brewer in the United States, began a cost-cutting campaign. It included reducing the quality of ingredients in their beers by switching to corn syrup and hop pellets and shortening the brewing cycle by 50 percent.

In the short term, it achieved higher returns on sales and assets than Anheuser-Busch (and the acclaim of Wall Street analysts). *Forbes* magazine stated, "Does it pay to build quality into a product if most customers don't notice? Schlitz seems to have a more successful answer." But customers do recognize inferior products. Soon after, market share and profits fell rapidly. By 1980 Schlitz's sales had declined 40 percent, the stock price fell from $69 to $5, and the company was eventually sold.

Differentiation

To achieve differentiation, a firm must be unique in its industry along some dimensions that are widely valued by customers. It selects one or more attributes that customers perceive as important and positions itself uniquely to meet those needs. As a result, it can command premium prices and achieve higher profits. Juran cites an example of a power tool manufacturer that improved reliability well beyond that of competitors.[5] Field data showing that the differences in reliability resulted in significantly lower operating costs were publicized, and the company was able to secure a premium price.

However, a firm that uses differentation as its source of competitive advantage cannot ignore cost. It must achieve a cost position on a par with its competitors and reduce costs in all areas that do not affect differentiation.

These issues apply to services as well. For example, Marriott's Fairfield Inn was designed to appeal to business travelers who wanted clean, comfortable rooms at inexpensive prices. Within this market, they are focused on cost leadership. On the other hand, the Ritz-Carlton hotels focus on differentiation (exceptional personal attention, twice-a day housekeeping service, and special amenities such as bathrobes and rooms with bay windows) and can command premium prices.

The Importance of Quality to Competitive Advantage

The role of quality in achieving competitive advantage was demonstrated by several research studies during the 1980s. PIMS Associates, Inc., a subsidary of the Strategic Planning Institute, maintains a data base of 1,200 companies and studies the impact of product quality on corporate performance.[7] PIMS researchers have found that

- Product quality is the most important determinant of business profitability.
- Businesses offering premium quality products and services usually have large market shares and were early entrants into their markets.
- Quality is positively and significantly related to a higher return on investment for almost all kinds of products and market situations. PIMS studies have shown that firms with products of superior quality can more than triple return on sales over products perceived has having inferior quality.
- A strategy of quality improvement usually leads to increased market share, but at a cost in terms of reduced short-run profitablity.
- High quality producers can usually charge premium prices.

General Systems Company, a prominent quality management consulting firm, has found that firms with TQM systems in place consistently exceed industry norms for return on investment. This is attributed to three factors:

1. TQM reduces the direct costs associated with poor quality.
2. Improvements in quality tend to lead to increases in productivity.
3. The combination of improved quality and increased productivity leads to an increase in market share.

These findings are summarized in Figure 10.1 and relate to both sources of competitive advantage—differentiation and low cost. The value of a product in the marketplace is influenced by the quality of its design. Improvements in performance, features, and reliability will differentiate the product from its competitors, improve a firm's quality reputation, and improve the perceived value of the product. This allows the company to command higher prices and achieve an increased market share. This, in turn, leads to increased revenues that offset the added costs of improved design.

Improved conformance in production leads to lower manufacturing and service costs through savings in rework, scrap, and warranty expenses. This viewpoint was popularized by Philip Crosby in his book *Quality is Free*.[8] As Crosby states:

> Quality is not only free, it is an honest-to-everything profit maker. Every penny you don't spend on doing things wrong, over, or instead of, becomes half a penny right on the bottom line. In these days of "who knows what is going to happen to our business tomorrow," there aren't many ways left to make a profit improvement. If you concentrate on making quality certain, you can probably increase your profit by an amount equal to 5 percent to 10 percent of your sales. That is a lot of money for free.

Figure 10.1 Quality and Profitability

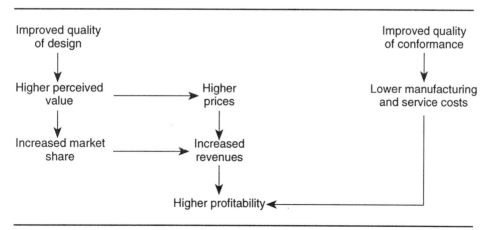

The net effect of improved quality of design and conformance is increased profits.

Today, many consumers are basing their purchasing decisions on *value*. Value can be defined as quality relative to price. When organizations provide less perceived value than their competitors, they lose market share. This is what happened to U.S. automakers in the 1970s and '80s. Thus, firms must focus their efforts at both improving the quality of design and service as well as reducing costs. No longer can firms focus their quality efforts solely on defect elimination. Today, the absence of defects is a "given" rather than a distinctive source of competitive advantage. Both Deming and Juran stress the need for never-ending cycles of market research, improved product development and design, production, and sales.

QUALITY AND DIFFERENTIATION STRATEGIES

Competitive advantage is gained from meeting or exceeding customer expectations—the fundamental definition of quality. A business may concentrate on any of several quality-related dimensions in order to differentiate itself from its competition. These key dimensions are

- superior product design,
- outstanding service,
- high flexibility and variety,
- continuous innovation, and
- rapid response.

Traditional management strategists advocated focusing on a single dimension. However, as consumers become more demanding, firms can no longer compete along only one dimension. Pursuing a strategy of total quality helps improve all of these dimensions. The following sections discuss these approaches to differentiation and the role of quality in each.

Competing on Superior Product Design

Among the most important strategic decisions a firm makes are the selection and development of new products and services. These decisions determine the growth, profitability, and future direction of the firm. Significant competitive advantage can be achieved by having products of superior design. In addition, products that are appealing, reliable, easy to operate, and economical to service give the consumer a perception of quality.

Basically, there are three types of products: custom products, option-oriented products, and standard products.[9] *Custom products*, generally made in small quantities, are designed to meet customers' specifications precisely. Two examples are a wedding gown or a machine tool designed to perform a specific, complex task. The production cost is relatively high and the assurance of quality requires careful attention at every step in the manufacturing process. Since custom products can only be produced upon demand, the customer must wait for the product to be made.

Option-oriented products are unique configurations of subassemblies that are designed to fit together. The customer participates in choosing the options to be assembled. A good example is a personal computer system in which the customer defines the types of disk drives, modem, memory configurations, and so forth. The subassemblies are made in relatively large quantities; therefore, costs are reduced, and quality is easier to achieve because of repetition. Since the manufacturer cannot anticipate all of the configurations a customer may desire, the customer sometimes must wait while the product is assembled to the desired configuration.

Standard products are made in larger quantities. Examples include radios, TVs, appliances, and most consumer goods found in department stores. The customer has no options to choose from, and quality is easiest to achieve because the product is made the same way every time. Since the manufacturer makes standard products in anticipation of customer demands, the customer will not have to wait for the product unless it is out of stock.

Standard products offer many advantages in terms of manufacturing efficiency, quality, and dependability. Mass-production on fixed assembly lines yields high levels of productivity. Thus, standard products are the basis for cost leadership. With fewer different parts to purchase, make, and assemble, quality is generally improved because there is less chance for error. Schedules are more predictable, so dependability is improved. Standard products also simplify purchasing and customer service. Orders of components are more consistent, and shipments can be scheduled more frequently, resulting in lower inventories.

Marketing personnel are concerned with sales and how to respond correctly and successfully in the market. They prefer products to be customized to the individual needs of customers. Custom and option-oriented products can be produced to meet customer expectations, whereas standard products offer little flexibility in meeting changing customer needs. Customer expectations can be incorporated only in the design stages. However, this leads to manufacturing efficiencies. This inherent conflict between manufacturing and marketing must be addressed from a strategic perspective.

In the quick-service restaurant industry, similar strategic choices are made. McDonald's, for example, produces a standard product and achieves an advantage in terms of service delivery. Burger King and Wendy's, on the other hand, produce option-oriented products. Although their selection may be greater, these companies sacrifice speed of service. Neither the standard nor the option-oriented approach is necessarily better; each firm must decide what trade-offs must be made with each approach and select the approach that best fits their overall strategic focus.

Many products begin as custom products and, over time, become standard products. For instance, Henry Ford was one of the first to standardize production of the automobile. Later, however, consumers demanded more variety of options, and the American automobile evolved into the classic option-oriented product. Customers can now choose from dozens of colors, seat types, engines, transmissions, tires, and other options.

Many German and Japanese automobile manufacturers have chosen a strategy that limits the number of options. Few options exist, and some are installed by the dealer, rather than the manufacturer. This strategy provides a distinct cost advantage and enables the factory to achieve higher levels of productivity. Flexibility is achieved by offering several model variations of the same car and frequent design changes. The Japanese can produce as many as seven models on a single production line. (Most U.S. manufacturers' production lines are dedicated to a single model.)

The product design function that traditionally was concerned solely with technical aspects of the product must now be concerned with manufacturing and marketing issues. Product designers must match the right products with the continually changing variety of customer needs. This requires great flexibility. At the same time, costs must be minimized, which demands attention to the manufacturing process during the design stage.

The quality of a product's design is influenced by several quality dimensions:[10]

- Performance—the primary operating characteristics of the product: the horsepower of an engine or the sound quality of a stereo amplifier.

- Features—the "bells and whistles" of a product: antilock brakes or a CD player in an automobile or surround-sound options in an amplifier.

- Reliability—the probability of a product's surviving over a specified period of time under stated conditions of use: the ability of a car to start consistently in all types of weather and the lack of failure of electronic components.

- Durability—the amount of use one gets from a product before it physically deteriorates or until replacement is preferable: the number of miles one would expect from an automobile with normal maintenance.

- Aesthetics—how a product looks, feels, sounds, tastes, or smells: the sleekness of an automobile's exterior and the black "high-tech" look of modern stereo components, for example.

The Role of Total Quality in Product Design

A firm must focus on the key product dimensions that reflect specific customer needs. If these expectations are not identified correctly or are misinterpreted, the final product will not be perceived to be of high quality by customers. Considerable marketing efforts are needed to ensure that the needs are correctly identified.

The Malcolm Baldrige Award criteria emphasize the importance of systematic processes to design and improve products and services. The award application requires evidence of how customer requirements are translated into product requirements; how quality requirements are addressed early in the design process; how designs are coordinated and integrated with production and delivery systems; and how key process performance characteristics are selected based on customer requirements.

A total quality focus in product design requires significant investment in engineering to ensure that designs meet customer expectations. *Quality engineering* is concerned with the plans, procedures, and methods for the design and evaluation of quality in goods and services. Useful techniques of quality engineering include:

- *concurrent engineering*, in which engineering and production personnel jointly develop product designs that are both functional and easy to manufacture, thus reducing opportunities for poor quality;

- *value analysis*, in which the function of every component of a product is analyzed to determine how it might be accomplished in the most economical fashion;

- *design reviews*, in which managers assess how well the design relates to customer requirements and how it might be improved prior to releasing it to production; and

- *experimental design*, in which formal statistical experiments are applied to determine the best combinations of product and process parameters for high quality and low cost. All of these efforts involve a high level of teamwork.

Competing on Service

Until rather recently, companies viewed service as secondary in importance to manufacturing. However, next to the quality of the product itself, service is perhaps the greatest key to success and a key source of competitive advantage. This may be due to the fact that as the average level of product quality increases, consumers turn to service as the primary means of differentiating among competing firms.

The importance of service was recognized in the early 1980s because of the book *In Search of Excellence* by Tom Peters and Bob Waterman.[11] One of their key themes was that excellent companies share an obsession with service. How important is it? A 1985 Gallup poll on the quality of American products and services found that the vast majority of consumers believe that quality is determined by employee behavior, attitudes, and competence. They also believe—to an even greater degree—that poor service quality is due to the same set of factors.

Service translates into dollars. Banking studies have found that 10 percent of customers leave each year,[12] and 21 percent of those leave because of poor service. Each customer contributes $121 per year in profit, and the cost to acquire a new customer is $150. If a bank has a base of 200,000 customers, this means that 4,200 will leave because of poor service. The arithmetic shows that the combined lost profit and replacement effort costs are more than $1 million. Similar studies in other industries have found a high correlation between customer retention and profitability.

Another important aspect of service is complaint resolution (an important criterion in the Baldrige Award). Research has shown that about 80 to 95 percent of unhappy customers (depending on the amount of loss) will purchase from a company again if their complaints are resolved quickly. This drops to around 20 to 45 percent if complaints are not resolved. Furthermore, of the majority of unhappy customers that do not complain at all, only about 10 to 40 percent will become repeat customers.

The Role of Total Quality in Service

Companies that have consistently provided superior service—such as IBM, Federal Express, Nordstrom, and many others—have certain elements in common:[13]

1. They establish service goals that support business and product line objectives.
2. They identify and define customer expectations for service quality and responsiveness.
3. They translate customer expectations into clear, deliverable, service features.
4. They set up efficient, responsive, and integrated service delivery systems and organizations.
5. They monitor and control service quality and performance.
6. They provide quick, but cost-effective response to customers' needs.

These ideas are embodied in the Malcolm Baldrige Award criteria on Customer Focus and Satisfaction. Among the areas addressed in this category are:

- *Customer Relationship Management.* This includes determining how relationships between employees and customers are built and maintained; how service standards are set, implemented, and tracked; how information and easy access are provided to enable customers to seek assistance, comment, and complain; how customer-contact employees are selected and trained; and how customer complaints and feedback are resolved and used as a source of improvement.
- *Commitment to Customers.* This seeks to determine what types of commitments the company makes to promote trust and confidence in its products and services to satisfy customers when failures occur, and how the company evaluates and improves its commitments and customers' understanding of them, to avoid gaps between expectations and delivery.

Much of the total quality concept is devoted to empowering front-line employees to provide the services that satisfy and exceed customer expectations. Because service usually occurs in direct contact with the customer, the attention to the human resource is critical. Most of this book focuses on these issues.

Competing on Flexibility and Variety

Flexibility is the capacity of a production system to adapt successfully to changing environmental conditions and process requirements. Variety refers to the ability to produce a wide range of products and options. Companies that can change product lines more rapidly in the face of changing consumer demands and exploit new technologies can gain a competitive advantage in certain markets.

Many firms use flexibility and variety as a competitive weapon. Some firms provide custom service on complex systems for low-volume customers and markets. They must be excellent at product design and responsiveness to customers. Other firms do little innovation themselves, but take product designs from customers and produce custom products on a low-volume basis. Both types of firms must have considerable flexibility in their production operations to produce low volumes and customized products. High quality is a must, as is delivery on schedule.

While the quality gap between U.S. and Japanese products narrows, many Japanese firms are focusing their strategies on flexibility and variety—more and better product features, factories that can change product lines quickly, expanded customer service, and continually improving new products. For instance, Toshiba's computer factory assembles 9 different word processors on the same production line and 20 varieties of laptop computers on another.[14] The flexible lines guard against running short of a hot model or overproducing one whose sales have slowed.

Nissan describes its strategy as "five anys:" to make anything in any volume anywhere at any time by anybody. Nissan's high tech Intelligent Body Assembly System can weld and inspect body parts for any kind of car, all in 46 seconds. As U.S. automakers think about dropping entire car lines, Nissan is gearing up to fill market niches with more models.

The value of flexibility and variety was illustrated by the "Honda-Yamaha war" in 1981. Honda, whose supremacy in motorcycles was being challenged by Yamaha, responded by introducing 113 new or revamped models in 18 months. Yamaha could only manage 37 model changes and finally announced that it was content to be number two.

The Role of Quality in Flexibility and Variety

The ability to develop the right products depends on a clear customer focus and determination of customer expectations. As these change, the company must be able to respond quickly. Being close to the customer is essential.

Equally important is the ability of different functions and groups of employees to work together as teams in designing and operating the type of production systems that require continuous change and improvement. Good supplier relations, a key issue in total quality, are critical as designs and volumes change. These issues will be addressed later in this book.

Competing on Innovation

Many firms focus on research and development as a core component of their strategy. Such firms are on the leading edge of product technology, and their ability to innovate and introduce new products is a critical success factor. Product performance, not price, is the major selling feature. When competitors enter the market and profit margins fall, these companies often drop out of the market while continuing to introduce innovative new products. These companies focus on outstanding product research, design, and development; high product quality; and the ability to modify production facilities to produce new products frequently.

As global competition increases, the ability to innovate has become almost essential for remaining competitive. National Cash Register, for example, clung to outdated mechanical technologies for years, while competitors developed innovative new electronic systems. The lack of innovation nearly destroyed the company.

Today leading companies do not wait for customers to change; they use innovation to create new customer needs and desires. At 3M, for example, every division is expected to derive 25 percent of its sales each year from products that did not exist five years earlier. This forces managers to think seriously about innovation. Such a spirit of continuous improvement not only will result in new products, but also will help managers to create better processes that improve quality.

The Role of Quality in Innovation

The Malcolm Baldrige Award criteria explicitly state that invention, innovation, and creativity are important aspects of delivering ever-improving value to customers and maximizing productivity. Innovation and creativity are crucial features in company competitiveness and can be applied to products, processes, services, human resource development, and overall quality systems.

The award criteria encourage innovation through several means:

- The criteria are nonprescriptive. They encourage creativity and breakthrough thinking because they channel activities toward the organization's purpose and are not focused on following specific procedures.

- Customer-driven quality emphasizes the "positive side of quality"—enhancement, new services, and customer relationship management. Success with the positive side of quality depends heavily on creativity, more so than on steps to reduce errors and defects that rely on well-defined techniques.

- Human resource utilization stresses employee involvement, development, and recognition, and encourages creative approaches to improving employee effectiveness, empowerment, and contributions.

- Continuous improvement and learning are integral parts of the activities of all work groups. This requires analysis and problem solving everywhere within the company. Emphasis on continuous improvement encourages change, innovation, and creative thinking in how work is organized and conducted.

- The focus on future requirements of customers encourages companies to seek innovative and creative ways to serve their patrons.

Competing on Time

In today's fast-paced society, people hate to wait. Time has come to be recognized as one of the most important sources of competitive advantage. The total time required by a company to deliver a finished product that satisfies customers' needs is referred to as the *product lead time*. This includes time spent on design, engineering, purchasing, manufacturing, testing, packaging, and shipping.

Short product lead times offer many advantages. First, they allow companies to introduce new products and penetrate new markets more rapidly. Being the first to market a new product allows a firm to charge a higher price, at least until competitive products are offered. For example, when first introduced, Kodak's Ektar film sold for 10 to 15 percent more than conventional film; Motorola's pocket-sized cellular telephone was 50 percent smaller than any competing Japanese product and sold for twice the price; and the Mazda Miata sold for up to $5,000 above sticker price.

Second, every month saved in development time can save a large company millions of dollars in expenses. Third, short lead times reduce the need to forecast long-term sales, allow more accurate production plans to be developed, and reduce inventory. Short lead times increase the flexibility of a company to respond to changing customer needs.

The Role of Quality in Time Competitiveness

The Malcolm Baldrige Award criteria emphasize the importance of reducing cycle times in all business processes. Success in competitive markets increasingly demands shorter cycles for new or improved product and service introduction. Also, faster and more flexible response to customers is a more critical requirement of business management.

Major improvements in response time often require work organizations, processes, and paths to be simplified and shortened. To accomplish this, more attention needs to be paid to time performance. This can be done by making

---

Domino's Pizza Changed the Rules[15]

Tom Monaghan, founder of Domino's Pizza, determined that customers ordering home-delivered pizza wanted their pizzas quickly because they were usually hungry when they ordered. He also understood that people anticipated having their pizzas delivered anywhere from 20 minutes to 2 hours after placing their orders. This wide variation in delivery was acceptable because people had been conditioned to accept that there were no other options available. Since fast, consistent delivery was not an option, customers placed their pizza orders based only on taste and price.

Monaghan changed all that by promising fast and consistent delivery—30 minutes or less—or it's free. Domino's exceeded customers expecations. Today, this "delighter/exciter" has become a satisfier, and consistently fast delivery is often the first criterion in the pizza-ordering decision process.

---

response time a key indicator for work unit improvement processes. Simplified processes reduce opportunities for errors, leading to improved quality.

Improvements in response time often result from increased understanding of internal customer-supplier relationships and teamwork. Cutting response time requires a significant commitment from all employees and leadership from top management. Such efforts must involve the entire organization and often require organizational redesign.

COMPETITIVE PERFORMANCE OF BALDRIGE WINNERS

Baldrige Award winners have demonstrated that quality leads to competitive advantage and improved business performance. A 1991 General Accounting Office study of Baldrige finalists explored four measurable areas of a company's operations that could demonstrate the impact of TQM practices on corporate performance:[17]

1. employee relations,
2. operating procedures,
3. customer satisfaction, and
4. financial performance.

In employee relations, significant improvements were realized in employee satisfaction, attendance, turnover, safety and health, and suggestions received. In operating procedures, favorable results were realized in reliability,

---

Northern Telecom Competes on Time[16]

In the late 1970s Northern Telecom introduced the first fully digital telephone switch to the market. By 1985 competing products had reduced their sales. To meet the demand for increasingly more sophisticated products, the company increased the speed with which they brought new products to market. As new products were developed, they found themselves making thousands of design changes that added little value to the product and accounted for more than 20 percent of manufacturing overhead. They considered such technological solutions as computer-integrated manufacturing and automation but concluded that such fixes would provide only short-term advantages over the competition. Instead, they redesigned their entire organization to conduct business faster.

To reach its three major strategic objectives of increasing customer satisfaction by at least 20 percent, reducing manufacturing overhead as a percentage of sales by one-half, and cutting inventory days by 50 percent, they needed the ability to do things faster than ever before. By focusing on manufacturing process improvement, the manner in which they develop new products, and procurement activities, Northern Telecom achieved significant results in a short period of time. For example, one product's manufacturing cycle dropped from 9 to 2.4 weeks, and another product's from 16 to 6 weeks. New product introduction times were reduced by as much as 20 to 50 percent. Finally, the receiving cycle was reduced by 97 percent—from 3 weeks to 4 hours!

---

timeliness of delivery, order-processing times, errors and defects, product lead time, inventory turnover, cost of quality, and overall cost savings. Overall customer satisfaction also improved, as customer complaints fell and customer retention rose. In the financial performance area, market share, sales per employee, return on assets, and return on sales all showed positive improvement for most companies.

The GAO developed a general framework for describing Total Quality Management and its effect on competitiveness (Figure 10.2.) The solid line shows how TQ processes lead to improved competitiveness, beginning with leadership dedicated to improving products and services, as well as quality systems. Improvements in these areas lead to customer satisfaction and benefits to the organization, both of which improve competitiveness. The dotted lines show the information feedback necessary for continuous improvement. The arrows in the boxes show the expected direction of the performance indicators.

Figure 10.2   General Accounting Office TQM Framework

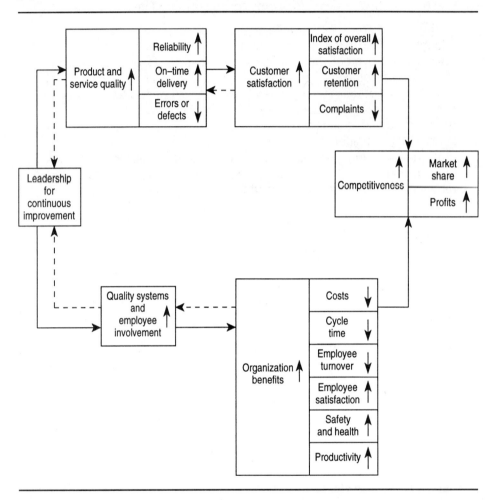

SUMMARY

Every business strives to achieve a competitive advantage. This is usually done through cost leadership or product/process differentiation that meets the needs and expectations of customers. Improved quality leads to lower costs and higher productivity, thus helping a firm to attain a cost leadership position. Similarly, differentiation strategies such as superior product design, outstanding service, high flexibility and variety, continuous innovation, and rapid response, are driven and improved by attention to total quality.

Many studies have shown that quality influences financial performance and competitive position. Achieving competitive advantage through quality requires a good strategy and good implementation. The next chapter discusses these issues.

REVIEW AND DISCUSSION QUESTIONS

1. Explain how a total quality perspective can support the six characteristics of competitive advantage introduced at the beginning of the chapter.

2. Discuss the two basic types of competitive advantage. Can a company achieve both?

3. List ten firms or businesses that you have read about or have personal experience with. Describe their sources of competitive advantage and how you believe that quality supports (or does not support) their strategy.

4. Prepare a report (using sources such as business periodicals, personal interviews, and so on) profiling a company that competes on each of the major dimensions of differentiation discussed in the chapter. What aspects of their total quality approach support their strategic focus?

5. Think of a product or service you have purchased recently. What aspects of the product or service made it attractive?

6. What is the importance of total quality to achieving competitive advantage?

7. Explain how quality affects profitability.

8. Discuss the key quality dimensions of differentiation strategies.

9. Explain the differences among custom, option-oriented, and standard products.

10. How might the dimensions of product design (performance, features, reliability, durability, and aesthetics) discussed in this chapter be applied to services?

11. Explain the purpose of quality engineering.

12. Describe one good and one bad service experience that you encountered. How did this change your perceptions of the company?

13. How are flexibility and variety sources of competitive advantage. What relationships do these dimensions have with quality?

14. What is the role of quality in innovation?

15. How can the tools of quality discussed in chapter 3 help in reducing cycle times?

16. Explain the General Accounting Office framework for TQM. Discuss specific cause-and-effect relationships of a total quality focus and the expected changes in performance indicators.

17. How might the principles of competitive advantage that we discussed be applied to the management of your college or university? How about a fraternity or student professional organization?

CASE

Case of the Rotary Compressor[18]

In 1981 market share and profits in General Electric's appliance division were falling. The company's technology was antiquated compared to foreign competitors. For example, making refrigerator compressors required 65 minutes of labor in comparison to 25 minutes for competitors in Japan and Italy. Moreover, GE's labor costs were higher. The alternatives were obvious: either purchase compressors from Japan or Italy or design and build a better model.

By 1983 the decision to build a new rotary compressor in-house was made, along with a commitment for a new $120 million factory. GE was not a novice in rotary compressor technology; they had invented it and had been using it in air conditioners for many years. A rotary compressor weighed less, had one-third fewer parts, and was more energy efficient than the current reciprocating compressors. The rotary compresor took up less space, thus providing more room inside the refrigerator and better meeting customer requirements.

Some engineers argued to the contrary, citing the fact that rotary compressors run hotter. This is not a problem in most air conditioners, because the coolant cools the compressor. In a refrigerator, however, the coolant flows only one-tenth as fast, and the unit runs about four times longer in one year than an air conditioner. GE had problems with the early rotary compressors in air conditioners. Although the bugs had been eliminated in smaller units, GE quit using rotaries in larger units due to frequent breakdowns in hot climates.

GE managers and design engineers were concerned about other issues. Rotary compressors make a high-pitched whine, and managers were afraid that this would adversely affect consumer acceptance. Many hours were spent on this issue by managers and consumer test panels. The new design also required key parts to work together with a tolerance of only 50 millionths of an inch. Nothing had been mass produced with such precision before, but manufacturing engineers felt sure they could do it.

The compressor they finally designed was nearly identical to that used in air conditioners, with one change. Two small parts inside the compressor were made out of powdered metal, rather than the hardened steel and cast iron used in air conditioners. This material was chosen because it could be machined to much closer tolerances, and reduced machining costs. Powdered metal had been tried a decade earlier on air conditioners but did not work. The design engineers who were new to designing compressors did not consider the earlier failure important.

A consultant suggested that GE consider a joint venture with a Japanese company that had a rotary refrigerator compressor already on the market. The idea was rejected by management. The original designer of the air conditioner rotary compressor, who had left GE, offered his services as a consultant. GE declined his offer, writing him that they had sufficient technical expertise.

About 600 compressors were tested in 1983 without a single failure. They were run continuously for two months under elevated temperatures and pressures that were supposed to simulate five years' operation. GE normally conducts extensive field testing of new products; their original plan to test models in the field for two years was reduced to nine months due to time pressure to complete the project.

The technician who disassembled and inspected the parts thought they did not look right. Parts of the motor were discolored, a sign of excessive heat. Bearings were worn, and it appeared that high heat was breaking down the lubricating oil. The technician's supervisors discounted these findings and did not relay them to upper levels of management. Another consultant who evaluated the test results believed that something was wrong because only one failure was found in two years and recommended that test conditions be intensified. This suggestion was also rejected by management.

By 1986, only 2.5 years after board approval, the new factory was producing compressors at a rate of 10 per minute. By the end of the year, more than 1 million had been produced. Market share rose and the new refrigerator appeared to be a success. But in July 1987 the first compressor failed. Soon after, reports of other failures in Puerto Rico arrived. By September the appliance division knew it had a major problem. In December the plant stopped making the compressor. Not until 1988 was the problem diagnosed as excessive wear in the two powdered-metal parts that burned up the oil. The cost in 1989 alone was $450 million. By mid-1990, GE had voluntarily replaced nearly 1.1 million compressors with ones purchased from six suppliers, five of them foreign.

Discussion Questions

1. What factors in the product development process caused this disaster? What individuals were responsible?
2. How might this disaster have been prevented? What lessons do you think GE learned for the future?
3. On what basis was GE attempting to achieve a competitive advantage? How did they fail?

ENDNOTES

1. S.C. Wheelwright, "Competing Through Manufacturing," in Ray Wild (ed.), *International Handbook of Production and Operations Management*, London: Cassess Educational, Ltd., 1989, pp. 15–32.

2. Michael E. Porter, *Competitive Advantage: Creating and Sustaining Superior Performance*, New York: The Free Press, 1985.

3. H. Lee Hales, "Time Has Come for Long-Range Planning of Facilities Strategies in Electronic Industries," *Industrial Engineering*, April 1985.

4. Bradley T. Gale, "Quality Comes First When Hatching Power Brands," *Planning Review*, July/August 1992, pp. 4–9,48.

5. J.M. Juran, *Juran on Quality by Design*, New York: The Free Press, 1992, p. 181.

6. Gale, "Quality Comes First."

7. *The PIMS Letter on Business Strategy*, The Strategic Planning Institute, Number 4, Cambridge, Mass., 1986.

8. Philip Crosby, *Quality is Free*, New York: McGraw-Hill, 1979.

9. Charles A. Horne, "Product Strategy and Competitive Advantage," *P&IM Review with APICS News*, 7, no. 12, December 1987, pp. 38–41.

10. David A. Garvin, "What Does Product Quality Really Mean?" *Sloan Management Review*, 26, no. 1, (1984), pp. 25–43.

11. Tom Peters and Bob Waterman, *In Search of Excellence*, New York: Harper & Row, 1982.

12. F.F. Reichheld and W.E. Sasser, Jr. "Zero Defections: Quality Comes to Services," *Harvard Business Review*, September–October, 1990.

13. Jeffrey Margolies, "When Good Service Isn't Good Enough," *The Price Waterhouse Review*, 32, No. 3, New York: Price Waterhouse, 1988, pp. 22–31.

14. Thomas A. Stewart, "Brace for Japan's Hot New Strategy," *Fortune*, September 21, 1992, pp. 62–73.

15. Joan Uhlenberg, "Redefining Customer Expectations," *Quality*, September 1992, pp. 34–35.

16. Roy Merrills, "How Northern Telecom Competes on Time," *Harvard Business Review*, July–August 1989, pp. 108–114. Copyright 1989 by the President and Fellows of Harvard College; all rights reserved.

17. U.S. General Accounting Office, "Management Practices: U.S. Companies Improve Performance Through Quality Effort," GA/NSIAD-91-190, May 1991.

18. Reprinted by permission of *The Wall Street Journal,* © 1990 Dow Jones & Company, Inc. All Rights Reserved Worldwide.

CHAPTER 11

Strategic Planning and Total Quality Implementation

Chapter Outline

Quality as a Strategy
    Strategy and the Baldrige Award
The Strategic Management Process
    Strategy Formulation
    Strategy Implementation
Implementing a TQ Strategy
    The Role of Management
    Common Implementation Mistakes
    Strategies for Success
    Best Practices
Summary
Review and Discussion Questions
Case

A firm has many options in defining its long-term goals and objectives, the customers it wants to serve, the products and services it produces and delivers, and the design of the production and service system to meet these objectives. *Strategic planning* is the process by which the members of an organization envision its future and develop the necessary procedures and operations to carry out that vision. *Strategy*—the result of strategic planning— is the pattern of decisions that determines and reveals a company's goals, policies, and plans to meet the needs of its stakeholders. An effective strategy allows a business to create a sustainable competitive advantage, as discussed in chapter 10. This chapter discusses the role of quality in strategy, and strategic issues of implementing total quality in organizations. This chapter will

- discuss quality as a generic business strategy,
- describe the role of quality in strategy formulation and implementation and introduce policy deployment as a means of implementation, and
- discuss approaches to implementing TQM strategies in organizations.

QUALITY AS A STRATEGY

The concept of strategy has different meanings to different people. Quinn characterizes strategy as follows:[1]

> A strategy is a pattern or plan that integrates an organization's major goals, policies, and action sequences into a cohesive whole. A well-formulated strategy helps to marshal and allocate an organization's resources into a unique and viable posture based on its relative internal competencies and shortcomings, anticipated changes in the environment, and contingent moves by intelligent opponents.

Formal strategies contain three elements:

1. goals to be achieved,
2. policies that guide or limit action, and
3. action sequences, or programs, that accomplish the goals.

Effective strategies develop around a few key concepts and thrusts that provide focus. The essence of strategy is to build a posture that is so strong in selective ways that the organization can achieve its goals despite unforeseeable external forces that may arise.

The traditional focus of business strategies has been finance and marketing. These parallel the two principal sources of competitive advantage discussed in chapter 10—cost and differentiation. Total quality leads to improvements in both areas. Therefore, quality can be viewed as a strategy in itself.

The role of quality in business strategy has taken two significant steps since 1980. First, many firms have recognized that a strategy driven by quality can lead to significant market advantages. Second, the lines between quality strategy and generic business strategies have become increasingly blurred. The current trend is to integrate quality planning within normal business planning; that is, to make TQM a basic operating philosophy.

For most companies, integration of TQM into strategic business planning is the result of a natural evolution. For most new companies—or those that have enjoyed a reasonable measure of success—quality takes a back seat to increasing sales, expanding capacity, or boosting production. Strategic planning usually focuses on financial and marketing strategies.

As a company begins to face increasing competition and rising consumer expectations, cost-cutting objectives take precedence. Some departments or individuals may champion quality improvement efforts, but quality is not integrated in the company's strategic business plan. In the face of market crises, which many U.S. firms experienced in the 1970s and 1980s, top management begins to realize the importance of quality as a strategic operating policy. In many cases, however, quality is considered separate from financial and marketing plans. Companies that aspire to world-class status reach the highest level of evolution where quality becomes an integral part of the overall strategic plan and is viewed as a central operating strategy.

Strategy and the Baldrige Award

The Baldrige Award recognizes the importance of integrating quality with overall business planning. The Strategic Quality Planning category examines the company's planning process and how all key quality requirements are integrated into overall business planning. This means that quality improvement objectives like increasing customer satisfaction, reducing defects, and reducing process cycle times should be given as much attention as financial and market share objectives.

The Baldrige Award criteria focus on means for developing superior products and lowering costs of operations—in short, producing superior overall value for customers. Delivering superior value is an important part of business strategy that supports other business strategies. For example, superior value offers the possibility of price premiums or competing via lower prices. Pricing decisions may enhance market share and may also contribute to improved financial performance. The award criteria and evaluation system take into account market share, customer retention, customer satisfaction, productivity, asset utilization, and other factors that contribute to financial performance.

The Baldrige Award criteria consider the development, deployment, and evaluation of business decisions and strategies, even though these may involve many factors other than product and service quality. Some examples include the following:

- the scope, validity, and analysis of the quality of information used in business decisions and strategy
- analysis of factors—societal, regulatory, economic, competitive, and risk—that may bear upon the success or failure of strategy
- development of scenarios built around possible outcomes of strategy or decisions, including risks and consequences of failures
- lessons learned from previous strategy developments—within the company or available through research.

Xerox's Strategy is Built on Quality

The introductory section of chapter 1 described the turnaround that Xerox experienced by developing a strategy based on quality. The Xerox Leadership Through Quality strategy is built on three elements:

1. Quality Principles
   - Quality is the basic business principle for Xerox to continue to be a leadership company.
   - We will understand our customers' existing and latent requirements.
   - We will provide all our external and internal customers with products and services that meet their requirements.
   - Employee involvement, through participative problem solving, is essential to improve quality.
   - Error-free work is the most cost-effective way to improve quality.

2. Management Actions and Behaviors
   - We will assure strategic clarity and consistency.
   - We will provide visible supportive management practices, commitment, and leadership.
   - We will set quality objectives and measurement standards.
   - We will establish and reinforce a management style of openness, trust, respect, patience, and discipline.
   - We will establish an environment in which each person can be responsible for quality.

3. Quality Tools
   - The Xerox quality policy
   - Competitive benchmarking and goal setting
   - Systematic defect and error-prevention processes
   - Training for leadership through quality
   - Communication and recognition programs that reinforce leadership through quality
   - A measure for the cost of quality (or its lack)

Following the formation of this strategy, senior executives at Xerox defined the goals they would strive to achieve and the activities necessary to implement these goals over the next five years.

THE STRATEGIC MANAGEMENT PROCESS

Strategic planning helps leadership mold an organization's future and manage change by focusing on an ideal vision of what the organization should and could be 10 to 20 years in the future. In contrast, the term "long range planning" may only mean one year in the future or the next budget submission in many organizations. Strategic plans are developed at the highest level of an organization and deployed throughout.

The strategic management process consists of two parts: formulation and implementation. Strategy formulation consists of defining the mission of the organization—the concept of the business and the vision of where it is headed; setting objectives—translating the mission into specific performance objectives; and defining a strategy—determining specific actions to achieve the performance objectives. Implementation focuses on executing the strategy effectively and efficiently, as well as on evaluating performance and making corrective adjustments when necessary.

Strategy Formulation

The organization's leaders first must explore and agree upon the *mission, vision,* and *guiding principles* of the organization; these form the foundation for the strategic plan.

The *mission* of a firm defines its reason for existence. For example, Federal Express describes its mission as "People, Service, Profit;" McDonald's is "Quality, Service, Cleanliness, Value." A firm's mission guides the development of strategies by different groups within the firm. It establishes the context within which daily operating decisions are made, and it sets limits on available strategic options. In addition, it helps to make trade-offs among the various performance measures and between short and long-term goals. At Federal Express, the fact that people and service come before profits sends a clear message about the company's priorities.

The *vision* describes where the organization is headed and what it intends to be. (See chapter 9 for a discussion of vision from a leadership perspective.) The Federal Express vision is to "produce outstanding financial returns by providing totally reliable, competitively superior global air-ground transportation of high priority goods and documents that require rapid, time-sensitive delivery."

The *guiding principles* direct the journey to that vision by defining attitudes and policies for all employees that are reinforced through conscious and subconscious behavior at all levels of the organization. Federal Express states that "We will be helpful, courteous, and professional to each other and the public. We will strive to have a completely satisfied customer at the end of each transaction."

To illustrate how the mission, vision, and guiding principles relate to strategy, let us consider the mission for a hypothetical consumer electronics company:

To design and manufacture miniature electronic products utilizing radio and microwave frequency technologies, digital signal processing technologies, and state-of-the-art surface mount manufacturing techniques.

The vision of this company might be stated as

We will provide exceptional value to our customers in terms of cost-effective products and services of the highest quality and superior value to our shareholders from their investment. We will provide a supportive work environment that promotes personal growth and the pursuit of excellence and allows all employees to achieve their full potential. We are committed to advancing the state-of-the-art in electronics miniaturization and related technologies and to developing market opportunities that are built upon our unique technical expertise.

Guiding principles might include the following:

- Quality—We are committed to a philosophy of Quality Without Exception in everything we do. We support customer-focus, continuous improvement, personal growth and learning, and the pursuit of excellence in products, processes, and people.

- Integrity—We are committed to integrity in all our promises and actions.

- Teamwork—We are committed to the principles of teamwork, respect for individuals, open communication, and cultural diversity.

The mission, values, and guiding principles serve as the foundation for strategic planning. The next step is to assess the gap between where the organization is now and where it wants to be as described in its vision. Then using this assessment, planners must develop goals, strategies, and objectives that will enable the organization to bridge this gap. Goals for our electronics company might be to embrace and implement Quality Without Exception throughout the company and to provide facilities, equipment, systems, and training that contribute to the accomplishment of our mission.

Strategies and objectives to achieve the first goal might include the following:

Strategy 1: Educate and train all employees in TQ principles.

        Objective 1.1: Provide introductory training to all employees.

        Objective 1.2: Identify and train TQM instructors, facilitators, and coordinators in each deparment.

        Objective 1.3: Develop and implement a continuous TQM education and training program.

This process is summarized in Figure 11.1. The final set of objectives defines the specific activites that must be accomplished to achieve the strategic goals.

Figure 11.1   Strategic Planning Process

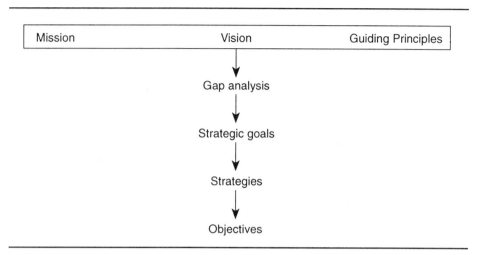

TQM and Strategy Formulation

Total quality can improve the strategy formulation process in several ways. First, it forces the organization to think in terms of its customers. Second, it places the expectation of leadership on senior management in developing and implementing the strategy. Third, the focus on measurement and objective reasoning introduces a reality check in determining the effectiveness of strategy and performance in meeting goals and objectives. Fourth, the focus on teamwork creates an expectation that everyone in the organization play a role in the formulation of the strategy. Finally, it supports the inclusion of quality as part of the fundamental strategy.

Strategy formulation is a process. Like any other process, it can be improved through the use of TQ methods. The final benefit of TQ in strategy formulation is the potential for improving this process each time it is undertaken. The aspects of this process that could be improved are the forecasting of future demand, assessment of internal capabilities, and integration of internal and external perspectives into the planning process.

TQM and Strategic Planning in Action[2]

The Total Quality Management program at the Stroh Brewery Company is based on the belief that employees hold the key to achieving a comprehensive focus on Service-Quality—an organized concerted effort to add value to products, including those processes through which services are delivered—that will enable Stroh to meet and exceed the expectations of its customers. Service-Quality means more than a quality product. It is defined through customers' perception of value. The customer judges Stroh not just by the reliability of their basic product, but by the total experience of doing business with them. Every encounter with a company system or a company employee is a "moment of truth" when the customer will judge the Service-Quality efforts of Stroh. This philosophy is reflected in the company's strategic plan:

Vision

Our vision of The Stroh Brewery Company is one of a growing and prospering company with a dynamic and motivated organization providing our shareholders with reasonable return on their investment.

Mission

To achieve this vision, our mission is to produce, distribute and market a variety of high-quality beers in a manner that meets or exceeds the expectations of our customers.

Values

Our company values provide a constant point of reference for all of our efforts and confirm our commitment to Stroh employees and to all of our customers. The core values of *Quality, Integrity*, and *Teamwork* will serve as the foundation upon which we will build success.

- *Quality*. We seek to continuously improve the level of quality in all that we do. We pursue having the finest products, efficient production and distribution facilities, innovative marketing and sales programs, and totally supportive administrative policies and procedures. These efforts are directed at meeting or exceeding our customers' expectations—both inside and outside the company.

- *Integrity*. We conduct all of our activities with integrity. We believe that the Stroh name stands for honesty and trust. We apply this belief to our relationship with all employees, our suppliers, wholesalers, and all others with whom we have business relationships. Our business activities will model our values, demonstrating that we are a responsible corporate citizen with a firm resolve to live up to our social and environmental responsibilities.

- *Teamwork*. Teamwork is essential to our mutual success. Stroh employees are a valuable asset. Every employee is given respect and trust, regardless of position in the organization. All employees are encouraged to share their views and suggestions. It is through mutual respect, cooperation, and sharing of ideas with employees, suppliers, wholesalers, and retailers that the full potential of the company will be realized. We will fully support the submission and discussion of new ideas from all of our associates (employees, wholesalers, and suppliers). Commitment and innovation will be viewed as actions worthy of praise and recognition.

Strategy Implementation

Top management requires a method to ensure that their plans and strategies are successfully executed within the organization. The Japanese deploy strategy through a process known as *hoshin planning*, or *policy deployment. Hoshin* means policy or policy deployment. Policy deployment is a systems approach to managing change in critical business processes. It emphasizes organization-wide planning and setting of priorities, providing resources to meet objectives, and measuring performance as a basis for improving performance. Policy deployment is essentially a TQ-based approach to executing a strategy. King describes it eloquently:[3]

> Imagine an organization that knows what customers will want five to ten years from now and exactly what they will do to meet and exceed all expectations. Imagine a planning system that has integrated [Plan, Do, Study, Act] language and activity based on clear, long-term thinking, a realistic measurement system with a focus on process and results, identification of what's important, alignment of groups, decisions by people who have the necessary information, planning integrated with daily activity, good vertical communication, cross-functional communication, and everyone planning for himself or herself, and the buy-in that results. That is *hoshin* planning.

With policy deployment, top management is responsible for developing and communicating a vision, then building organization-wide commitment to its achievement.[4] This vision is deployed through the development and execution of annual policy statements (plans). All levels of employees actively participate in generating a strategy and action plans to attain the vision.

At each level, progressively more detailed and concrete means to accomplish the annual plans are determined. The plans are hierarchical, cascading downward from top management's plans. There should be a clear link to common goals and activities throughout the organizational hierarchy. Policy deployment provides frequent evaluation and modification based on feedback from regularly scheduled audits of the process. Plans and actions are developed based on analysis of the root causes of a problem, rather than only on the symptoms.

Planning has a high degree of detail, including the anticipation of possible problems during implementation. The emphasis is on the improvement of the process, as opposed to a results-only orientation.

An example of policy deployment is provided by Imai:[5]

> To illustrate the need for policy deployment, let us consider the following case: The president of an airline company proclaims that he believes in safety and that his corporate goal is to make sure that safety is maintained throughout the company. This proclamation is prominently featured in the company's quarterly report and its advertising. Let us further suppose that the department managers also swear a firm belief in safety. The catering manager says he believes in safety. The pilots say they believe in safety. The flight crews say

they believe in safety. Everyone in the company practices safety. True? Or might everyone simply be paying lip service to the idea of safety?

On the other hand, if the president states that safety is company policy and works with his division managers to develop a plan for safety that defines their responsibilities, everyone will have a very specific subject to discuss. Safety will become a real concern. For the manager in charge of catering services, safety might mean maintaining the quality of food to avoid customer dissatisfaction or illness.

In that case, how does he ensure that the food is of top quality? What sorts of control points and check points does he establish? How does he ensure that there is no deterioration of food quality in flight? Who checks the temperature of the refrigerators or the condition of the oven while the plane is in the air?

Only when safety is translated into specific actions with specific control and check points established for each employee's job may safety be said to have been truly deployed as a policy. Policy deployment calls for everyone to interpret policy in light of their own responsibilities and for everyone to work out criteria to check their success in carrying out the policy.

Figure 11.2 shows the general *hoshin* planning process. Policy deployment starts with the senior managers of the company. The senior managers establish the vision and core objectives of the company. An example of an objective might be "to improve delivery," which supports the long-term vision of "To be the industry leader in customer satisfaction." Middle management negotiates with senior management regarding the goals that will achieve the objectives. Goals specify numerically the degree of change that is expected. These should be challenging, but people should feel that they are attainable.

Strategies specify the means to achieve the goals. They include more specific actions to be taken. Middle managers are responsible for managing the resources to accomplish the goals. Middle management then negotiates with the implementation teams regarding the performance measures that are used to indicate progress toward accomplishing the strategies.

Measures are specific checkpoints to ensure the effectiveness of individual elements of the strategy. The implementation teams are empowered to manage the actions and schedule their activities. Senior management then uses a review process to understand both the progress of the implementation teams and the success of their planning system. The Seven Management and Planning Tools described in chapter 3 are used extensively in the process.

Although policy deployment bears some similarity to management by objectives (MBO), an approach condemned by Deming, there are some important differences. First, typical MBO focuses on the performance of individual employees rather than on improvement of the organization as a whole. Attainment of objectives is closely tied to individual performance evaluation and rewards. This tends to promote actions that optimize the individuals' gain, rather than that of the organization. Second, MBO objectives generally are not supportive of the company's vision but are set independently. Third, MBO is primarily used as a means of management control; in practice most subordi-

Figure 11.2 *Hoshin kanri* model

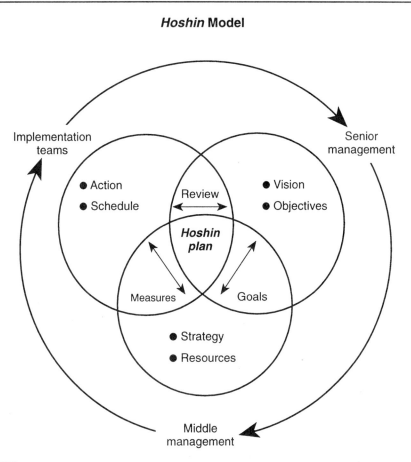

Hoshin Model

Source: From *Hoshin Kanri: Policy Deployment for Successful TQM,* by Yoji Akao (ed.), English translation copyright © 1991 by Productivity Press, Inc., Portland, OR, 1-800-394-6868. Reprinted by permission.

nates succumb to their supervisor's wishes. Finally, MBO objectives are often not used in daily work, but are resurrected only during performance reviews. However, many different MBO approaches exist in the United States, and MBO is practiced differently in Japan. Many smaller organizations that have good internal communication have used MBO successfully.

IMPLEMENTING A TQ STRATEGY

A total quality strategy has several elements:[6]

1. a customer-focused vision,
2. a concept of the voice of the customer,
3. a way of learning from outstanding companies,
4. an expression of caring for employees,
5. a means of removing the barriers to achieving quality, and
6. a measurement plan.

These elements can be implemented in any organization, provided the organization has made a commitment to quality. The Ritz-Carlton Hotel Company, a 1992 winner of the Baldrige Award, is one example (see box).

A common approach that has been used successfully to implement TQM is steering committees of senior managers; Juran terms such committees quality councils. The AT&T Network Operations Group, for example, has an Executive Quality Council, Vice President Quality Councils, Director Quality Councils, and Division/District Manager Quality Councils, all of which are networked together. Quality councils assume the responsibilities for planning and deployment and incorporate TQM into the company's strategic planning process.

Roles in Implementing a Quality Strategy

Senior management, middle management, and the workforce each have a critical role to play in the implementation process. Senior managers must ensure that their plans and strategies are successfully executed within the organization. Middle managers provide the leadership by which the vision of senior management is translated into the operation of the organization. In the end, it is the workforce that delivers quality and must have not only empowerment, but also a true commitment to quality for TQM to succeed.

Senior Management   Senior managers must ensure that the organization is focusing on the needs of the customer. They must promote the mission, vision, and values of the company throughout the organization. Senior managers must identify the critical processes that need attention and improvement and the resources and trade-offs that must be made to fund the TQM activity. They must review progress and remove barriers to implementation. Finally, they must improve the processes in which they are involved (strategic planning, for example), both to improve the performance of the process and to demonstrate their ability to use quality tools for problem solving.[7]

Middle Management   Middle management has been viewed by many as a direct obstacle to creating a supportive environment for TQM.[8] Middle manag-

---

Ladies and Gentlemen Serving Ladies and Gentlemen

This eloquently expresses the vision of the Ritz-Carlton. It is based on service through people, with the utmost respect for the customer. A guest profiling computer system, maintaining individual preferences of more than 240,000 guests who have stayed at their hotels at least three times, helps them to understand the voice of the customer and to provide uniquely tailored services (such as down pillows and other amenities) to each guest. The Ritz benchmarks other competitors such as the Four Seasons Hotel Company and other world-class organizations to learn how to improve its services.

Employees receive more than 100 hours of quality training, and nearly 90 percent have attended at least one quality seminar. Turnover is less than half of the industry average. The company listens to and acts upon employee feedback. Cross-functional teams solve quality problems, and employees are empowered to make customer-based decisions.

Measurements are taken throughout the company, from the time to clean a room, to the cost of guest-dissatisfaction, and even the waiting time of elevators. These measurements are used to solve quality problems and to improve the system. As for walking the talk, the CEO and top executives work beside cooks and housekeepers for a full week before opening a new hotel. Ninety percent of the work week of senior staff is spent with employees and customers.

---

ers are often seen as feeding territorial competition, stifling information flow, not developing and/or preparing employees for change, and feeling threatened by continuous improvement efforts. However, middle management's role in creating and sustaining a TQM culture is critical. Middle managers improve the operational processes that are the foundation of customer satisfaction; they can make or break cooperation and teamwork; and they are the principal means by which the workforce prepares for change.

Mark Samuel suggests that transforming middle managers into change agents requires a systematic process that dissolves traditional management boundaries and replaces them with an empowered and team-oriented state of accountability for organizational performance.[9] This process involves the following:

1. Empowerment. Middle managers must be accountable for the performance of the organization in meeting objectives.

2. Creating a common vision of excellence. This vision is then transformed into critical success factors that describe key areas of performance that relate to internal and external customer satisfaction.

3. New rules for playing the organizational game. Territorial walls must be broken, yielding a spirit of teamwork. One new approach is interlocking accountability, in which all managers are accountable to one another for their performance. The second is team representation, in which each manager is responsible for accurately representing the ideas and decisions of the team to others outside the team.

4. Implementing a continuous improvement process. These projects should improve their operational systems and processes.

5. Developing and retaining peak performers. Middle managers must identify and develop future leaders of the organization.

The Workforce The workforce must develop ownership of the quality process. Ownership and empowerment gives employees the right to have a voice in deciding what needs to be done and how to do it.[10] It is based on a belief that what is good for the organization is also good for the individual and vice versa. At Westinghouse they define ownership as "...taking personal responsibility for our jobs...for assuring that we meet or exceed our customers' standards and our own. We believe that ownership is a state of mind and heart that is characterized by a personal and emotional commitment to approach every decision and task with the confidence and leadership of an owner." Self-managed teams, discussed in chapter 7, is one form of ownership.

Ownership is prevalent among Baldrige winners. At Cadillac, for example, some teams have "cradle to grave" responsibility for products. Milliken employees are responsible for team member role assignment and election of team leaders and are becoming involved in the initial employee selection decision. At Zytec, employees are engaged in the design of many of their tools and workstations. Training, recognition, and better communication are key success factors for transferring ownership to the workforce. With increased ownership, however, comes a flatter organization—and the elimination of some middle managers. Increased ownership also requires increased sharing of information with the workforce and a commitment to the workforce in good times and in bad. This might mean reducing stock dividends and executive bonuses before laying off the workforce during economic downturns. This is what Japanese companies do when the business climate turns south.

Union/Management Relations

A major stumbling block in implementing TQM in the United States has been the traditional adversarial relationship between unions and management.[11] For example, in 1986 General Motors introduced a team concept for quality improvement in Van Nuys, California, which passed a union membership vote with only 53 percent in support. Since then, the opposition has worked against the concept. In many cases, management must share the responsibility in working with unions as equal partners. Both union and management have important roles in TQM.

Labor's role is to recognize the need for changing its relationship with management and then to educate its members as to how cooperation will affect the organization. This includes what its members can expect and how working conditions and job security might change. Labor must carefully select members for such a program and have a positive attitude. TQM programs must be separated from collective bargaining.

Management must realize that it needs the skills and knowledge of all employees to improve quality and meet competitive challenges and must be willing to develop a closer working relationship with labor. Management must be ready to address union concerns and cultivate trust. Both sides should receive training in communication and problem solving skills. Union and management should have equal representation on committees and have total trust and commitment. External consultants can play an important role as facilitators and mediators in such efforts.

Common Implementation Mistakes

A wide range of quality implementation strategies exist, many of which have serious pitfalls. For example, the general manager of a large defense electronics contractor unveiled a major program, then plunged into dealing with the unit's plummeting revenues and layoffs. Quality went nowhere. At Florida Power and Light, John J. Hudiburg drove hard to win the Deming Prize, but created a large bureaucracy in which morale fell as workers and managers had to compile hundreds of pages of analysis. The new CEO reduced the scope of the quality effort. Alcoa's CEO scrapped the company's decade-long continuous improvement strategy, calling it a "major mistake," focusing instead on "quantum" improvements.[12]

Implementation of TQM is often attempted without a full grasp of its nature, and certain mistakes are made repeatedly. The most frequent errors are as follows:[13]

1. TQM is regarded as a program, despite rhetoric to the contrary.
2. Short-term results are not obtained. There may be no attempt to get short-term results, or management may believe that measurable benefits lie *only* in the distant future.
3. The process is not driven by a focus on the customer, strategic business issues, and senior management.
4. Structural elements in the organization—such as compensation systems, promotion systems, accounting systems, rigid policies and procedures, specialization and functionalization, and status symbols such as offices and perks—block change.

5. Goals are set too low. Management does not shoot for stretch goals or use outside benchmarks as targets.

6. The organizational culture remains one of "command and control," and is driven by fear or game-playing, budgets, schedules, or bureaucracy.

7. Training is not properly addressed. There is too little training of the workforce. Training may be of the wrong kind; for example, providing only classroom training without on-the-job reinforcement, or focusing on the mechanics of tools and not on identifying problems.

8. The focus is mainly on products, not processes.

9. Little real empowerment is given and what is given is not supported in actions.

10. The organization is too successful and complacent. It is not receptive to change and learning and clings to the "not invented here" syndrome.

11. The organization fails to address three fundamental questions: Is this another program? What's in it for me? How can I do this on top of everything else?

12. Senior management is not personally and visibly committed and actively participating.

13. The use of teams to solve cross-functional problems is overemphasized to the neglect of individual efforts at local improvements.

14. The belief prevails that more data are always desirable, regardless of relevance—"paralysis by analysis."

15. Management fails to recognize that quality improvement is a personal responsibility at all levels of the organization.

16. The organization does not see itself as a collection of interrelated processes making up an overall system. Both the individual processes and the overall system need to be identified and understood.

Although this list is extensive, it is by no means exhaustive. It reflects the still immature development of TQM. TQM requires a new set of skills and learning, including interpersonal awareness and competence, teambuilding, encouraging openness and trust, listening, giving and getting feedback, group participation, problem solving, clarifying goals, resolving conflicts, delegating and coaching, empowerment, and continuous improvement as a way of life.[14] The process must begin by creating a set of feelings and attitudes that lead to lasting values.

Strategies for Success

Studies of Deming Prize and Baldrige Award winners have suggested that certain key practices have contributed to their success:[15]

- Successful companies have a sharp focus on quality through planning. Deming Prize winners have developed detailed, well-communicated plans and reinforced them by visual aids posted throughout the company. These firms have specific annual objectives, with frequent review of progress. Goals include both defensive goals (such as cost reduction) and offensive goals (such as building market share).

- Top management is heavily involved. Senior managers are personally involved in the process. It is not uncommon for the top executives to make numerous field visits to customers and divisions.

- Customer satisfaction is integrated across functions. Customer satisfaction drives the quality effort. Specific tasks and responsibilities are assigned to all departments. Many companies use techniques such as quality function deployment.

- Employee participation is high, especially among Deming Prize winners. As we discussed elsewhere in this book, suggestion systems have much greater importance in Japan than in the West. Training is steady and continuous and involves everyone in the company.

A comprehensive research study—called the International Quality Study[SM]—conducted by the American Quality Foundation and Ernst & Young was designed to measure quality practices across four major industries (automotive, computer, banking, and health care) and four countries (Japan, Germany, Canada, and the U.S.) to help understand how quality practices affect market performance. The study shows differences among countries, particularly Japan and the United States. The following are among the key findings:

1. A significantly larger percentage of businesses in the U.S. than in Japan do not evaluate quality at all or do so less than once each year. However, the use of quality performance as a measure for compensating senior management is expected to rise in all countries.

2. More emphasis is placed on incorporating consumer research in new product and service design in Japan than in the United States. Technology is used more extensively in Japan in meeting customer expectations.

3. Japan uses process simplification and cycle-time reduction efforts more than any other country as a means of gaining competitive advantage.

4. Japanese companies have the highest rate of employee participation regarding quality. However, businesses in other countries expect this to increase.

This study suggests that Japanese managers typically take the time necessary to examine the issues and then carefully select elements of a quality program that fit their overall mission. In the West, managers usually are impatient and seek immediate successes, often by imitation. Joshua Hammond of the American Quality Foundation urges business leaders in the U.S. to develop approaches that maximize their own cultural strengths. How we implement quality programs should be built on American strengths, not imitations of Japanese programs. Business leaders should consider what the strengths are upon which quality can be built. This requires strategic planning and integration. It is not surprising that these are two of the key themes underlying the Baldrige Award.

Although some universal principles apply, a successful quality strategy needs to fit within the existing organization culture. This is why the Baldrige Award guidelines are nonprescriptive; there is no magic formula that works for everyone. At Zytec, for instance, Deming's 14 Points were chosen as the cornerstone of the quality improvement culture. They established a Deming Steering Committee to guide the Deming process and champion individual Deming Points and act as advisors to three Deming Implementation Teams. Motorola, on the other hand, invited numerous consultants to propose quality plans, but in the end decided to develop a quality program tailored to their specific needs.

One study of Baldrige winners concluded that each has a unique "quality engine" that drives the quality activities of the organization.[16] These are summarized in Figure 11.3. This is not to suggest that all other aspects of TQM are ignored; they are not. The quality engine customizes the quality effort to the organizational culture and provides a focus for all quality efforts.

Best Practices

Imitation, while the sincerest form of flattery, may not always be the best strategy for TQM. In fact, it can actually hurt, wasting time and money on the wrong things. In 1992 the International Quality Study published research results that provides a factual basis for this claim.[17] The study suggests that best practices depend on the current level of performance of a company. Two measures of performance are the ROA (return on assets—aftertax income divided by total assets) and VAE (value added per employee—sales less the costs of materials, supplies, and work done by outside contractors divided by the number of employees).

Low performers, those with less than 2 percent ROA and $47,000 VAE, can reap the highest benefits by concentrating on fundamentals. This includes identifying processes that add value, simplifying them, and improving response to customer and market demands. In addition, training and team-work—particularly in resolving customer complaints—can lead to significant improvements. More advanced concepts, like self-managed teams, take too much preparation and time to be worthwhile for these companies. Other suggestions including benchmarking competitors, not world-class companies, listening to the customer for ideas, selecting suppliers mainly for price and reliability, buying turnkey technology for reducing costs, and rewarding front-line workers for teamwork and quality.

Figure 11.3 Quality Engines of Baldrige Award Winners

- Market Driven Quality—Focus on customer needs early in the planning and design process (IBM Rochester)
- Process Control—Focus on defect prevention, such as six-sigma quality (Motorola)
- Product Development—Focus on integrating manufacturing and design and partnering with customers and suppliers (Cadillac)
- Benchmarking—Focus on competitive and best-in-class benchmarks (Xerox)
- Technology—Focus on using technology to speed processes and improve customer service (Federal Express)
- Employee Empowerment and Involvement—Use self-managed teams and active participation of employees in all aspects of the business (Milliken)
- Strategic Planning—Involvement of cross-functional teams, customers, and suppliers in the planning process (Zytec)
- Management by Data and Facts—Focus on the use of measurements to track and improve quality (Westinghouse)

Medium performers, those with ROA from 2 percent to 6.9 percent and VAE between $47,000 and $73,999, achieve the most benefits from meticulously documenting gains, further refining practices to improve value added per employee, time to market, and customer satisfaction; and encouraging employees at every level to find ways to improve their jobs. A separate quality assurance staff is recommended. These companies should emulate market leaders and selected world-class companies; use customer input, formal market research, and internal ideas for new products; select suppliers by quality certification, then price; find ways to use facilities more flexibly to produce a wider variety of products and services; and base compensation for workers and middle managers on contributions to teamwork and quality.

High performers, with ROA and VAE exceeding 7 percent and $74,000 respectively, gain the most from using self-managed teams and cross-functional teams that focus on horizontal processes such as logistics and product development and from benchmarking product development, distribution, and customer service against world-class firms. Additional training, except for new hires, is of limited value. In addition, new products should be based on customer input, benchmarking, and internal research and development. Suppliers should be chosen primarily for their technology and quality. Strategic partnerships should be considered to diversify manufacturing. Senior managers should be included in compensation schemes pegged to teamwork and quality. Finally, these firms should further refine practices to improve VAE, market response, and customer satisfaction.

Strangely, the IQS Best Practices Report has been interpreted by many in the news media as a criticism of TQM[18]. On the contrary, the results are the first significant effort to develop a prescriptive theory (back to Deming again) of TQM implementation, rather than relying on intuition and anecdotal evidence. We are now in a position to begin to understand how TQM can best be applied. The findings contradict the notion that there is one magic quick fix for quality. Rather, companies advance in stages along a learning curve and must design their TQM initiatives carefully to optimize their effect.

SUMMARY

Many organizations now recognize that quality is a viable strategy to achieve competitive advantage. Moreover, a total quality focus within an organization can make the strategic planning and implementation processes more effective, particularly if policy deployment principles are applied.

Successful implementation of TQ-based strategies depends on the commitment and involvement of all constituents: senior management, middle management, and the workforce, including union leadership. Doing so is not easy, and many mistakes can be made. However, we are continually learning what practices lead to successful strategies and implementation. This suggests that today's managers cannot cling to past practices, but must constantly improve their approaches to meet competitive challenges.

REVIEW AND DISCUSSION QUESTIONS

1. What is a strategy? What elements does a formal strategy contain?

2. What factors have led companies to pursue a strategy based on quality?

3. Research some of the background of recent Baldrige winners. How do they integrate quality into their business strategies? Discuss different approaches that these firms use.

4. Discuss the process of strategy formulation. How can TQM improve this process?

5. Interview managers at some local companies to determine if their businesses have well-defined missions, visions, and guiding principles. If they do, how are these translated into strategy? If not, what steps should they take?

6. What is *hoshin* planning, or policy deployment? Explain how this approach is used in organizations.

7. What are the differences between policy deployment and management by objectives?

8. Does your university or college have a mission and strategy? How might policy deployment be used in a university setting?

9. Describe the roles of senior managers, middle managers, and the workforce in implementing a quality strategy.

10. How can TQM be implemented in unionized companies? What role should the union play?

11. Discuss the common implementation mistakes that many organizations make when trying to implement TQM.

12. For each of the common implementation mistakes cited in the chapter, develop a remedy or process for helping an organization to avoid them.

13. What strategies for success have been found to be especially useful in implementing TQM?

14. Do the results of the Best Practices report make sense? What might happen in companies that try to implement TQ practices that are beyond their abilities?

CASE

Stroh Brewery's Strategy[19]

The strategy of The Stroh Brewery Company (whose vision, mission, and values were introduced in this chapter) follows.

Strategy

In support of our vision and mission, the following strategies will be employed to achieve our Service-Quality goal. WE WILL:

- Maintain a competitive brand portfolio that allows us to capture unique market opportunities and strive to realize the potential of our present brands and new product introductions. Our goal is to increase unit volume. This does not mean, however, that every brand will experience unit growth every year. We will manage each brand based on its long-term growth potential, its strategic relevance, and its relationship to the company's overall business strategy.

- Invest heavily in the development of our human resources through orientation and training, which will enable our employees to make better decisions and to improve processes. We will hire individuals who have the job-related skills and abilities that support Stroh's Service-Quality mode of operation.

- Develop and introduce line extensions, new brands, and new packages, seeking to create innovative breakthroughs. New products are a critical element to Stroh's overall success. We will develop new products with a sense of urgency while maintaining a commitment to sound product concepts, excellent sales execution, and appropriate marketing support.

- Maintain a flexible approach in the balance between national and regional marketing and sales efforts. Although there are aspects of marketing our products that have relevance to all markets (e.g. national advertising), we will always to try to find ways to capitalize on regional strengths and opportunities.

- Pursue opportunities to develop international markets. Our focus for the future extends to international markets where we believe there are significant opportunities to market our products both directly and in partnership with others.

- Commit to maintaining the best distribution network in the industry along with our full support of the three-tier system. Our distribution system will function around the guiding principles of Service-Quality.

- Strive to control production and administrative expenses which allow us to provide the maximum funds to market our products. We will do this by constantly seeking ways to improve our method of completing tasks necessary to our business.

- Consider acquiring assets to build synergies and to reduce production costs. The acquisition of additional brands, manufacturing facilities, and other businesses that will improve the company's overall strategic position is viewed as highly desirable.

- Invest in plant equipment and new technologies to produce new products and to maintain our production facilities to remain competitive.

- Be comfortable with change. We will pursue change as a strategic weapon. There is no safety in standing still, nor is there any advantage in abiding by the rules set by our competitors. Change will not be pursued for its own sake, but neither will change be avoided because it is uncomfortable or because of the risks associated with change.

- Be market and service driven. We will develop systems and processes to facilitate this strategy.

Questions for Discussion

1. Who are the customers of Stroh's?
2. What aspects of Stroh's vision, mission, values, and strategy support the fundamental principles of TQM described in chapter 1?

ENDNOTES

1. James Brian Quinn, *Strategies for Change: Logical Incrementalism*, Homewood Ill.: Richard D. Irwin, 1980.

2. Adapted with permission from "TQM," The Stroh Brewing Company.

3. Bob King, *Hoshin Planning: The Developmental Approach*, Methuen, Mass.: GOAL/QPC, 1989, pp. 2–3.

4. The Ernst & Young Quality Improvement Consulting Group, *Total Quality: An Executive's Guide for the 1990s,* Homewood, Ill.: Dow Jones-Irwin, 1990.

5. M. Imai, *Kaizen: The Key to Japan's Competitive Success*, New York: McGraw-Hill, 1986, pp. 144–145. Reproduced with permission of McGraw-Hill.

6. Richard C. Whiteley, *The Customer-Driven Company: Moving from Talk to Action,* New York: Addison-Wesley, 1991.

7. Arthur R. Tenner and Irving J. DeToro, *Total Quality Management: Three Steps to Continuous Improvement,* Reading, Mass.: Addison Wesley, 1992.

8. Mark Samuel, "Catalysts for Change," *The TQM Magazine*, (1992).

9. Samuel, "Catalysts for Change."

10. James H. Davis, "Who Owns Your Quality Program? Lessons from the Baldrige Award Winners," College of Business Administration, University of Notre Dame (n.d.).

11. John Persico, Jr., Betty L. Bednarczyk, and David P. Negus, "Three Routes to the Same Destination: TQM, Part 1," *Quality Progress*, January 1990, pp. 29–33.

12. *Business Week*, "Where Did They Go Wrong?" October 25, 1991.

13. Leadership Steering Committee, *A Report of The Total Quality Leadership Steering Committee and Working Councils,* (Procter & Gamble Total Quality Forum) November 1992.

14. Thomas H. Patten, Jr., "Beyond Systems—The Politics of Managing in a TQM Environment," *National Productivity Review*, 1991/1992.

15. George H. Labovitz and Y.S. Chang "Learn from the Best," *Quality Progress*, 1990, pp. 81–85; J.M. Juran, "Strategies for World Class Quality," *Quality Progress*, March 1991, pp. 81-85.

16. Davis, "Who Owns Your Quality Program?"

17. American Quality Foundation and Ernst & Young, *International Quality Study Best Practices Report*, 1992; *Business Week*, "Quality," November 30, 1992.

18. Cyndee Miller, "TQM's Value Criticized in New Report," *Marketing News*, 1992.

19. "TQM," The Stroh Brewing Company.

Bibliography

This bibliography is a sampling of the hundreds of books that have been published in response to the quality revolution. They are arranged in the following categories:

1. Malcolm Baldrige National Quality Award
2. Deming philosophy
3. Employee involvement/human resources
4. General reference
5. Management
6. Case studies of quality practices
7. Service organizations
8. Tools

MALCOLM BALDRIGE NATIONAL QUALITY AWARD

Brown, M.G. *Baldrige Award Winning Quality: How to Interpret the Malcolm Baldridge Award Criteria*. White Plains, N.Y.: Quality Resources and ASQC Quality Press, 1991.

Haavind, R. *The Road to the Baldrige Award*. Boston: Butterworth-Heinemann, 1992.

Ross, J.E. *Total Quality Management: Text, Cases and Readings*. Delray Beach, Fla.: St. Lucie Press, 1993.

Steeples, M.M. *The Corporate Guide to the Malcolm Baldridge National Quality Award: Proven Strategies for Building Quality into Your Organization*. Milwaukee: ASQC Quality Press and Business One Irwin, 1992.

DEMING PHILOSOPHY

Aguayo, R. *Dr. Deming: The American Who Taught the Japanese About Quality*. New York: Simon & Schuster, 1990.

Deming, W.E. *Out of the Crisis.* Cambridge, Mass.: Massachusetts Institute of Technology Center of Advanced Engineering Study, 1982.

Gabor, A. *The Man Who Discovered Quality: How W. Edwards Deming Brought the Quality Revolution to America—The Stories of Ford, Xerox, and GM.* New York: Times Books, 1990.

Killian, C.S. *The World of W. Edwards Deming.* Washington, D.C.: CEEPress Books, 1988.

Mann, N.R. *The Keys to Excellence: The Story of the Deming Philosophy.* Los Angeles: Prestwick Books, 1989.

Neave, H.R. *The Deming Dimension.* Knoxville: SPC Press, 1990.

Scherkenbach, William W. *Deming's Road to Continual Improvement.* Knoxville, Tenn.: SPC Press, 1991.

Walton, M. *Deming Management at Work.* New York: G.P. Putnam's Sons, 1990.

EMPLOYEE INVOLVEMENT/HUMAN RESOURCES

Cooksey, Clifton, Richard Beans, and Debra Eshelman. *Process Improvement: A Guide for Teams.* Arlington, Va.: Coopers & Lybrand, 1993.

Grazier, P.B. *Before It's Too Late: Employee Involvement...An Idea Whose Time has Come.* Chadds Ford, Pa.: Teambuilding, Inc., 1989.

Kinlaw, Dennis C. *Developing Superior Work Teams.* Lexington, Mass.: Lexington Books, 1991.

Kohn, A. *No Contest: The Case Against Competition.* Boston: Houghton Mifflin, 1986.

Ryan, K.D., and D.K. Oestreich. *Driving Fear Out of the Workplace: How to Overcome the Barriers to Quality, Productivity, and Innovation.* San Francisco: Jossey-Bass Publishers, 1991

Scholtes, P.R. *The Team Handbook.* Madison, Wisc.: Joiner and Associates, 1988.

Wellins, Richard S., William C. Byham, and Jeanne M. Wilson. *Empowered Teams.* San Francisco: Jossey-Bass, 1991.

GENERAL REFERENCE

Evans, J.R., and W.M. Lindsay. *The Management and Control of Quality* (2nd ed.). St. Paul: West Publishing Company, 1993.

Feigenbaum, A.V. *Total Quality Control* (3rd ed., revised), New York: McGraw-Hill Book Company, 1991.

Forsha, H.I. *The Pursuit of Quality Through Personal Change.* Milwaukee: ASQC Quality Press, 1992.

Johnson, R.S., and L.E. Kazense. *TQM: The Mechanics of Quality Processes.* Milwaukee: ASQC Quality Press, 1993.

Juran, J.M., and F.M. Gryna. *Juran's Quality Control Handbook* (4th ed.). New York: McGraw-Hill Book Company, 1988.

Juran, J.M. *Juran on Planning for Quality*. New York: The Free Press, 1988.

Juran, J.M. *Juran on Quality by Design*, New York: The Free Press, 1992.

Shetty, Y.K. and V.M. Buehler. *The Quest for Competitiveness*. New York: Quorum Books, 1991.

Tenner, A.R., and I.J. DeToro. *Total Quality Management: Three Steps to Continuous Improvement*. Reading, Mass.: Addison Wesley, 1992.

Townsend, P.L. and J.E. Gebhardt. *Quality in Action: 93 Lessons in Leadership, Participation, and Measurement*. New York: John Wiley & Sons, 1992.

Walsh, L., R. Wurster, and R.J. Kimber (eds.) *Quality Management Handbook*. New York: Marcel Dekker, Inc. and ASQC Quality Press, 1986.

MANAGEMENT

Berry, T.H. *Managing the Total Quality Transformation*. New York: McGraw-Hill, 1991.

Bowles, J., and J. Hammond. *Beyond Quality: How 50 Winning Companies Use Continuous Improvement*. New York: G.P. Putnam's Sons, 1991.

Brocka, B. and M.S. Brocka. *Quality Management: Implementing the Bset Ideas of the Masters*. Homewood, Ill.: Irwin, 1992.

Dixon, G., and J. Swiler. *Total Quality Handbook: The Executive Guide to the New American Way of Doing Business*. Minneapolis, Minn.: Lakewood Books, 1990.

Dobyns, L., and C. Crawford-Mason. *Quality or Else: The Revolution in World Business*. Boston: Houghton Mifflin Company, 1991.

Eureka, W.E., and N.E. Ryan. *The Customer-Driven Company: Managerial Perspectives on QFD*. Dearborn, Mich.: ASI Press, 1988.

Garvin, D.A. *Managing Quality: The Strategic and Competitive Edge*. New York: The Free Press, 1988.

Hradesky, J.L. *Productivity and Quality Improvement: A Practical Guide to Implementing Statistical Process Control*. New York: McGraw-Hill Book Company, 1988.

Hudiburg, J.J. *Winning with Quality: The FPL Story*. White Plains, N.Y.: Quality Resources, 1991.

Imai, M. *Kaizen: The Key to Japan's Competitive Success*. New York: McGraw-Hill Publishing Company, 1986.

King, B. *Hoshin Planning: The Developmental Approach*. Methuen, Mass.: GOAL/QPC, 1989.

Schmidt, Warren H. and Jerome P. Finnigan. *The Race Without a Finish Line*. San Francisco: Jossey-Bass, 1992.

Senge, P.M. *The Fifth Discipline: The Art and Practice of the Learning Organization*. New York: Doubleday Currency, 1990.

Shecter, E.S. *Managing for World-Class Quality: A Primer for Executives and Managers*. New York: Marcel Dekker, Inc. and ASQC Quality Press, 1992.

Whiteley, R.C. *The Customer-Driven Company: Moving from Talk to Action*. New York: Addison-Wesley Publishing Company, Inc., 1991.

PRACTICES

American National Standard: Guide for Quality Control Charts, Control Chart Method of Analyzing Data, Control Chart Method of Controlling Quality During Production. Milwaukee: American Society for Quality Control, 1985.

Hiam, A. *Closing the Quality Gap: Lessons From America's Leading Companies,* Englewood Cliffs, N.J.: Prentice-Hall, 1992.

International Quality Study: A Definitive Report on International Industry-Specific Quality Management Practices (Automotive Industry Report). Cleveland, Ohio: Ernst & Young and American Quality Foundation, 1992.

International Quality Study: A Definitive Report on International Industry-Specific Quality Management Practices (Banking Industry Report). Cleveland, Ohio: Ernst & Young and American Quality Foundation, 1992.

International Quality Study: A Definitive Report on International Industry-Specific Quality Management Practices (Computer Industry Report). Cleveland, Ohio: Ernst & Young and American Quality Foundation, 1992.

International Quality Study: A Definitive Report on International Industry-Specific Quality Management Practices (Health Care Industry Report). Cleveland, Ohio: Ernst & Young and American Quality Foundation, 1992.

Lefevre, H. *Government Quality and Productivity—Success Stories.* Milwaukee: ASQC Quality Press, 1990.

Peters, T., and N. Austin. *A Passion for Excellence: The Leadership Difference.* New York: Random House, 1985.

Peters, T.J., and R.H. Waterman, Jr. *In Search of Excellence: Lessons from America's Best-Run Companies.* New York: Harper & Row Publishers, 1982.

SERVICE

Baker, R.H. *Serve Yourself: Customer Service from the Inside Out.* Amherst, Mass.: Human Resource Development Press, Inc., 1992.

DiPrimio, A. *Quality Assurance in Service Organizations.* Radnor, Pa.: Chilton Book Company, 1987.

Drewes, W.F. *Quality Dynamics for the Service Industry.* Milwaukee: ASQC Quality Press, 1991.

Heskett, J.L., W.E. Sasser, Jr., and C.W.L. Hart. *Service Breakthroughs: Changing the Rules of the Game.* New York: The Free Press, 1990.

Lash, L.M. *The Complete Guide to Customer Service.* New York: John Wiley & Sons, 1989.

Lele, M.M., and J.N. Sheth. *The Customer is Key: Gaining an Unbeatable Advantage Through Customer Satisfaction.* New York: John Wiley & Sons, Inc., 1987.

Lefevre, H.L. *Quality Service Pays: Six Keys to Success.* Milwaukee: ASQC Quality Press and Quality Resources, 1989.

Rosander, A.C. *The Quest for Quality in Services.* Milwaukee: ASQC Quality Press and Quality Resources, 1989.

Rosander, A.C. *Deming's 14 Points Applied to Services.* New York: Marcel Dekker, Inc. and ASQC Quality Press, 1991.

Spechler, J.W. *When America Does It Right: Case Studies in Service Quality.* Norcross, Ga.: Industrial Engineering and Management Press, 1988.

Tschohl, J. *Achieving Excellence Through Customer Service,* New York: Prentice-Hall, 1991.

Zeithaml, V.A., A. Parasuraman, and L.L. Berry. *Delivering Quality Service: Balancing Customer Perceptions and Expectations.* New York: The Free Press, 1990.

TOOLS

Automotive Division: Statistical Process Control Manual. Milwaukee: American Society for Quality Control, 1986.

Basic Training in TQM Analysis Techniques. Springfield, Va.: U.S. Department of Commerce, National Technical Information Service, 1989.

Brassard, Michael. *The Memory Jogger Plus+.* Methuen, Mass.: GOAL/QPC, 1989.

Clements, R.B. *Handbook of Statistical Methods in Manufacturing.* Englewood Cliffs, N.J.: Prentice-Hall, 1991.

DataMyte Handbook: A Practical Guide to Computerized Data Collection for Statistical Process Control (3rd ed.). Minnetonka, Minn.: DataMyte Corporation, 1987.

Evans, James R. *Statistical Process Control for Quality Improvement: A Training Guide to Learning SPC.* Englewood Cliffs, N.J.: Prentice-Hall, 1991.

Gitlow, H., S. Gitlow, A. Oppenheim, and R. Oppenheim. *Tools and Methods for the Improvement of Quality.* Homewood, Ill.: Irwin, 1989.

Harrington, H.J. *The Improvement Process: How America's Leading Companies Improve Quality.* New York: McGraw-Hill Book Company, 1987.

Ishikawa, K. *Guide to Quality Control.* Tokyo: Asian Productivity Organization, 1982.

Leebov, W., and C.J. Ersoz. *The Health Care Manager's Guide to Continuous Quality Improvement.* American Hospital Association 1991.

Marsh, S., J.W. Moran, S. Nakui, and G. Hoffherr. *Facilitating and Training in Quality Function Deployment.* Methuen, Mass.: GOAL/QPC, 1991.

Mazur, G., J.B. ReVelle, and S. Nakui. *Quality Function Deployment: Advanced QFD Application Articles.* Methuen, Mass.: GOAL/QPC, 1991.

Miller, G.L. and L.L. Krumm. *The Whats, Whys, and Hows of Quality Improvement.* Milwaukee: ASQC Quality Press, 1992.

Mizuno, S. (ed.) *Management for Quality Improvement: The Seven New QC Tools.* Cambridge, Mass.: Productivity Press, 1988.

Moran, J.W. R.P. Talbot, and R.M. Benson. *A Guide to Graphical Problem-Solving Processes*. Milwaukee: ASQC Quality Press, 1990.

Morse, W.J., H.P. Roth, and K.M. Poston. *Measuring, Planning, and Controlling Quality Costs*. Montvale, N.J.: National Association of Accountants, 1987.

Nikkan Kogyo Shimbun, Ltd./Factory Magazine, ed. *Poka-Yoke: Improving Product Quality by Preventing Defects*. Cambridge, Mass.: Productivity Press, 1988.

Ott, E.R. *Process Quality Control: Troubleshooting and Interpretation of Data*. New York: McGraw-Hill Book Company, 1975.

Participant Guide for Total Quality Management (TQM) Quantitative Methods Workshop. Springfield, Va.: U.S. Department of Commerce, National Technical Information Service, May 1990.

Pyzdek, T. *Pyzdek's Guide to SPC: Volume One/Fundamentals*. Tucson: Quality Publishing, Inc. and ASQC Quality Press, 1990.

_____. *Pyzdek's Guide to SPC: Volume One/Fundamentals (Workbook)*. Tucson: Quality Publishing, Inc. and ASQC Quality Press, 1989.

_____. *Pyzdek's Guide to SPC: Volume One/Fundamentals (Workbook for Services)*. Tucson: Quality Publishing, Inc. and ASQC Quality Press, 1992.

_____. *An SPC Primer: Programmed Learning Guide to Statistical Process Control Techniques*. Tucson: Quality America, Inc., 1987.

Wilson, P.F., L.D. Dell, and G.F. Anderson. *Root Cause Analysis*. Milwaukee: ASQC Quality Press, 1993.